Unholy
Alliance

Unholy Alliance

Radical Islam and the American Left

David Horowitz

Since 1947
REGNERY
PUBLISHING, INC.
An Eagle Publishing Company • Washington, DC

Library of Congress Cataloging-in-Publication Data

Horowitz, David, 1939-
  Unholy alliance : radical Islam and the American left / David
Horowitz.
    p. cm.
  Includes index.
  ISBN 0-89526-076-X (hardcover)
  ISBN 0-89526-026-3 (paperback)
  1. Radicalism--United States. 2. Islam--United States. 3. Islam and
politics--United States. 4. Right and left (Political science) I.
Title.
  HN90.R3H583 2004
  320.53'0973--dc22

                                    2004018257

First paperback edition published in 2006

Published in the United States by
Regnery Publishing, Inc.
An Eagle Publishing Company
One Massachusetts Avenue, NW
Washington, DC 20001

Visit us at www.regnery.com

Distributed to the trade by
National Book Network
4720-A Boston Way
Lanham, MD 20706

Manufactured in the United States of America

10 9 8 7 6 5 4 3 2 1

Books are available in quantity for promotional or premium use. Write to Director
of Special Sales, Regnery Publishing, Inc., One Massachusetts Avenue, NW, Washington, DC 20001, for information on discounts and terms or call (202) 216-0600.

*To the brave young men and women
risking their lives in Afghanistan and Iraq for ours*

Contents

Hatred of America is a powerful and a very destructive force in the world today. Some of that hatred is caused by America's mistakes, though that is not true of the rage of Islamic nihilists, a minority that nothing can assuage. For all its faults, American commitment and American sacrifice are essential to the world. As in the twentieth century, so in the twenty-first, only America has both the power and the optimism to defend the international community against what really are forces of darkness.

—WILLIAM SHAWCROSS, 2004

Introduction

This is a book about the political Left in America, its problematic allegiances with Islamic radicals, its influence on the Democratic Party, its opposition to the war in Iraq, and its impact on the war on terror.

Of the opposition to the war in Iraq, it can be said that never in American history has so formidable an opposition been mobilized against an American war so admirable in its aims; nor has there ever been such an opposition mobilized before the onset of a war itself.

Unlike the Vietnam conflict, which dragged on for years with mounting casualties and no result, the American military action in Iraq succeeded in toppling the Saddam regime in six weeks with minimal loss of human life. Unlike the Vietnam conflict, the war in Iraq was not waged to defend a dictatorial ally, but to overthrow an oppressive enemy regime.

"Operation Iraqi Freedom" was authorized by large majorities in both political parties. It destroyed a dictatorship universally regarded as one of the most tyrannical and lawless in modern times. When American forces entered Iraq on March 20, 2003, the Iraqi regime had invaded two sovereign states and was currently in violation of

seventeen Security Council resolutions, including a unanimous ultimatum on November 8, 2002, to disarm in thirty days or face "serious consequences"—a diplomatic euphemism for the invasion that
actually took place.

Opponents of the war in Iraq were unmoved by these compelling
facts. Before the outset of hostilities their movement had grown to
a size and scope comparable to the anti-Vietnam protests of the late
1960s, which occurred only after the Tet offensive had caused many
Americans to lose faith that the war could be won. Moreover, resistance to America's war in Iraq did not stop with the military victory
over Saddam's armies. Instead, it went on to oppose America's efforts
to consolidate the peace and to establish a sovereign and democratic government in Baghdad. Never before in American history has
there been an American movement to oppose the establishment of
a democratic government in another country.

Despite its radical agendas, the "anti-war" movement is not a
fringe phenomenon. The anti-war Left has already exerted a critical
influence on the politics of the Democratic Party, re-defining its
presidential campaign in the 2004 election. The opposition to Operation Iraqi Freedom has affected the struggle for a postwar peace in
Iraq and impacted the conduct of the war on terror.

There is a troubling wisdom in the linking of the conflicts in
Vietnam and Iraq. One lesson of Vietnam on which all sides can
agree is that when Americans are sufficiently divided, their government is significantly weakened in its ability to exert its will on international actors and events.

Opponents of American power will rejoice in this reality. But
those who believe that the exercise of that power is a bulwark of
security at home and a pillar of international order abroad will not
be so sanguine. In the context of the war on terror, in which the
enemy has access to chemical, biological, and possibly nuclear

weapons, and has exhibited no restraint in the killing of civilians, these issues are far from academic.

The opposition to the war in Iraq has been largely—though not exclusively—a posture of the political Left. There is a paradox embedded in this reality since the political Left has traditionally opposed American power on the grounds that it is a conservative force, "constantly... interested in the maintenance of 'order' in every corner of the terrestrial globe," as the Communist leader Leon Trotsky once remarked. Yet this claim is obviously at odds with recent events. America's wars in Afghanistan and Iraq were anything but conservative in nature and purpose. Their express intent was to overthrow reactionary regimes and replace them with democratic governments, guaranteeing human rights. In fact, it is precisely the nonconservative character of the war in Iraq and its agenda of "preemptive" regime change that has been the focus of its critics' primary distress.

These critics are both radical and liberal. Following the liberation of Baghdad, historian Arthur Schlesinger Jr. wrote, "President George W. Bush has made a fatal change in the foreign policy of the United States. He has repudiated the strategy that won the Cold War—the combination of containment and deterrence.... The Bush Doctrine reverses all that. The essence of our new strategy is military: to strike a potential enemy, unilaterally if necessary, before he has a chance to strike us."[1]

Bush had already answered this criticism before Schlesinger articulated it. Deterrence, the president maintained, was meaningless when dealing with "shadowy terrorist networks with no nation or citizens to defend." Containment was impossible "when unbalanced dictators with weapons of mass destruction can deliver those weapons on missiles or secretly provide them to terrorist allies."[2] The Bush Doctrine was thus more than just a military strategy to preempt terrorist attacks. It was—as its critics protested—a political strategy of regime change that was designed to disarm terror-supporting states and create an international environment that would be inhospitable to terrorist agendas.

This was indeed a departure from past American policies in the Middle East, which had preferred "containment" to "liberation." The United States had traditionally tolerated internal repression in these states and focused instead on their external policies. Ironically, during the Cold War this realpolitik had aroused the ire of the Left, which was perennially outraged by Washington's engagement with despotic rulers who supported America's anti-Communist agendas. Thus, Washington's defense of its authoritarian ally the shah of Iran had earned the passionate contempt of radicals and liberals alike.

A further irony of these complaints was that the shah had been, in fact, a modernizer who promoted education and the equality of women. His social progressivism was the very cause of the Islamic revolution that overthrew him. President Jimmy Carter's liberal aversion to the shah's authoritarian rule helped to undermine his regime and pave the way for the reign of the Ayatollah Khomeini and the Islamic revolution. While American radicals welcomed the revolution of the ayatollahs, their regime was far more reactionary and repressive than the government of the shah, and it both created and inspired the Islamic radicals who confront America as enemies today.

Why has the American Left made alliances of convenience with Islamic radicals who have declared war on the democratic West and whose own values are reactionary and oppressive? Why have American radicals actively obstructed the War on Terror, thereby undermining the defense of the democracies of the West? Why have liberals opposed Operation Iraqi Freedom, whose goals are the overthrow of tyranny and the establishment of political democracy and human rights—agendas that coincide with their own? Why have Democrats turned against the policy of regime change, which they had supported during the Clinton administration in both Kosovo and Iraq? Why has the Democratic Party declared political war on the president's war and thus made foreign policy a point of partisan conflict for the first time since the end of World War II? What does this fracture of the American consensus mean for the future of America's War on Terror?

These are the questions the current inquiry seeks to address. In doing so, it necessarily must confront others: What is the nature of the American Left? How does it think about the world? How did it come to ally itself with Islamic jihad? How significant is the threat posed by its opposition to the War on Terror? How powerful is its presence in the Democratic Party? What is its role in shaping the American future?

Today the war abroad is the most pressing concern for Americans who care about the security of their nation. But America can win a war against any external foe. Consequently, it is the war at home that will ultimately decide America's fate, which is the real subject of this text.

Before embarking on this inquiry, it should be said that this book is not about everyone who opposed the war in Iraq for whatever reason. Criticism of national policy and even of war policy is a basic American right, and the reasons for such criticism may be patriotic or not. Not all criticism is equal, however. There is a difference between healthy dissent and conducting a political war against a war while it is still in progress. This is not a book about war critics as such, but about the leaders of the organized anti-war movement and the practical support they are willing to give to America's enemies and their agendas.

PART ONE:
A Defining Moment

*"Every nation, in every region, now has a decision to make.
Either you are with us, or you are with the terrorists."*

—President George W. Bush, September 20, 2001

*"Here is our answer: We refuse to allow you to speak for all
the American people. . . . We refuse to be party to these wars
and we repudiate any inference that they are being waged
in our name or for our welfare. We extend a hand to those
around the world suffering from these policies; we will
show our solidarity in word and deed."*

—"Not In Our Name," advertisement
New York Times, September 19, 2002

1

9/11

On the morning of September 11, 2001, Islamic radicals commandeered two hostage-filled airliners and rammed them into the World Trade Center, turning its twin towers into a thermal nightmare. Within minutes, these imposing monuments of global commerce were engulfed by the inferno, collapsing in a hailstorm of ashes and dust. Three thousand innocent civilians were killed. It was an epoch-defining moment, which reflected in its horror the sudden vulnerability of a superpower previously thought to be immune to external foes. In an eyeblink, America had been turned into a pathetic victim, its citizens hunted in their own cities, its economy momentarily in shambles, its government on the run.

This was a day of infamy even more unsettling than Pearl Harbor, which had been the only site of an enemy attack on American territory in nearly two hundred years. While the Japanese war machine had targeted a military base three thousand miles from the American mainland, the Islamic terrorists had struck defenseless civilians in America's most populous city, choosing an hour to strike when the maximum number of victims—perhaps more than fifty thousand—might be unsuspectingly at work. It was the signature of an enemy that gave no quarter, and would provide no warning of its next attack.

From this day into the foreseeable future, America would be the prey of an invisible enemy whose agendas were genocidal and non-negotiable. Among the victims of 9/11 were individuals from eighty countries who were at work in the World Trade Center on the morning of the attack, a fact that accurately reflected the wounded nation's image of itself. The rage of the enemy was directed at a nation that was in its very conception pluralistic and inclusive, a country founded by people who had imagined themselves building a "city on a hill," a microcosm of all humanity—in its very inclusiveness an exemplar to the world. "America was targeted for attack," its president explained in an address afterward, "because we're the brightest beacon for freedom and opportunity in the world."

The improbable agenda of the Islamic radicals who perpetrated the 9/11 attacks was to restore the imperial caliphate of Islam and spread its empire across the globe. In the eyes of the terrorist vanguard, America was the "Great Satan" that embodied worldly evil, had invaded the Islamic *umma*, and prevented the global establishment of Islamic law. "We declared jihad against America," Osama bin Laden told a CNN interviewer in 1997, "because America is unjust, criminal, and tyrannical."[1] In 1998, he issued the following explanatory edict:

> We—with God's help—call on every Muslim who believes in God and wishes to be rewarded to comply with God's order to kill the Americans and plunder their money wherever and whenever they find it. We also call on Muslim *ulema*, leaders, youths, and soldiers to launch the raid on Satan's U.S. troops and the devil's supporters allying with them, and to displace those who are behind them so that they may learn a lesson.

The ruling to kill the Americans and their allies—civilians and military—is an individual duty for every Muslim who can do it in any country in which it is possible to do it, in order to liberate the al-Aqsa Mosque and the holy mosque [Mecca] from their grip, and in order for their armies to move out of all the lands of Islam, defeated and unable to threaten any Muslim.[2]

As xenophobic and murderous as this declaration was, a movement immediately arose within the United States to resist its own defense. Within days of 9/11, with the images of the fallen towers and the innocent dead still fresh in mind, radicals launched a campaign to protest *in advance* any military response America might contemplate to answer the unprovoked attack. By the radicals' own account, there were 247 "anti-war" demonstrations in the United States and in countries overseas between September 11 and September 30, before a shot was fired in response to the World Trade Center attack. Approximately 150 "peace vigils" and "teach-in" protests were held on university campuses across the country, and in the nation's capital.[3]

In the face of the nation's grief, without knowing when the next terrorist attack might occur,[4] prominent American leftists seized the occasion to state that the attacks had "root causes." In other words, America was to no small degree guilty for what had happened, just as the terrorists proclaimed. "Where is the acknowledgement that [the 9/11 strike] was not a 'cowardly' attack on 'civilization' or 'liberty' or 'humanity' or 'the free world,'" asked Susan Sontag, one of America's leading literary intellectuals in one of its leading intellectual journals, "but an attack on the world's self-proclaimed superpower, undertaken as a consequence of specific American alliances and actions?"[5] Sontag then proceeded to name such an action: "How many citizens are aware of the ongoing American bombing of Iraq?"

Sontag was referring to the fact that the United States for some years had been engaged in a low-intensity war in Northern Iraq, which was itself unfinished business of Saddam's war of aggression against Kuwait. In implying that these defensive efforts were an *American* aggression, Sontag was merely echoing Iraqi propaganda. The United States was conducting flights over Iraq to protect four million Kurds from the savagery of a regime that had already subjected them to aerial poison gas attacks. The American and British flights were also to enforce U.N. resolutions calling on Iraq to adhere to the terms of the truce it had signed to end the Gulf War. In effect, Sontag was suggesting that enforcing a signed truce was a crime to be weighed alongside the mass murder committed on 9/11.

Sontag continued, "And if the word 'cowardly' is to be used, it might be more aptly applied to those who kill from beyond the range of retaliation, high in the sky, than to those willing to die themselves in order to kill others. In the matter of courage (a morally neutral virtue): whatever may be said of the perpetrators of Tuesday's slaughter, they were not cowards." In fact, the opposite is true. Converting hostage-packed commercial airliners into bombs and targeting tens of thousands of innocent civilians without means to defend themselves is cowardice. On the other hand, bombing enemy aircraft installations and military depots, whatever the altitude, is not.

Other verbal assaults on the American victims were even more intemperate. As citizens attempted to recover a sense of security and their government set about defending them, American flags were flown in profusion as symbols of national solidarity. The Stars and Stripes were soon fluttering from homes, draped from office windows, waved from automobiles, and perched on the taxicabs driven by New York's multiethnic workforce, including immigrants from Afghanistan, Pakistan, and other Muslim countries. The effect was contagious, buoying the shaken national spirit and rallying a population still conscious of its vulnerability but regaining its confidence and finding comfort in defiance.

This provoked the Left to further recriminations. In an op-ed piece in the national press on September 25, best-selling novelist Barbara Kingsolver asked, "Who are we calling terrorists here?" and described her dismay that her daughter had come home from kindergarten announcing that the next day they would all have to wear red, white and blue:

> "Why?" I asked, trying not to sound wary. "For all the people that died when the airplanes hit the buildings." I fear the sound of saber-rattling, dread that not just my taxes but even my children are being dragged to the cause of death in the wake of death. I asked quietly, "Why not wear black, then? Why the colors of the flag, what does that mean?" "It means we're a country. Just all people together." So we sent her to school in red, white, and blue, because it felt to her like something she could do to help people who are hurting. And because my wise husband put a hand on my arm and said, "You can't let hateful people steal the flag from us." He didn't mean terrorists, he meant Americans.

In fact her husband meant the "hateful" Americans who were waving the flag in self-defense and out of a patriotic concern for their targeted countrymen and love for country. In Kingsolver's eyes this was menacing and repellent: "Patriotism threatens free speech with death. It is infuriated by thoughtful hesitation, constructive criticism of our leaders, and pleas for peace. It despises people of foreign birth who've spent years learning our culture and contributing their talents to our economy. It has specifically blamed homosexuals, feminists, and the American Civil Liberties Union. In other words, the

American flag stands for intimidation, censorship, violence, bigotry, sexism, homophobia, and shoving the Constitution through a paper shredder."

Kingsolver was not alone. Five days earlier, in an editorial in *The Nation*—the flagship publication of American radicalism—Katha Pollitt wrote of her own instruction to her wayward daughter, which she titled, "Put Out No Flags."[6] "My daughter, who goes to Stuyvesant High School only blocks from the World Trade Center, thinks we should fly an American flag out our window. Definitely not, I say: The flag stands for jingoism and vengeance and war."

Rhetorically, Pollitt made a pass at compromise with both daughter and country: "In a way we're both right: The Stars and Stripes is the only available symbol right now." But in practice she could find nothing to say that was positive about the symbol. On the one hand the flag expressed America's grief for her fallen citizens, but on the other it expressed America's bigotry and criminality. "It has to bear a wide range of meanings, from simple, dignified sorrow to the violent anti-Arab and anti-Muslim bigotry that has already resulted in murder, vandalism, and arson around the country and harassment on New York City streets and campuses." The charge was a wild exaggeration. Led by a president who declined even to identify the terrorists as Islamic radicals, the American people by and large did exactly the opposite of what Pollitt claimed. They showed relative restraint and tolerance for the Muslim community. While there were a number of episodes—some indeed violent—these were isolated and minimal in the circumstances, and inevitable in a diverse nation of 300 million.[7]

By the time Pollitt's article appeared, the White House had announced its plans to retaliate and, more important, forestall another attack. It intended to remove the Taliban regime in Afghanistan, which was providing the terrorists with their military base. Pollitt denounced this American response. "Bombing Afghanistan to 'fight terrorism' is to punish not the Taliban but the victims of the Taliban, the people we should be supporting." Pollitt did not indicate how people oppressed by the Taliban could be supported without attacking the Taliban, but continued her anti-American screed: "At the same time, war would reinforce the worst elements in our own society—the flag-wavers and bigots and militarists."

Another opinion from the Left was offered by Columbia professor Eric Foner, whose concerns were also focused on America's possible response rather than the actual Islamic attacks. In a widely circulated column, the past president of both the American Historical Association and the Organization of American Historians said:

> I'm not sure which is more frightening: the horror that engulfed New York City or the apocalyptic rhetoric emanating daily from the White House. "We will rid the world of evil-doers," President Bush announces as he embarks on an open-ended "crusade" (does he understand the historical freight this word carries?) against people who "hate us because we are free." This Manichean vision of the world, so deeply rooted in our Puritan past and evangelical present, is daily reinforced by the media as an emblem of national resolve.[8]

Foner's concern about the word "crusade" was highly selective. The Crusades were themselves a *response* to the Muslim sacking of Jerusalem, while bin Laden and his al Qaeda terrorists had defined *their* war as a jihad against "Crusaders and Zionists," a historically-freighted reference that elicited no comparable comment. Foner's concern was beside the point, moreover, since the hypersensitive White House had already retracted the word.

On the other hand, the president's "Manichaean" observation that the terrorists hated us because we were a free people standing in the way of the theocratic empire they hoped to establish was accurate to the letter. "America is the head of heresy in our modern world," an al Qaeda manifesto explained, "and it leads an infidel democratic regime that is based upon separation of religion and state and on ruling the people by the people via legislating laws that contradict the way of Allah and permit what Allah has prohibited. This compels the other countries to act in accordance with the same laws in the same ways . . . and punishes any country [that rebels against these laws] by besieging it, and then by boycotting it. By so doing [America] seeks to impose on the world a religion that is not Allah's."[9]

Bush had laid down the guidelines for the War on Terror in a formal speech to Congress on September 20. Far from being open-ended, as Foner claimed, his demands were specific. He called on the Taliban to surrender bin Laden and the al Qaeda terrorists: "These demands are not open to negotiation or discussion. The Taliban must act, and act immediately. They will hand over the terrorists, or they will share in their fate." The actual statement that Bush made was in fact practical rather than evangelical, and was as remote as could be imagined from the Puritan intolerance about which Foner had complained:

I also want to speak tonight directly to Muslims throughout the world. We respect your faith. It's practiced freely by many millions of Americans, and by millions more in countries that America counts as friends. Its teachings are good and peaceful, and those who commit evil in the name of Allah blaspheme the name of Allah. The terrorists are traitors to their own faith, trying, in effect, to hijack Islam itself. The enemy of America is not our many Muslim friends; it is not our many Arab friends. Our enemy is a radical network of terrorists, and every government that supports them.

As Bush took pains to make clear, America's war was not a crusade against "evil-doers" in general but was specifically directed against organized global terrorists and the states that harbored them: "Our war on terror...will not end until every terrorist group *of global reach* has been found, stopped and defeated." (emphasis added) Bush's definition of the war utterly refuted Foner's accusations: "This is not, however, just America's fight.... This is the fight of all who believe in progress and pluralism, tolerance and freedom."[10]

2

Striking Back

In the beginning of October, the United States began air strikes against the Taliban regime. The goal was to destroy the ability of the Afghanistan-based al Qaeda forces to strike again. Such considerations were irrelevant to leftists opposing the strikes, such as Berkeley Congresswoman Barbara Lee. In voting against the president's request for an authorization to use force, Lee declared, "As we act, let us not become the evil that we deplore." The implication was that if Americans used force to defend themselves, they would be no better than the terrorists who attacked them. Lee was returned to Congress by her Democratic constituents the following year.

Protesters echoed Lee's sentiments in campus demonstrations across the country. At the University of North Carolina, teach-ins featured professors attacking America as a "rogue state" and a greater terrorist threat than al Qaeda. At the City University of New York, professors condemned "American imperialism."[11] At Brown University, students and professors went on strike chanting, "One, two, three, four, we don't want a racist war."[12] Within weeks of the most heinous attack on America in its history, radicals had turned their own country into the villain.

The refusal to concede that Americans had a right to defend themselves was difficult to understand. Equally incomprehensible was the Left's willingness to defend a fundamentalist theocracy that oppressed women, homosexuals, and non-Muslims and that consequently should have been repellent to its own values. From both angles, the protesters' decision to oppose the war in Afghanistan was a defining moment for the American Left, analogous to its response to the signing of the Nazi-Soviet Pact in 1939.

At the time the Nazi-Soviet Pact was consummated, American Communists and progressive "fellow travelers" had considered themselves anti-fascists and anti-imperialists. But when Moscow signed the "Non-Aggression Pact" with the Nazi state, they embraced it. For the next two years—until Germany attacked Soviet Russia in June 1941—the Communists opposed the defense policies of the democracies and denounced what they referred to as an "inter-imperialist war."[13] When it came to choosing between the interests of the Soviet state and their "progressive agendas"—even their opposition to Fascism—American Communists and their progressive allies did not hesitate to choose the former. The subtext of their reaction to the Nazi-Soviet entente was clear: their loyalty to the Soviet state overrode their loyalty to any other principle, however progressive it might seem. This kind of calculus led Stalin's great antagonist, Leon Trotsky, to condemn the parties of the Communist International and their progressive fellow travelers as "frontier guards for the Soviet Union."[14]

Like Hitler's Reich, the Taliban regime was morally repulsive to the political left, a position expressed in Katha Pollitt's post-9/11 editorial. "Feminists and human-rights groups have been sounding the alarm about the Taliban since they took over Afghanistan in 1996.... The Taliban—far from being their nation's saviors, enforcing civic peace with their terrible swift Kalashnikovs—are just the latest oppressors of the miserable population." Given such an assessment, the readiness of a large segment of the Left to actively oppose America's war against the Taliban indicated that their opposition to America was greater than their support for "progressive" values. In short, they had become frontier guards for any opponent of American power.

Operation Enduring Freedom—the name given to the American war in Afghanistan—frustrated the predictions of its opponents. Dire warnings of terrorist eruptions in Muslim countries, "hundreds of thousands" of civilian casualties, a "quagmire" similar to Vietnam, and a "silent genocide" of "three to four million" Afghans through famine that would allegedly be caused by American policies—all failed to materialize.[15] The war lasted less than ten weeks, there was no quagmire, and the numbers of civilian casualties were minimized by the precision strikes of America forces. When American troops entered the capital, there was rejoicing among the liberated population. Women in particular were the beneficiaries of the new American dispensation. As the *New York Times* editorialized on November 24:

> America did not go to war in Afghanistan so that women there could once again feel the sun on their faces, but the reclaimed freedom of Afghan women is a collateral benefit that Americans can celebrate. After five years of Taliban rule, women in Afghanistan are uncovering their faces, looking for jobs, walking happily with female friends on the street and even hosting a news show on Afghan television.

In his September 20 address to Congress, the president had warned that there would be no "swift conclusion" to the War on Terror, that the nation should not expect "one battle" but "a lengthy campaign, unlike any we have ever seen. We will starve terrorists of funding, turn them one against another, drive them from place to place, until there is no refuge or no rest. And we will pursue nations that provide aid or safe haven to terrorism. Every nation, in every region, now has a decision to make. Either you are with us, or you are with the terrorists. From this day forward, any nation that continues to harbor or support terrorism will be regarded by the United States as a hostile regime."

Confronted by global terrorist organizations like al Qaeda, the president's either/or ultimatum was a security imperative. Afghanistan had shown that if only one nation was willing to provide sanctuary for the terrorists, Americans would not be safe. But the speech was also not unlike the Truman Doctrine, which had been promulgated more than fifty years earlier at the outset of the Cold War. Confronted by an expanding Soviet empire, President Truman had declared that every nation had to "choose between alternative ways of life," between democracy and totalitarianism. (Undoubtedly Professor Foner would consider this Manichaean as well.) Truman threw down the gauntlet to the totalitarian forces and proclaimed that it would be "the policy of the United States to support free peoples who are resisting attempted subjugation by armed minorities or by outside pressures. . . . We must assist free peoples to work out their own destinies in their own way."

By the time American troops marched into Kabul in December 2001, the next phase of the War on Terror was already in motion and the next level of opposition as well.

3

The War for Iraq

On January 30, 2002, with Hamid Karzai, the new leader of Afghanistan, sitting in the House chamber, President Bush reflected on the military victory in his State of the Union address. America had "rid the world of thousands of terrorists, destroyed Afghanistan's terrorist training camps, saved a people from starvation, and freed a country from brutal oppression." But there were dangers ahead. "Iraq continues to flaunt its hostility toward America and to support terror. The Iraqi regime has plotted to develop anthrax, and nerve gas, and nuclear weapons for over a decade." It was "a regime that [had] already used poison gas to murder thousands of its own citizens—leaving the bodies of mothers huddled over their dead children." States like Iraq constituted an "axis of evil" that threatened the peace. "By seeking weapons of mass destruction, these regimes pose a grave and growing danger. They could provide these arms to terrorists, giving them the means to match their hatred. They could attack our allies or attempt to blackmail the United States. In any of these cases, the price of indifference would be catastrophic."

To prevent future catastrophes, Bush declared that the United States would "work closely with our coalition to deny terrorists and their state sponsors the materials, technology, and expertise to make and deliver weapons of mass destruction." He made it clear that going to war with nations and specifically with Iraq was a considered option: "We'll be deliberate, yet time is not on our side. I will not wait on events, while dangers gather. I will not stand by, as peril draws closer and closer. The United States of America will not permit the world's most dangerous regimes to threaten us with the world's most destructive weapons."

In the shadow of 9/11, the fact that the 1991 Gulf War with Saddam Hussein had not been resolved acquired ominous overtones. Saddam's regime was a hostile power that had demonstrated its willingness to develop and use chemical and biological weapons against defenseless populations. It seemed determined to evade the U.N. resolutions designed to prevent it from developing new weapons programs. The dictator's desire for revenge for his defeat in the Gulf War was manifest in his abortive attempt to assassinate the president's father for leading the Gulf coalition. The technical mastermind of the first World Trade Center bombing in 1993 had been an Iraqi named Ramzi Yousef. Abdul Rahman Yasin, the one conspirator who escaped after the 1993 attack, had fled to Iraq, where Saddam protected him for years.[16] Saddam's pleasure at 9/11 and the series of terrorist attacks that followed was ill-concealed.[17] Saddam had harbored international terrorists like Abu Abbas and Abu Nidal, and was a financial sponsor of suicide bombings in the Middle East. No American security official could afford to be sanguine about these facts.

Under the terms of the Gulf War truce, Saddam had agreed to cease his internal repression and dismantle his weapons of mass destruction along with the programs to build them. He had further agreed to permit U.N. weapons inspectors access to any suspected sites at which violations might be taking place. From the outset, however, the Iraqi regime had demonstrated its determination to ignore and circumvent these terms, to the extent that it could, short of reopening the war itself.

For seven years Saddam played a cat-and-mouse game of defiance with the U.N. weapons inspectors. Then, in the fall of 1998, he expelled them, in effect breaking the cease-fire agreement and challenging the United States and the United Nations to respond. At the request of the Clinton administration, legislators in Congress drafted the Iraqi Liberation Act as an expression of the government's determination to seek "regime change" in Iraq. Among the crimes of Saddam's regime listed in the Act were Iraq's invasions of Iran and Kuwait, its use of chemical weapons, and its failure to dismantle its weapons of mass destruction or to allow verification of their destruction as required by the terms of the 1991 cease-fire conditions. It concluded by pointing out that Iraq had "ceased all cooperation" with the U.N. inspectors and that "the Government of Iraq is in material and unacceptable breach of its international obligations." On October 31, President Clinton signed the bill, which declared: "That it should be the policy of the United States to seek to remove the Saddam Hussein regime from power in Iraq and to replace it with a democratic government."[18] The vote to adopt the policy of regime change and use of force in Iraq was unanimous in the Senate. In the House, the act passed by an overwhelming majority (360–38) with 202 Republicans supporting and 9 opposed and 157 Democrats supporting and 20 opposed.[19]

Two weeks later, the Clinton administration took military action. Embroiled in the Monica Lewinsky affair, it could not undertake an invasion of Iraq but instead launched Operation Desert Fox, which consisted of four days of military strikes. Despite the brevity of the attack, the United States and Britain flew 650 bombing sorties and fired 415 cruise missiles into Iraq, a greater quantity than during the entire Gulf War.[20]

Thus, when President Bush began pressing for military action against Iraq in the summer of 2002, a reasonable expectation would have been equally broad and unified support from both political parties. This seemed even more likely because of the attack on 9/11 and the successful military campaign in Afghanistan. But fissures had already begun to develop in the bipartisan coalition behind the War on Terror. These became ever deeper as the Bush administration began to lock down a final deadline for Saddam's compliance.

In July, the American press reported that the administration was developing war plans for Iraq. To parry the American move, Baghdad invited U.N. weapons inspection chief Hans Blix to come to Iraq on August 1. The purpose of his visit was to review the progress of disarmament since the Gulf War, to discuss "remaining issues," to "study and assess" them, and to "decide upon the measures to resolve them when the inspection regime returns to Iraq." To some it looked like a new opening. To others it looked instead like a resumption of the cat-and-mouse game Saddam had been playing for years. Its immediate impact was political, offering an opening to the opponents of a military solution.

On September 12, Bush appeared before the U.N. General Assembly and called on its members to conclude a decade of toothless resolutions, give Iraq an ultimatum, and if necessary end the stalemate through action. "We know that Saddam Hussein pursued weapons of mass murder even when inspectors were in his country. Are we to assume that he stopped when they left? The history, the logic, and the facts lead to one conclusion: Saddam Hussein's regime is a grave and gathering danger." The remedies that had been tried in the past had not worked. "We've tried sanctions. We've tried the carrot of oil for food,[21] and the stick of coalition military strikes. But Saddam Hussein has defied all these efforts and continues to develop weapons of mass destruction."[22]

Iraq's refusal to comply with the U.N. resolutions was, in the president's words, "a threat to the authority of the United Nations, and a threat to peace." Iraq had answered "a decade of U.N. demands with a decade of defiance." Consequently the U.N. faced a "defining" test: "Are the Security Council resolutions to be honored and enforced, or cast aside without consequence? Will the United Nations serve the purpose of its founding, or will it be irrelevant?"

Iraq had also been given an ultimatum: Either its government would "immediately and unconditionally forswear, disclose, and remove or destroy all weapons of mass destruction," and "end all support for terrorism and act to suppress it," or it would suffer the consequences, which clearly meant war.

Four days later, Iraq responded by inviting the weapons inspectors to return for the first time in four years. Commentators noted, however, that Iraq's offer was not "unconditional." Iraq demanded that its "dignity," "sovereignty," and "territorial integrity" be respected and that "practical arrangements" be discussed for achieving this. These were requirements that had been used in the past to deny the inspectors access to civilian sites where weapons had been hidden. The cat-and-mouse game had resumed. In the words of the U.N.'s chief biological weapons inspector in Iraq, Saddam's offer was a "faux capitulation" and the proposed inspections "designed for failure." This testimony was especially troubling since according to the same writer, "from its inception in the 1970s, Iraq's biological weapons program included both military and terrorist applications," and there was no way to trace the biological agents in a terrorist attack to their source.[23]

Despite its disingenuousness, Iraq's offer had a predictable impact on domestic politics in the United States: it galvanized those segments of the Left that had held back during the war against al Qaeda. Following the president's U.N. appearance, the size of the anti-war demonstrations grew and many segments of the Left that had not participated in the previous protests began to publicly attack the administration's policies in Iraq. These included leaders of the Democratic Party who had muted their doubts during the war in Afghanistan and now began to openly voice their concern, often using the Afghanistan War itself as a cover for their attacks.

In an op-ed piece for the *Washington Post* called "The Troubling New Face of America," former President Jimmy Carter departed from two long-standing American political traditions to issue an unusually severe dissent from the administration's foreign policies and specifically from its policy toward Iraq. In the face of the warnings by his own government to the contrary, Carter asserted "there is no current danger to the United States from Baghdad." He ascribed White House Iraq policy to the machinations of "a core group of conservatives who are trying to realize long-pent-up ambitions under the cover of the proclaimed war against terrorism." He did not specify what the ambitions were.[24] Carter also accused the United States of siding with Israel in the Middle East conflict, a standard complaint of America's Islamic adversaries, and of "abandoning any sponsorship of substantive negotiations" for peace. He called the present state of affairs a "radical departure from policies of every administration since 1967." Carter agreed with the president that "we cannot ignore the development of chemical, biological or nuclear weapons," but warned that "a unilateral war with Iraq is not the answer."

Carter's demarche was followed by a broadside from former vice president Al Gore. Gore declared that he was "deeply concerned that the policy we are presently following with respect to Iraq has the potential to seriously damage our ability to win the war against terrorism and to weaken our ability to lead the world in this new century." By focusing on Iraq instead of al Qaeda and the postwar stabilization of Afghanistan, the president was distracting the nation from this more urgent task, "simply because it is proving to be more difficult and lengthy than predicted." Worse still, the president's misguided policy had set the world against us (in this Gore echoed Carter): "By shifting from his early focus after September 11 on war against terrorism to war against Iraq, the president has manifestly disposed of the sympathy, good will and solidarity compiled by America and transformed it into a sense of deep misgiving and even hostility."

Gore was distressed that the president now wanted to put the matter of war and peace to a vote of Congress before the November elections. "He is demanding in this high political season that Congress speedily affirm that he has the necessary authority to proceed immediately against Iraq and for that matter any other nation in the region."[25] On the other hand, what could be more appropriate to a democracy than, in effect, submitting a vote on war and peace to the electorate itself?

Other Democrats, including Senators Daschle and Kennedy, echoed Gore and Carter, but on October 3, the congressional debate and vote took place nonetheless. The result was overwhelming support for the war policy, albeit grudgingly on the Democratic side. The Senate passed a joint resolution authorizing the use of force against Iraq by a vote of 77–23. Seven days later the House passed the same resolution, Republicans supporting it 215–6, while House Democrats opposed it 126–81.

On November 8, the U.N. Security Council unanimously passed its own war resolution (1441), giving Iraq a month to provide "an accurate full, final, and complete disclosure" of its weapons programs and "immediate, unconditional, and unrestricted access" for the inspectors. The course for war was now set.

4

The Left's Response

As in Afghanistan, the United States was undertaking a regime change in Iraq that the Left might be expected to support. Saddam Hussein's Ba'ath Party was modeled on the Nazi Party,[26] and his policies were as bloody as those of any living tyrant. Saddam was a mass murderer who had invaded two countries, and also a terrorist against his own people, having used poison gas against Kurds and Shi'ites. He had made Iraq a safe harbor for terrorists and had embraced radical Islam to curry favor with al Qaeda and other Islamic terrorists.[27]

But when the moment of decision arrived, these facts did not seem to matter to the Left in the slightest. Whereas some factions of the Left had supported the war against Afghanistan, when it came to Iraq the Left acted on its core belief that America was the threat. The first demonstrations against the looming war took place at the end of September 2002, in anticipation of the congressional vote to authorize the war policy. The Iraq issue was added to the agenda of demonstrations already planned to coincide with the second anniversary of the Al-Aqsa intifada, the Palestinian terror campaign of suicide bombings that had followed the breakdown of the

Oslo "peace process." The September "anti-war" demonstrations were organized by International ANSWER (Act Now to Stop War and End Racism) as an expression of "solidarity" with the Palestinian terror campaign. They were coupled with a call issued by Arab radicals and European leftists for "International Days of Protest Against Occupation and Empire from Palestine to Iraq to the Philippines to Cuba and Everywhere." Al Qaeda was not a target of the demonstrations. The protesters' twin enemies were Israel and the United States.

Although the war in Iraq would not begin for six months, by the end of October the demonstrations had already swelled to the hundreds of thousands domestically, and even greater numbers, internationally.[28] These numbers were larger than those that had been achieved in the first six years of protest against the Vietnam War, which had not exceeded ten thousand for any demonstration until the student draft was instituted in 1964. Another striking difference between the early protests against the Vietnam War and the protests in anticipation of the conflict with Iraq was the rapidity and vehemence with which the protesters denounced the American government and its allegedly imperialist agendas.[29] This was particularly notable in light of the facts that the War on Terror had begun with an attack on American soil and the war in Iraq was months away. There was little evidence of pacifism in the slogans and speeches at the anti-Iraq demonstrations. Spokesmen denounced America as a "rogue state" and a "terrorist state," likened the president to Adolf Hitler, equated the CIA with al Qaeda, described America's purpose as "blood for oil," and called for "revolution." At a demonstration on the National Mall, a black American imam from the mosque Masjid al-Islam, declaimed, "It's revolution time, brothers and sisters. We have to get rid of greedy murderers and imperialists like George Bush in the White House." The imam then led the crowd in the chant *Allahu Ahkbar!* which is a traditional Muslim prayer but is also the ritual last cry of suicide "martyrs" as they reach targets like the World Trade Center.[30]

Speakers at the Washington demonstration were not drawn exclusively from the political fringe. The crowd was also addressed by Representative John Conyers, the ranking Democrat on the House Judiciary Committee. Charles Rangel, the ranking Democrat on the House Ways and Means Committee, sent a letter of support that was read from the platform. A Democratic city councilman from New York, Charles Barron, told the crowd, "If you're looking for the Axis of Evil, then look inside the belly of this beast."[31]

When American troops entered Iraq on March 21, the Democratic Party and most mainstream critics of White House policy closed ranks behind the war. On that day both houses of Congress passed a resolution "expressing the support and appreciation of the nation for the president and the members of the armed forces who are participating in Operation Iraqi Freedom." The vote in the Senate was unanimous. In the House only eleven members—all Democrats, including Conyers and Rangel—voted no. Twenty-one members—twenty Democrats and one Republican[32]—voted present, in effect withholding their support.

Television talk-show host Alan Colmes, who had been a vocal critic of the war policy in the period leading up to hostilities, explained his own decision to put his views on hold once the flag had been committed and while the troops were in the field: "The time to debate going to war was before the fact. Once American men and women were in harm's way, that debate was over and lost by those of us who opposed the intervention."[33]

But organizers of the "anti-war" movement were undaunted by such considerations. A month earlier, Leslie Cagan, the leader of a newly organized "moderate" anti-war group, had warned, "If marches do not work, we will have to do things to disrupt the normal flow of life in this country."[34] Hundreds of demonstrations followed this warning in cities across America, including the nation's capital. Many were part of the "No Blood for Oil! Resistance Campaign," whose expressed intent was to break the law, obstruct traffic, and tie up police and other Homeland Security officials. A typical instruction explained, "These [protests] will be direct action oriented, unpermitted demonstrations to interrupt Business as Usual in the Capital of Capital and to raise the social costs of the U.S. Government to Wage war on Iraq and the world."[35]

At Columbia University, less than a week into the fighting, a group of thirty professors held a "teach-in" against the war, one of hundreds of similar events. For six hours, before three thousand members of the Columbia community, the professors made their case against the war. A professor of Iranian studies contrasted the "C" students who he claimed were running the war with the "A" students who had come to protest it. A professor of international affairs denounced the "naked, open, shameless lies" of the American government. A professor of political science attacked media coverage of the war by CNN and other networks, concluding "the watchdog of government has become its lapdog." Another called American policy "a new form of colonialism," while a third lumped America and Israel, calling their policies "acts of colonialism" led by "crude military men."[36]

But it was an anthropology professor named Nicholas De Genova who drew national attention to the event when he called for "a million Mogadishus," a reference to the 1993 defeat and humiliation of American soldiers in Somalia by an al Qaeda warlord. De Genova explained, "Peace is not patriotic. Peace is subversive, because peace anticipates a very different world than the one in which we live—a world where the U.S. would have no place. U.S. patriotism is inseparable from imperial warfare and white supremacy. U.S. flags

are the emblem of the invading war machine in Iraq today. They are
the emblem of the occupying power. The only true heroes are those
who find ways that help defeat the U.S. military."

Another aspect of the spreading protests was their international
character, a product of the Internet network that "antiglobalization"
and "social justice" activists had already established.[37] From the first
demonstrations in September, held in conjunction with the "International Days of Protest," the anti-war effort transcended national
borders, and by January, demonstrations in Paris, Madrid, Rome,
London, and other cities in Europe, and in Asia and Latin America, had reached collective levels exceeding a million protesters.
These demonstrations were reminiscent of the international protests
organized by the Communists during the Cold War, including the
"nuclear freeze" movement of the 1980s, in which many of the organizers had participated, and more recently the "antiglobalization"
demonstrations, which culminated in a riot in Seattle two years
before the World Trade Center attack.

Six weeks later the war was over and Iraq had been liberated. The
swift and relatively bloodless victory of American forces, however,
had no effect on the views of its internal adversaries. When the
smoke had cleared, the dire predictions of the critics of Operation
Iraqi Freedom proved as groundless as the fears the Left had raised
in advance of the war against the Taliban. The victory was relatively
painless (insofar as any military victory can be said to be painless)—
not even Saddam's vaunted Republican Guard had the will to defend
the dictator. American and Iraqi civilian casualties were minimal.
There was no eruption on the Arab streets. There was no explosion
of terrorist incidents. The war against al Qaeda was not inter-
rupted—indeed many top al Qaeda operatives were captured during
the conflict. Saddam Hussein had not unleashed a chemical attack.
He had not been able to create an environmental disaster by setting

fire to Iraq's oil fields as he had done at the end of the Gulf War. But these achievements led to no second thoughts on the part of the demonstrators or by the president's Democratic critics in Congress.

On April 9, American soldiers liberated Baghdad to the cheers of its citizens, while remnants of the forces loyal to Saddam Hussein began a rearguard resistance to the occupation forces. Thousands of jihad warriors, including al Qaeda, poured into the country from neighboring Syria, Jordan, and Iran to take up the fight. Iraq, as the president said, was now "the central front in the war on terror." But at home the internal opposition to America's war continued.

Less than a week after American and British forces had liberated Iraq—after the victors had opened Saddam Hussein's prisons, dismantled the torture chambers, begun to dig up the mass graves, shipped in vast quantities of food and medicine, and announced plans to create the first Iraqi regime in history that would not be a monarchy, a military junta, or a fascist dictatorship—the faculty senate of UCLA voted to "condemn" the "United States invasion of Iraq." It was a move that reflected widespread sentiment among college professors nationally. The extraordinary session of the academic senate was convened just for the purpose of expressing the condemnation, which passed by a vote of 180–7. The professors also voted to "deplore the doctrine of preventive war the president has used to justify the invasion" and to "oppose the establishment of the American protectorate in Iraq," even though the president actually justified Iraq's liberation under U.N. Resolution 1441 and no American "protectorate" was ever contemplated.

The professorial resolution was only one of many indications in the months ahead that the political war at home would go on. The boilerplate on a bulletin board for demonstrations worldwide provided a map of the battles ahead:

The war against terrorism threatens to be an unending war yet we see little progress in addressing the actual causes of terrorism, violence, and war. Join protests to stop the endless war. We must stop this war and start addressing the real causes of terrorism.[38]

Addressing the "real causes" of timeless phenomena like "terrorism, violence, and war" was a code for the utopian agendas of the Left. It was a declaration of war against the War on Terror, and it was only one of many to come. Wherever American and British forces proposed to engage terrorism or the state sponsors of terrorism, the international Left would be there to interpose its own political forces between them and the agents of terror. The international left had become frontier guards for Saddam and the Islamic jihad.

PART TWO:
THE MIND OF THE LEFT

"Peace is not patriotic [but] subversive. . . . Peace anticipates a very different world than the one in which we live—a world where the U.S. would have no place."

—PROFESSOR NICHOLAS DE GENOVA
REMARKS AT A COLUMBIA UNIVERSITY TEACH-IN.

5

Patriotism

Professor De Genova's arresting formulation is a good starting point for understanding the global perspective of anti-war radicals and goes to the heart of the questions raised by the anti-war demonstrations. How could so many Americans be inspired to oppose their own country in its response to an indiscriminate, unprovoked attack? How could "progressives" who claim to abhor religious fundamentalism, to support democracy and women's rights, and to oppose "imperialism" find the terrorist, misogynist, and expansionist state of Saddam Hussein less culpable than the democracy they live in? How could they regard Saddam as the *victim*? How could they oppose a war for Iraqi freedom? And how could they actively obstruct the war once American troops were in harm's way?

Almost as instructive as De Genova's remarks in providing answers to these questions were the rebukes he received from other speakers at the teach-in. These rebukes, which were entirely fraternal, came from critics who were concerned by the public relations impact of his remark that peace was "unpatriotic." De Genova, they believed, had gone a phrase too far, exposing their positions to

41

unfriendly fire. The most significant voice among these critics belonged to Columbia's most famous radical professor, Eric Foner. While De Genova was an obscure assistant professor, Foner was an academic lion, a former head of both professional historical associations and the Columbia history department, and winner of the Bancroft Prize. Foner was also a founding member of Historians Against the War.[1]

"I refuse to cede the definition of American patriotism to George W. Bush," declared Foner, distancing himself from De Genova's remark. "I have a different definition of patriotism, which comes from Paul Robeson: *The patriot is the person who is never satisfied with his country.*"

The invocation of Robeson as a patriotic emblem was itself revealing. Paul Robeson was an icon of the Communist Left, a winner of the Stalin Peace Prize (while Stalin was alive) whose passport had been confiscated by the State Department because of his loyalty to the Soviet enemy during the Cold War. At a time when Soviet tanks were creating police states in Eastern Europe, Robeson led a Communist campaign to distract attention from the Kremlin's latest crimes, including Stalin's anti-Semitic purges. Robeson charged the United States with "genocide" against American Negroes, climaxing with a petition presented to the U.N. in 1949. In the same year that Stalin's agents engineered a coup in Czechoslovakia and the Red Army instituted the Berlin Blockade, Robeson declared that American Negroes would not fight for the United States in a war with the Soviet Union.[2] Robeson was an interesting choice to provide a definition of patriotism.

Throughout his career, Robeson's attitude toward the liberties and opportunities offered by America was as unrelentingly negative as his attitude toward the oppression in the Soviet bloc was forgiving and blind. In this he resembled his admirer, who could trace his own intellectual roots to American Communism. Eric Foner grew up in a family of Communists. His uncle Philip was the Party's labor historian and editor of the speeches and writings of the Black Panthers and of Robeson himself; another uncle was a Communist union leader (SEIU). Foner began his own political career writing for the *National Guardian*, a paper that had a Maoist editorial line.

In a long review of Foner's subsequent academic work, the liberal intellectual historian John Diggins wrote, "[Eric] Foner... is both an unabashed apologist for the Soviet system and an unforgiving historian of America."[3] Foner's history of the United States, *The Story of American Freedom*, was caustically dismissed by historian Theodore Draper, who called it a work more accurately described as "the story of unfreedom." Writing in the *New York Review of Books*, Draper characterized Foner as "a partisan of radical sects and opinions" and described his narrative as "a tale of hopeful efforts that failed and of dissident voices that cried out in the wilderness." A distinctive feature of Foner's history was his attempt "to rehabilitate American Communism." Draper summed up: "From [Foner's] account it would be hard to understand why so many millions of immigrants should have come to the United States for more freedom."[4]

This background is helpful for understanding Foner's definition of patriotism as "never being satisfied with [one's] country." But it also leads to a further question. Since radicals like Robeson are dissatisfied with their country to the point that they are unwilling to defend it, under what conditions—if any—would Foner and the other Columbia protesters be willing to defend America against its enemies? How fundamental are the changes they would seek before a sense of loyalty would take hold? How does their idea of patriotism square with De Genova's comment that America as we know it would not exist in a peaceful world? Not one of the Columbia protesters—Foner included—spoke to this issue at the time, or has spoken to it since.

Were there changes America had not made *or could not make*, that would cause radicals like De Genova and Foner to decide it should not be defended after 9/11? Can any radical identify with America to an extent that would provide them reason to defend it? De Genova's vision of a world in which "the U.S. would have no place" is a clear statement that there is no such identification for radicals like him.

6

The Communist Forerunners

Samuel Johnson's famous scoundrel who finds a last refuge in patriotic fervor has a counterpart in radicals like De Genova and Foner, who cloak their revolutionary agendas in the flag and values they intend to subvert. A generation of American Communists, Paul Robeson among them, rationalized their disloyalty to America (and fealty to the Soviet Union) as a higher commitment to socialism that would one day transform America itself. By defending Soviet Communism, they were in their own minds actually building "a better America." In the 1930s, the Communist Party's leader, Earl Browder, made this fantasy a party slogan: "Communism is Twentieth Century Americanism."

Through this distorted lens, American Communists viewed their loyalty to the Soviet Union as loyalty to an ideal America, which would be built on Communist principles. Opposition to Communism and the Soviet Union could then be viewed as a form of treason to America itself.

Albert Lannon was a Communist leader who was tried under the Smith Act for conspiring to teach the overthrow of the American government. His first loyalty was to the Soviet Union. When he appeared before the court, however, he was able with complete sincerity to invert the values normally associated with patriotism:

> I consider disloyal and traitors those who foment war, those who try to deprive Americans of their democratic rights, those who live on the blood and sweat of the American working class, those who have instigated this and other trials of Communists and progressives to stifle the great voice of my beloved Communist Party.[5]

Obviously not every critic of American policy—even wartime policy—has treasonous intent. This is a distinction easily blurred in times of national peril, a fact that has led to well-known abuses during both world wars and the McCarthy era of the Cold War. The fact that leftists were on the receiving end of these abuses, on the other hand, did not prevent the Communist Party from accusing those who disagreed with it of treason. Thus, during the Second World War, when America and the Soviet Union had a common enemy, the Communist Party denounced both labor leader John L. Lewis and civil rights leader A. Philip Randolph as "American traitors," because they refused to sacrifice the interests of workers and civil rights to the war effort.[6]

Moreover, many American Communists were in fact traitors. They worked as agents and spies for the Soviet Union through secret apparatuses that the American Communist Party had set up to serve Soviet interests.[7] Some American leftists have belatedly owned up to these facts: "Among the most remarkable revelations that emerged from the [opening of the Soviet archives]," write two of them, "was the extent to which the Communist Party USA was itself embroiled in Soviet espionage. That individual spies like Julius Rosenberg were Communists is not exactly news. But that the party helped on a regular basis to recruit spies and vet their political reliability did come as a surprise, as did the indication that some of its top leaders, including the wartime general secretary, Earl Browder, actually ran espionage operations."[8]

Why did these Americans willingly betray their country? Many of them were European immigrants who had come to America to find refuge from persecution abroad. Why were they willing to work for the enemies of a nation that had given them refuge and opportunity, and the benefits of a society that was relatively free?

Many students of the Left have reflected on this question,[9] but few as astutely as the philosopher Gerhardt Niemeyer. Niemeyer observed that "in Communist eyes, the future is more real than the present," and that for Communists the future is "closed."[10] In other words, radicals imagine the future as already determined. In the radical view, once human beings have been freed from institutional oppressions, their natural goodness asserts itself and the traditional dilemmas of power no longer exist. It is a future in which "social justice" prevails and there are no troubling questions about the dispensations of authority. Therefore the questions of process and means are no longer important. There is only the end result, which justifies everything. There is the revolution and then there is the perfect future, which for Communists was already a *fait accompli* in the Soviet Union.

This explains why American Communists were willing to betray their country. They were convinced that their comrades in the Soviet Union had already created the just society. The Soviet Union was "a heaven...brought to earth,"[11] the American Communist Tillie Olsen wrote in 1934. For radicals who shared this belief, the fate of the progressive future lay in the success of the Soviet state. For Communist progressives, the interests of the Soviet state were the interests of mankind itself. To serve one meant advancing the other. As one Communist Party text instructed its adherents, "The USSR is the stronghold of the world proletariat; it cannot be looked on as merely a nation or a country; it is the most advanced position of the world proletariat in the struggle for a socialist world."[12]

For progressives who held these beliefs, betraying their country was easily justified as benefiting their countrymen at the same time. It was a higher form of "patriotism." "Treason" to America was loyalty to humanity. It was fidelity to a truer American self. (The same idea has been extended by radicals to include racial issues: "Treason to whiteness is loyalty to humanity" is the motto of the magazine *Race Traitor*, which is edited by Harvard leftists and which Princeton professor and political consultant Cornel West has called "the most visionary courageous journal in America."[13])

In his memoir *Witness*, Whittaker Chambers described the Communist movement he had served as a new development in the annals of betrayal:

> Other ages have had their individual traitors—men who from faintheartedness or hope of gain sold out their causes. But in the twentieth century, for the first time, men banded together by the millions in movements like Fascism and Communism, dedicated to the purpose of betraying the institutions they lived under. In the twentieth century, treason became a vocation whose modern form was specifically the treason of ideas.[14]

Chambers was wrong in maintaining that treason for an idea was an entirely new phenomenon. Benedict Arnold could reasonably be considered a traitor motivated by an idea—in his case, loyalty to the Crown of England, his first allegiance. By the same token, America's revolutionary founders were traitors to their king in the name of an idea. This is why—having created a democracy—they made treason such a difficult crime to establish.

Chambers was right, however, in the sense that Communists and Fascists betrayed the actual institutions they lived under in the name of an abstraction, whereas the others had not. Benedict Arnold and other loyalists to the Crown acted to preserve the system they lived under. So did the American founders who fought to defend what they considered "the rights of Englishmen," which they believed the Crown had denied them. They fought for a reality they knew, while invoking abstract ideals to justify their rebellion and to articulate the principles they for the most part lived by. But Communists and Fascists were not defending any reality. Like contemporary radicals, they were motivated by an abstraction—the vision of a future that did not exist and had never existed, but which they were convinced they could create.

It is this abstraction, this *monde idéal* that accounts for the otherwise incomprehensible fact that for Communists "the future is more real than the present." The belief in this "reality" is the reason radicals discount the freedoms, and benefits of the actual world they live in. Their eyes are fixed on the revolutionary future that is perfect and just. Measured by this impossible standard, any actually existing society—including America's—is easily found deficient, even to the point where it is worthy of destruction.[15]

It is only the radicals' impossible dream that explains the extravagant hatred they feel toward their own privileged circumstances. It is the expression of their total rejection of the existing world. Examining the writings of Marx—which still provide the wellspring of the radical "critique"—Niemeyer observed that Marxism is not a criticism of particular wrongs in the social order but a "total critique of society" itself.

"Marx's indictment condemns not this or that concrete choice or a pattern of civil actions, but the entire historical condition of human existence [under capitalism]." Niemeyer observes that this is not so much a "moral" critique as an "ontological" one—a critique that affects the entire social reality. "All that which has gone under the name of reality appears to Marx as a nullity."[16] Not only is the radical's revolution *not* about the reform of a social reality, and therefore its preservation, it is the opposite. It is about the total destruction of one: "By force of the overall definition, in the present society *all* laws are unjust, *all* consciousness is false, *all* relations must be corrupt, *all* institutions appear oppressive."[17] In Marx's chilling phrase in *The Eighteenth Brumaire*, "Everything that exists deserves to perish." A total critique requires an equally total solution.

This is the perspective that informs the critiques not only of Marx and his followers but also those of post-Communist radicals, including the anti-war Left. For those who define the world in this totalitarian way, the problem of determining the morality or justice of particular human actions and particular institutions no longer exists. Because America is an unjust society, all its wars are also unjust by virtue of that fact alone. America's reasons for entering the war in Iraq are thus tainted before the fact.

It does not matter to the radical whether the use of force was authorized by the elected representatives of the American people, as the Iraq war was. In the radical's perspective the electoral system is itself a fraud and cannot be a source of legitimacy for any action (except those the Left favors for other reasons). Formal political democracy merely masks the domination of a corporate ruling class whose interests the state is alleged to serve. It doesn't matter to the anti-American radical if America is the nation attacked, because America is itself the corporate ruler of the "global system"—the system that is responsible for the conditions that create the terrorists. In other words, whatever the details and regardless of the facts, America is the root cause of the attacks on itself.

In the radical perspective, every aspect of human activity is shaped by the injustice of the prevailing global order. The radical's universe is thus Manichaean, a world divided between good and evil; his political actions are always a choice between an oppressive present and the progressive future. This is a religious conception rather than a political one. Radicals see themselves as the army of the saints and their opponents as the party of Satan, a fact that explains their passionate hatred for the opponents of their faith.

Aileen Kraditor is the foremost scholar of the worldview of American Communists. A New Left historian and former member of the Communist Party herself, she has written a classic study of the mental world of rank-and-file American Communists. An entire chapter of her book on the subject is devoted to "The Rationale of Hate," as the predominant emotion the party attempted to instill in its members.[18] (From similar observations, George Orwell, in his futuristic novel about Communism, *1984*, made the "Five-Minute Hate" program, a daily ritual in his totalitarian state.)

One party leader tasked with instilling these attitudes was its "chief theoretician," Herbert Aptheker, to whom Kraditor devotes several pages. In a text published in 1949, Aptheker described the global capitalist system as "so putrid . . . that it no longer dares permit the people to live at all." In a review of Cleveland Amory's book on America's wealthy, he wrote, "These are the rules as depicted by a court-scribe. They [the members of America's ruling class] have the morals of goats, the learning of gorillas and the ethics of—well of what they are: racist, war-inciting, enemies of humanity, rotten to the core, parasitic, merciless—and doomed."[19]

Aptheker's rhetorical style was typical of party functionaries and has been characteristic of the pronouncements of hard-core radicals ever since. In 1951, at the height of the Cold War, the Party's general secretary William Z. Foster, expressed a view of the conflict that in sentiment and tone was not dissimilar to those voiced from anti-war platforms fifty years later:

> It is nauseating to listen to the self-righteous big capitalists and their mouthpieces hypocritically blathering about their "moral leadership of the world." Goebbels . . . is a novice compared with the war propagandists of the United States. . . . American imperialism, which is the organization of the most ruthless gang of fascist-minded capitalists on earth, is insolently pictured by its orators and pen-pushers as the champion of democracy, the defender of world peace, the moral guardian of mankind.[20]

Foster died before the Cold War was over, but Herbert Aptheker lived to see its end, remaining an unrepentant Communist all his life. His ideological venom would only be of historical interest if it were not for the fact that the next generation of radicals—including the organizers of the anti-war movement—has embraced him as an intellectual model. In the 1990s Aptheker was given appointments as a visiting professor at Bryn Mawr and at the University of California's Boalt Hall, one of the nation's most prestigious law schools. His historical writings have been praised by the leading figures of the historical profession in its leading professional journals. Before his death in 2003, he was formally honored as a scholar by the Columbia University history department through the auspices of his friend and admirer Eric Foner.[21]

One can see the core elements of Aptheker's political perspective present in the demonstrations against the war in Iraq: the demonization of the Bush administration as a terrorist regime and as "the real axis of evil," and their extreme slogans, such as "Bush is the Disease, Death is the Cure," and "We Support Our Troops When They

Shoot Their Officers." And one can hear it in their speeches. "The president wants to talk about a terrorist named bin Laden," declaimed a keynote speaker at the Capital anti-war demonstration. "I don't want to talk about bin Laden. I want to talk about a terrorist called George Washington. I want to talk about a terrorist called Rudy Giuliani. The real terrorists have always been the United Snakes of America."[22]

One could also see these elements present in the fact that the "anti-war" movement was created in the wake of 9/11, thereby defining itself as a movement to attack one's country when one's country was attacked.

7

Neo-Communism I: The Transition

The collapse of the Communist system, which brought the Cold War to an end, was a watershed event in the life of the international Left. The catastrophe of Communism included the creation of a totalitarian state; the reintroduction of slave labor on an epic scale; and politically induced famines and government-created poverty of unprecedented proportions; political purges and mass executions resulting in the deaths of an estimated 100 million people.[23]

These were the direct results of a system based on socialist theories, which provided no rational method for allocating resources and no effective work incentives, and no guarantees of individual rights. The unique cause of the system's failure was in fact the socialist theories that inspired its creation and that had produced a continent-size society that did not work.[24]

A Czech writer, Joseph Svorecky, asked, "Has there ever been a case in history of a political system collapsing overnight, not as an aftermath of a lost war or bloody revolution but from its own inner rottenness?"[25] The answer was, there had not. The Soviet system and its political empire were the products of a self-conscious effort to create a social order based on false intellectual doctrines. It was this artificial nature of the regime that explained the unprecedented circumstances of its fall.

In other words, the Soviet catastrophe should have been a moment of reckoning for the progressive movements, which had based their hopes on the socialist future and shaped their movement according to its theoretical perspectives. But the paramount fact—overriding all others—was that it was not. Although their "solution" had failed, progressives continued to embrace the political culture that had produced it, and to guide their political actions by the same ideas. In the universities they had come to dominate, Stalinists like Antonio Gramsci, Gyorgy Lukacs, Walter Benjamin, Herbert Marcuse, and Eric Hobsbawm were iconic names. The Cuban Stalinist Che Guevara became a saint of the popular culture, along with the Rosenberg spies, who were elegized as martyrs in the literary culture including a celebrated theatrical epic, *Angels in America*, which won the Pulitzer Prize. Its dramatist, Tony Kushner, was, not surprisingly, a signer of the "Not In Our Name" denunciation of the war in Iraq.

For seventy years, the international progressive Left had supported the efforts of Soviet Marxists to create socialist states in Russia, China, Cuba, and Vietnam, and despite the acknowledgment that "mistakes" had been made, continued to keep the Communist tradition alive. In the international Left, there had been one significant exception to this rule, which was the Second Socialist International, whose member organizations, particularly the British Labour Party and Germany's Social Democrats, played important roles in bringing down the Soviet regime. The head of NATO, the principal anti–Soviet bloc-alliance, was in fact a Belgian socialist named Paul-Henri Spaak. But in the United States, anti-Communist socialists remained marginal factions of the political Left, grouped around tiny political magazines like *Dissent*, and had no effect on the direction of its mainstream.

Among mainstream radicals, a New Left had emerged in Europe and America after Khrushchev's denunciation of the crimes of Stalin in 1956. Hoping to escape the taint of the Stalinist past, these leftists rejected what they regarded as Communist deformations of the socialist dream, but not the Marxian theories that had led to them. Unlike the socialists of the Second International, they refused to embrace anti-Communist politics or support the democratic West in its Cold War conflict. New Leftists proclaimed themselves "anti-anti-Communists" to emphasize their continuing antagonism to the capitalist world. Their support for Communist revolutions, along with their steadfast opposition to America's Cold War agendas, reflected their primary hostility to the democratic West and their continuing commitment to the fantasy that they could finally make socialism work.[26]

In the normal course of events, the collapse of the Communist states and the bankruptcy of their Marxist economies ought to have thrown the Left into a profound crisis of faith. It should have caused radicals to rethink their Marxist critiques of democratic capitalism and socialist ideas about the revolutionary future. It should have caused them to reevaluate their opposition to American policy and their support for regimes that had murdered tens of millions and oppressed tens of millions more.

But such reassessments did not take place. Instead, in articles, manifestos, and academic texts, leftists the world over claimed that the Marxist economies they had supported and defended[27] did not represent "real socialism" and therefore were not what they had meant to defend. The system that had dominated world events and their own political imaginations for nearly a century was dismissed as merely "actually existing socialism" and not "real socialism,"[28] therefore of no particular interest to them now that it was gone and irrelevant to their political agendas. Jutta Ditfurth, a member of Germany's Green Party, expressed this universal radical attitude with admirable directness: "There simply is no need to re-examine the validity of socialism as a model. It was not socialism that was defeated in Eastern Europe and the Soviet Union because these systems were never socialist."[29]

Absent second thoughts, leftists continued to shape their political agendas according to the same Marxist premises about capitalism that history had discredited. Even when they recognized the need for reappraisals, they avoided the reality of what had happened. After the Soviet regime fell, Samuel Bowles, a professor of economics at the University of Massachusetts Amherst, told the *Wall Street Journal*, "Marx wrote almost nothing about socialism and communism"; therefore there was a need for a lot of "rethinking about socialist economies but little about capitalist economies."[30]

But of course the entire edifice of Marxist theory and its critique of capitalism had been erected on the premise that a socialist economy was practical, that a viable "revolutionary" alternative existed to the democratic societies of the West. This was the presumption that the Soviet experience had utterly discredited. The socialist ideal provided Marxists with their standard for measuring every shortcoming and failure of capitalist societies and for explaining what was wrong with them. The falsification of Marxist theories of socialism could hardly be separated from the Marxist view of capitalism, since they were two sides of the same analytical coin. If Marx's economic theories do not work in a socialist economy, how can they be said to explain *any* economy? Or be the basis for criticizing any society?

If socialism is not a viable system and capitalism is the only system that can produce wealth and freedom in a modern technological environment, what does this say about the revolutionary project itself? In the absence of a practical alternative, the revolutionary project is nihilism, the will to destroy without a concept of what to do next.

The persistence of the revolutionary illusion without the revolutionary fact has given rise to a Neo-Communist movement, which has learned nothing from the failures of Communism but has not forgotten the cause itself. Contemporary radicals have added new dimensions of oppression, like racism and sexism to the Marxist model. But theirs is the same Marxist model that divides the world into oppressors and oppressed, identifies capitalism as the root cause of global problems, and America as the system's guardian-in-chief. Consequently, like the Communist model it has replaced, the contemporary radical outlook opposes America's wars and opposes America's peace.

All that really distinguishes this Neo-Communist perspective from its Communist predecessor is its ad hoc attitude towards the revolutionary future, and the nihilistic agendas that follow. The contemporary Left defines itself and organizes its unity as a movement *against* rather than *for*. Its components may claim to be for egalitarian futures in which racism, sexism, and corporate dominance no longer exist and "social justice" prevails. But unlike Communists, contemporary leftists are not committed to even a rudimentary blueprint that they share in common as to what such an order might entail. It is this lack of programmatic consensus that leads some leftists to even deny that there is a "Left" and makes it possible for a fragmented coalition of Neo-Communists—including anarchists, eco-radicals, radical feminists, "queer" revolutionaries, Maoists, Stalinists, and vaguely defined "progressives"—to operate in improbable coalitions like the anti-war movement. It is why they can do so in ways that benefit such unlikely allies as Islamic radicals and the Ba'athist fascism of Saddam Hussein.

Neo-Communists may or may not reject the Leninist idea of a vanguard party; they may depart from particular aspects of the Communist future like the "dictatorship of the proletariat" or the "central plan." But they are inspired by the same hostility to private property and the market economy, and to the corporate structures that produce society's wealth. It is this animosity that unites them in the battles they engage, whether against the structures of "globalization" or the War on Terror. The continuity between the generations of the Communist and Neo-Communist Left is, in fact, seamless. It is the product of a leftist culture that embraces the political traditions and anticapitalist perspectives of the discredited Communist past.

An illustrative example of this mentality is provided in the career of Eric Hobsbawm, an icon of the contemporary intellectual Left. Hobsbawm was a lifelong Communist who joined the party in 1930, letting his membership lapse only after the fall of the Berlin Wall.[31] An unremitting apologist and devoted servant of the most oppressive and repellent empire in history, Hobsbawm is today one of the most honored professional historians in the universities of Europe and America.[32]

Hobsbawm's last historical work, *The Age of Extremes*, is probably the most highly praised effort to understand the twentieth century and the events about which he was so profoundly wrong. Hailed as the final volume of his tetralogy on industrial capitalism—"a *summa historiae* of the modern age"[33]—it has been published in thirty-seven languages. This in itself is a testament to the vitality of Neo-Communism in the contemporary political culture.

The Age of Extremes appeared in 1995, four years after the fall of Communism, and is an elaborate defense of the twin illusions in whose name the Communist Left wreaked so much havoc during the twentieth century: the inherent evil of capitalist democracies and the humanitarian promise of the socialist future. The *Age of Extremes* is in fact an elaborate and perverse defense of the very illusions that sustained the Communist cause.[34]

Although this cause left a greater trail of victims than any other in historical memory, Hobsbawm's attitude toward its enormities remains, revealingly, one of sadness and "nostalgia" rather than outrage and guilt. In an autobiography published in 2002, Hobsbawm told his readers, "To this day I notice myself treating the memory and tradition of the USSR with an indulgence and tenderness."[35] These are his feelings toward a regime that enslaved and slaughtered tens of millions, and reduced hundreds of millions to lives of inconceivable misery. Imagine a historian expressing the same sentiments toward the memory and tradition of Nazi Germany, which inflicted its damage over a twelve-year period rather than seventy years. Such an intellectual would be a moral pariah in the world of letters. Yet the opposite is true of Hobsbawm, to whom tribute is paid in the highest reaches of the academic culture, while his denial and nostalgia are, in fact, the widely shared attitudes of the intellectual Left.[36]

It was in Berlin in the 1930s that the young Hobsbawm joined the Communist Party and embraced a faith that has never left him. "The months in Berlin made me a lifelong Communist, or at least a man whose life would lose its nature and its significance without the political project to which he committed himself as a schoolboy, even though that project has demonstrably failed, and as I know now, was bound to fail. The dream of the October Revolution is still there somewhere inside me."[37]

Hobsbawm's reflection is striking in a way that provides profound insight into the mindset of the radical Left. Even though he now "knows" that the Communist project "was bound to fail," the dream of Communism still lives inside him. In other words, the belief in an alternate world to replace the one into which he has been born is not really connected to any reality. Even worse, the belief in the utopian future is impervious to its failure in practice, even at the cost of a hundred million lives.

This is to acknowledge, in effect, the religious dimension of radical belief. In Hobsbawm's own words, his life would "lose its nature and its significance" without the revolutionary project. Without, that is, the project of first destroying the world he has been born into. The destruction is justified by the desire to create an alternative future, notwithstanding that the practicality of that future is not an important issue for Hobswbawm or for the millions of leftists like him, who proceed with the destruction without regard for what will follow. So strong is the psychological need for the utopian illusion and its project of destruction that it does not matter to Hobsbawm (and to radicals like him) that the noble future to which he actually dedicated his life did not work and could not have, and in fact created monstrous injustice in its place. Although it is all over now and the corpses of the victims have been laid to rest, Hobsbawm still clings to his revolutionary fantasy and remains a dedicated enemy of the system it intended to destroy. Even though the utopian future is only an impossible dream, and has been the cause of immeasurable tragedy, it is still the center of his intellectual and political life.[38]

For radicals like Eric Hobsbawm, the revolutionary project is less about creating the future than it is about a war against the present. *This* is what gives their lives and their actions meaning. By his own account, Hobsbawm had doubts about the Soviet system all along the way. But his antagonism toward the capitalist democracies (despite the fact that they provided him with a privileged life) was greater than his doubts. Hobsbawm's admissions confirm this salient fact: Ungrounded hostility toward the present is the practical inspiration of the radical faith.

In 1991, the year that ended the Soviet nightmare, Hobsbawm wrote down his reflections on the event. He called the article "After the Fall" and in it expressed his concern that the Soviet Union's oppressive empire was now a thing of the past. In his eyes, the Soviet Union was the lesser evil, and it was the greater evil that had emerged victorious:

> Capitalism and the rich have, for the time being, stopped being scared. Why should the rich, especially in countries like ours where they now glory in injustice and inequality, bother about anyone except themselves? What political penalties do they need to fear if they allow welfare to erode and the protection of those who need it to atrophy? This is the chief effect of the disappearance of even a very bad socialist region from the globe.[39]

In Hobsbawm's perspective, the "chief effect" of the disappearance of a system that killed 100 million people, triggered a nuclear arms race, and imposed dictatorship and terror on a billion souls is this: The capitalist democracies of the West and the rich who rule them no longer have the Soviet empire to check their predatory designs. "The world may yet regret," Hobsbawm concludes, "that faced with Rosa Luxemburg's alternative of socialism or barbarism, it decided against socialism."[40]

In this view, capitalism—the system that underpins the democracies of the West and has raised the living standards of billions of human beings many millions to levels that only royalty enjoyed in the past—is *barbarism*. The identical conclusion ends Hobsbawm's "*summa historiae* of the modern age."

> We have reached a point of historic crisis. . . . If humanity is to have a recognizable future, it cannot be by prolonging the past or the present. If we try to build the third millennium on

that basis we shall fail. And the price of failure, that is to say
the alternative to a changed society, is darkness.

In short, the choice before mankind is exactly what Rosa Luxemburg thought it was in 1917—socialism or capitalist barbarism.

Hobsbawm's views identify the core belief of the Neo-Communist Left. Even after the fall of Communism, its members believe
that Western market societies are societies whose destruction is
required in the name of humanity and its survival.

An illuminating parallel to Hobsbawm's perspective is found in
the work of historian Gerda Lerner, a pioneer of radical feminism
and a bridge between the New Left and the Old. Like Hobsbawm,
Lerner began her political career as a Communist in Central
Europe, but emigrated to the United States in the late 1930s to
escape Nazism. Unlike Hobsbawm, she eventually withdrew her
membership from the Communist Party twenty years later and
joined the New Left to become one of its intellectual leaders. As a
professor of history at the University of Wisconsin, Lerner was a
shaping influence on New Left feminism, writing one of its
canonic texts, *The Creation of Patriarchy* and in 2003, during the
conflict in Iraq, one of the founding members of Historians
Against the War.[41]

Lerner abandoned the Communist Party in 1956 following
Khrushchev's revelations about the crimes of Stalin (which were, of
course, revelations only to Communists). But awareness of these
crimes—monstrous as they were—did not cause Lerner to rethink
her commitment to the revolutionary cause itself. Instead she continued her radical career as an "anti-anti-Communist." She went on
condemning the democracies of the West, opposing the Cold War
against the Soviet Union, and pursuing the same revolutionary agendas she had before.

Lerner's career is especially instructive because it spans three radical generations and, because, unlike Hobsbawm, she made the transition to each new revisionist version of the progressive cause. Thus, more than thirty years after being apprised of Stalin's crimes and joining the New Left, she experienced a second metaphysical lurch when the entire socialist enterprise collapsed. In 1991, the fall of the Soviet Union and the opening of the Soviet archives forced her to examine the lies that had governed her life for more than fifty years. In a memoir, published in 2002, she acknowledged this: "Had I written this account twenty years ago, I would have focused on the rightness of my position and on explaining to the post-Vietnam generation that the Old Left has been unduly maligned and its achievements have been forgotten. That still seems partially true to me, but now everything has become far more complex and disturbing."[42]

As a historian Lerner felt she could not simply shrug off the complexities that recent events had created. "I have striven to lead a conscious, an examined life, and to practice what I preach. It now appears that, nevertheless, I failed in many ways, for I fell uncritically for lies I should have been able to penetrate and perceive as such." But like others who went through the same crisis and did not give up their political faith, Lerner is unwilling to confront the lies she has lived by for so long. When it comes to what she refers to as "disturbing" realities, her text becomes minimalist and fails to make any serious attempt to deal with them. The entire passage of her self-examination occupies a mere four pages of her 373-page book, which she describes as a "political autobiography."

Lerner only manages to confront one particular lie she fell for and promoted in her service to the progressive cause. This was her acceptance of the Nazi-Soviet Pact, a traumatic event for activists who had regarded themselves as standing on the front line of the struggle against Nazism. It should have been difficult for a Jew, in particular, to swallow this lie, but when the Kremlin signed a "nonaggression" pact with Hitler, Gerda Lerner adapted to the new political reality overnight. Lerner and her comrades rationalized the alliance with Hitler as a necessary political measure. They formed an anti-war Left in the Western democracies to oppose what they referred to as the "militarist" policies of allied nations like Britain and the United States who were attempting to resist the Axis powers.[43]

In Lerner's account of her about-face, none of the ironies of her current opposition to an Anglo-American coalition fighting a fascist dictatorship in Iraq are apparent to her. Instead, she focuses exclusively on the past, recalling her studied disregard for the evidence available at the time, which showed that Stalin actively colluded with Hitler in dividing up Poland. These facts were easily accessible in the contemporary pages of the *New York Times* and fifty years later in the history of those events recorded in Harrison Salisbury's book on the siege of Leningrad, which she admits she had read but did not believe. It is only when the Soviet archive was opened and she was presented with official Soviet documentation of the collusion that she was finally able to recognize and acknowledge the truth. In other words, even though she left the Communist Party in 1956, she had to wait thirty-five years for an imprimatur from the defunct Soviet state to accept the facts. For progressive religionists like Gerda Lerner, any other source about these events was tainted by its association with capitalist institutions.

So powerful is the progressive faith that Lerner was never able to break its hold, despite the fact that it has been the basis for her lifelong commitment to a monstrous cause. "Like all true believers, I believed as I did because I needed to believe: in a utopian vision of the future, in the possibility of human perfectibility.... *And I still need that belief, even if the particular vision I had embraced has turned to ashes.*"[44]

After a lifetime of lies, her political choices are the same: hostility to the capitalist democracies of the West and faith in a utopian future. This is the illusion that led to her commitment to Communism in the first place, still undisturbed by the earth-shattering events of seventy years. She clings to her faith even though she now knows, like Hobsbawm, that Communism was never the solution she believed and argued it was, and even though the Communist state no longer exists. Notwithstanding that the West and her anti-Communist enemies were right all along, Gerda Lerner is still a determined and passionate enemy of America and the West. In the conflict in Iraq it does not matter to her that Saddam Hussein did not even pretend to advance the cause of "social justice," as Stalin did. It just matters that his antagonist is the Great Satan itself.

Lerner's current politics are still based on the irrational hope that the next revolution will turn out differently from the ones that failed. Even though she can't identify or describe the utopia of her dreams, she is still convinced that there is a "socially just" system that can replace the capitalist democracies she is determined to destroy. Since her belief in the Soviet Union and in the socialist-bloc states never was grounded in reality, there can be little difference between the beliefs that inspire her activities in the present and those that inspired her Stalinist agendas in the past. Or her New Left causes. At the end of a long political life, she is entirely unself-conscious in pledging her allegiance to what she herself concedes is an irrational creed.

This utopian longing—the need for an alternate reality to supply values that are "truly human" and social orders that are "socially just"—is the religious wellspring of the Communist Left and of its Neo-Communist successor.[45] It underpins their hope for a world informed by these ideals and contempt for the actual world that lacks them. It is the utopian fantasy that inspires in Lerner and her political comrades their otherwise incomprehensible revulsion toward the society they live in. Asked by an interviewer whether she saw any parallels between the Nazism she experienced in her youth and the realities of post-9/11 America, she is as ready as ever to conflate the noxious realities of the Hitler dictatorship with democracy in the United States:

> I see many very frightening signs. I see us creating a deviant 'out-group' once again. For example, the treatment of the Afghan prisoners, whom we are taking halfway across the world without a trial, without investigation. We are removing them from their homeland, we are putting them in open cages, like animals. It's horrible. And I think the only reason for doing it is that the government wishes to create this terror group as the new scapegoat for everything that's wrong with society. It is very dangerous. I also see the automatic, knee-jerk 'patriotism,' in quotation marks, in response to the terrorist attacks, and the immediate demand for conformity, so that anyone who questions whether bombing Afghanistan was the proper response will be treated as a traitor. That's familiar ground, I've been there before.[46]

What has this historian learned from the perverse incarnation of her Communist dreams and their self-implosion? By her own account, almost nothing. "I have called myself a post-Marxist," she writes (pointedly eschewing the term *ex*-Marxist). "I came to that stance as soon as I became a feminist. Ever since the late 1950s I believed that the so-called errors of Communist leadership in the Soviet Union were structural and built into the very fabric of Marxist doctrine." At first, this might seem like the prelude to a systematic revision of her false beliefs. But when Lerner explains her revision, it is evident that she is capable of no such thing: "Basically, I came to the conclusion that Marxist thought was in error in regard to race and ethnicity in its insistence that class subsumed these categories. As for gender, Marxist thought, while giving lip service to the 'woman question'...reduced patriarchal dominance to economic dominance."[47] This is the extent of her second thoughts. In other words, Lerner regards the failure of Communism as consisting of a gap in its indictment of capitalism.

In Lerner's view, Marxism failed to provide a proper map to the future not because it was based on false economic assumptions or utopian delusions about human possibilities, or a failure to understand the link between liberty and property, but because Marxist theory gave inadequate attention to race and gender oppression. How this accounts for the human catastrophe of Soviet Communism she doesn't even attempt to explain. There is no lack of thoughtful analysis available on the question of why the socialist idea turned out so badly.[48] But despite her academic credentials, Lerner seems entirely ignorant of this literature and wholly uninterested in addressing the issues herself. The remarks cited on gender and race are all she has to say about the failure of a system to which she dedicated fifty years of effort and which destroyed hundreds of millions of lives.

Far from instilling humility in progressives like Gerda Lerner, the collapse of socialism has revived their self-righteousness and reenergized their assault on the democratic West. The disappearance of the Soviet bloc has had only one consequence of note. It has lifted the burden of having to defend—however critically—an indefensible regime. Because the utopian vision is no longer anchored in the reality of an actually existing socialist state, the Left can now indulge its nihilistic agendas without restraint.

8

Neo-Communism II:
The New Left

Gerda Lerner was in her thirties when the New Left was launched in the wake of Khrushchev's report on the crimes of Stalin in 1956. She was young enough to join its political generation and become one of its mentors, as the sixties radicals shook off the burdens of their Stalinist past and went back on the attack. Her easy assimilation to its attitudes and doctrines reflected its continuities with the Communist past.

The New Left began officially in 1962 with the "Port Huron" statement, whose authors were determined to "speak American" and which employed terms like "participatory democracy" in place of "Soviet power," a concept that was identical in meaning.[49] The sixties radicals intended to create an indigenous radicalism that would avoid the foreign loyalties that had discredited their predecessor when Soviet crimes became inescapable. Yet, by the end of the decade, this "new" Left had become indistinguishable from the old. It, too, was a reliable ally of international Communism, while employing a political diction virtually indistinguishable from that of the Communist states.[50]

By the end of the sixties, the New Left was recognized by its opposition to the anti-Communist Cold War and its Marxist

71

analyses of American society. Like their Communist predecessors, New Leftists viewed America as an imperialist state, the guardian of a global system that plundered the poor. Their politics was distinguished by its warm embrace of the Stalinist regimes in Cuba and North Vietnam, and by its "critical support" (its own term of choice) for the Soviet bloc that—like Hobsbawm—it regarded as a check on the imperial ambitions of the United States.

These attitudes continued through the 1980s and 1990s as the Left focused its energies on "solidarity" organizations to aid Communist regimes and movements in Central America, and on "peace movements" to disarm the West in the face of the continuing Soviet threat. The continuity of this Left is crystallized in the career of one of its architects in the 1960s and the coauthor of the UCLA faculty resolution denouncing America's "invasion" of Iraq more than forty years later.

In 1960, Maurice Zeitlin was a Berkeley Marxist and a founding editor of *Root and Branch*, one of three radical journals that helped to launch the new radical movement.[51] With fellow editor Robert Scheer (later a columnist at the *Los Angeles Times* and a prominent opponent of the war in Iraq), Zeitlin wrote one of the first books hailing the triumph of the Communist revolution in Castro's Cuba.[52] Zeitlin had visited Cuba in 1960, the second year of the revolution. While there, he had conducted an interview with Che Guevara, the minister of trade unions and the number-two man in the Communist regime. The interview was published in *Root and Branch*.[53]

In this interview, Zeitlin challenged Guevara's policies toward the unions, particularly their independence from the revolutionary state. As a New Leftist, he was concerned that the socialist movement would not repeat the "mistakes" of the Stalinist past. He questioned Guevara about the control of the unions by the state, and asked him about the role he thought they should play in a socialist society. Should unions be independent of the state or appendages, as Lenin, and then Stalin, had made them in Soviet Russia? In asking the question, Zeitlin reminded Guevara that the elimination of independent unions had paved the way for the Soviet police state and its infamous gulags.

The question angered Guevara. He refused to criticize the Soviets or even discuss their policies, and abruptly changed the subject. Zeitlin had put Guevara to the test and the Cuban leader had failed. Guevara's reaction indicated that he was a Stalinist himself.

Zeitlin and the other *Root and Branch* editors understood exactly the significance of what Guevara had said, and its implications as well. The intention of Cuba's own leaders was to make Cuba a totalitarian state. Yet despite their own commitment to a *new* Leftism that would break with the Stalinist past, Zeitlin and the *Root and Branch* editors continued to support the Cuban dictatorship. Despite Guevara's clear commitment to a Stalinist state, the editors rationalized their support by telling themselves that it was America's opposition to the Cuban revolution that was forcing the Castro regime to take its totalitarian course, even though the interview had taken place before the Bay of Pigs and before the regime had declared itself a socialist state.[54]

This incident was emblematic of the politics of the New Left, which applied a double standard to Western democracies and the Soviet bloc, and restricted its criticisms of Communist regimes in Cuba, Vietnam, Nicaragua, North Korea, and the Soviet Union to verbal effects. When "revolutionary" regimes came into conflict with the United States, the New Left's political allegiances were always clear, its attitudes invariably defensive of the Communist side. At the end of the 1960s, Zeitlin wrote a critique of the Castro government's repressive practices for the New Left magazine *Ramparts*. But like his progressive comrades, he continued to support the Castro dictatorship and defend it against Washington's efforts to promote freedom for the Cuban population.

When the Communist empire collapsed in 1989, Zeitlin remained committed to the utopian cause and to the anti-American agendas that were its consequence.[55] Cuba survived the Soviet collapse but under Castro's rule went into a steady economic decline. More than forty years after the revolution, Cuba's *caudillo* was the longest-surviving dictator in the world and its economy had slid from being the second richest in Latin America in per capita income to a place as the second poorest, slightly above Haiti and below Honduras and Belize.[56] In these years, Zeitlin had become a professor of sociology at UCLA, specializing in Chile and writing about its "dominant classes." In 1997, he spoke at a UCLA symposium on twentieth-century utopias, where he returned to the subject of Che Guevara. Thirty years earlier, Guevara had resigned his position in the Cuban dictatorship to take up arms as a revolutionary in Bolivia, where he eventually was killed. His purpose in instigating this guerrilla campaign, as he announced in a famous 1967 declaration, was to incite an international civil war, creating "two, three . . . many Vietnams." Despite the catastrophes of Soviet and Cuban socialism, Zeitlin used the occasion of the UCLA seminar to declare his continuing faith in the Communist cause for which Guevara had died: "Che [Guevara] was above all a revolutionary socialist and a leader of the first socialist revolution in this hemisphere," Zeitlin told his college audience. "His legacy is embodied in the fact that the Cuban revolution is alive today despite the collapse of the Soviet bloc . . . No social justice is possible without a vision like Che's."[57]

More than forty years after his confrontation with Che Guevara over the totalitarian future of the Cuban revolution, Zeitlin was celebrating the totalitarian himself as a hero of "social justice" and the socialist future. In other words, despite the bankruptcy and collapse of the Communist bloc, despite the failure of every Marxist program and regime that Guevara had supported, including Cuba's totalitarian state, despite the opening of the Soviet archives, which confirmed the mass murders and economic failures of its Marxist regime, Zeitlin remained—like Hobsbawm, Lerner, and an entire generation of New Left radicals—a small-c communist: a fantasist of the socialist future and a determined opponent of the democratic West. While praising the Communist future, Zeitlin was simultaneously leading the attack on America's "invasion of Iraq," blind to the fact that Iraqis were celebrating in the streets of Baghdad pulling down the statues of the former dictator and welcoming the American troops that had come to liberate them.

Zeitlin's return to his Communist roots is instructive precisely because he was once a highly intelligent and authentic dissenter from that past, and thus a core member of what started out to be a "new" Left. Other leftists were never embarrassed by that past and continued its agendas as Communists proper, Maoists, and members of various Trotskyist sects.[58] It was a prominent member of these Communist sects, named Leslie Cagan, who was to emerge in the anti-Iraq protests as the primary leader of the "moderate" peace coalition.[59]

Cagan was selected to head the Coalition United for Peace and Justice by a group of left-wing activists meeting under the auspices of People for the American Way. According to the participants themselves, the organization was created as a public relations effort to deflect criticism that the peace movement was run by the hardline Communists of International ANSWER, self-styled "Bolsheviks" aligned with North Korea, who had organized all of the national demonstrations to that point.[60]

Leslie Cagan was a sixties radical who became an activist in the Communist movement in college, breaking American laws to travel to the Communist World Youth Festival in Bulgaria in 1968. The following year she joined the First Venceremos Brigade, a project of Cuban intelligence that recruited American leftists to help with the sugarcane harvest. Cagan was a leader in other institutions of the Left, including the extreme-left Pacifica radio network, and was an organizer of demonstrations for a nuclear freeze and for solidarity with Communists in Central America in the 1980s and against the Gulf War of 1991. For seven years Cagan was the director of the Cuba Information Project, which promoted the Communist dictatorship and worked closely with its official agencies. In 1997 she coordinated the U.S. delegation to the World Youth Festival in Cuba, once again in defiance of U.S. law.[61]

Cagan's view of America is as permanently dark as those of Hobsbawm and Lerner, with whom she shares a political lineage. In 1998, the sixth year of the Clinton administration, Cagan wrote, "I cannot recall a period in my lifetime as bad as this. The accelerated concentration of wealth and power in everything from the mass media to manufacturing to health-care and banking; the ever-widening gap between the world's poor and wealthy; the global environment crisis; xenophobia, racial and religious violence; an epidemic of violence against women, children and sexual minorities; the influence and power of religious fundamentalism in all its variations."[62]

Cagan was not exactly candid when she identified "religious fundamentalism in all its variations" as one of her nightmare fears. If religious fundamentalism took an anti-American turn, as it did in the politics of radical Islam, she and her comrades were quite prepared to form alliances with forces they otherwise professed to abhor. For Cagan and her comrades, the anti-American imperative defined the unwavering party line. Anti-Americanism is the core of their revolutionary agenda and takes precedence over all others, allowing them to make a *de facto* alliance with an Iraq regime that was self-consciously fascist and Islamo-fascist—an alliance they would not think of making with their own country despite the fact that it is a democracy and its values are progressive. [63]

9

Neo-Communism III: The Utopian Idea

The worldview of the radical Left is shaped by a Manichaean dualism that unifies its disparate factions and shapes its common agendas. At the heart of this worldview is the psychologically indispensable belief in a utopian future that embodies the idea of "social justice." It is this utopian vision that provides radicals with the standard of judgment that condemns the actually existing world, no matter how decent it may be.

Professor Todd Gitlin was one of the speakers at the Columbia teach-in against the war in Iraq. A former president of Students for a Democratic Society, Gitlin is a typical veteran of the New Left. In the 1960s, Gitlin was a self-declared "anti-anti-Communist," choosing not to support the West in its Cold War against the Communist states. After the 9/11 attacks, however, Gitlin draped an American flag from his New York apartment window and felt a tinge of patriotism for the first time in his political life, suffering the disdain of his leftist comrades for his gesture.

In an essay titled, "Varieties of Patriotism,"[64] Gitlin examined his feelings about this episode and attempted to explain it. During the Cold War, he had not identified with the Soviet Union, but expected the utopian idea to be realized in Vietnam or Cuba or some other revolutionary state. His alienation from his own country and rejection of any patriotic feeling came not from a positive identification with America's enemies but from a negative revulsion inspired—as he described it—by the Vietnam War.

According to Gitlin, Vietnam was something like an American original sin. "The war went on so long and so destructively, it felt like more than the consequence of a wrong-headed policy. My country must have been revealing some fundamental core of wrongness by going on, and on, with an indefensible war."[65] Because of this "fundamental core of wrongness," Gitlin writes, "The American flag did not feel like my flag, even though I could recognize—in the abstract—that it made sense for others to wave it in the anti-war cause."

According to Gitlin, he "argued against waving the North Vietnamese flag[66] or burning the Stars and Stripes," or at least he did at first. "But the hatred of a bad war, in what was evidently a pattern of bad wars—though none so bad as Vietnam—turned us inside out. It inflamed our hearts. You can hate your country in such a way that the hatred becomes fundamental. A hatred so clear and intense came to feel like a cleansing flame. By the late 60s, this is what became of much of the New Left."

Gitlin summarizes the anti-American feelings of his generation of radicals in these words: "For a large bloc of Americans, my age and younger, too young to remember World War II—the generation for whom 'the war' meant Vietnam and possibly always would, to the end of our days—the case against patriotism was not an abstraction. There was a powerful experience underlying it: as powerful an eruption of our feelings as the experience of patriotism is supposed to be for patriots. Indeed, it could be said that in the course of our political history we experienced a very odd turn about: The most powerful public emotion in our lives was *rejecting* patriotism."

Gitlin's reflections are rare among leftists for their introspection and frankness. But they are disingenuous nonetheless. The rejection of patriotism, the identification with the Communist enemy, and the broad condemnation of American democracy were staple attitudes of the Left long before the Vietnam War and thus cannot have been caused by American actions in the war. It was not negative actions by the United States in Vietnam or anywhere else that inspired this alienation; it was the power of the utopian dream.

Unlike Leslie Cagan, Gitlin was brought up in a liberal household, and while still impressionably young was drawn into the radicalism of the 1960s. The shapers of this movement, its intellectual leaders and leading institutions, were already anti-American and had rejected patriotism long before Todd Gitlin came of age. During the early Cold War years, they had supported Stalin and then Mao and finally Fidel and Ho, whom they defended according to the usual double standards employed by the Left. In their eyes, the Vietnamese Communists, for example, were "national patriots" and bearers of "rice roots democracy" to a people "oppressed" by American imperialism.

There was, in fact, nothing inherent in the Vietnam War that should have caused any American to turn against his country. Every year that has passed since the war's end has brought new testimonies to this fact. The most eloquent of these come from disillusioned leaders of the victorious side who confirm what the postwar slaughter had already revealed: North Vietnam had planned a conquest, not a liberation of the South; far more North Vietnamese soldiers were involved early in the conflict than even Washington had claimed; the National Liberation Front was a creation and instrument of Hanoi, and far from bringing democracy to South Vietnam, the conquerors imposed a ruthless, reactionary, and oppressive regime.[67] Hardly an "indefensible war," as Gitlin—still ensnared by false memories and false consciousness—describes it, America's involvement in Vietnam reflected honorable objectives. America's failure to win the war—a failure abetted by Gitlin and the Left—was a tragedy for the *Vietnamese*.

This is clear from the testimony of Colonel Bui Tin, a leader of the Communists' "liberation" campaign (and an architect of the Ho Chi Minh Trail), who wrote in 1995, "Nowadays the aspiration of the vast majority of the Vietnamese people, both at home and abroad, is to see an early end to the politically conservative, despotic, and authoritarian regime in Hanoi so that we can truly have a democratic government of the people, by the people, for the people."[68]

In understanding the mind of the anti-American Left, it is interesting to note how once the United States was defeated in the war, the Vietnamese, whom leftists had claimed to love with all the passion they denied their own country, disappeared from their consciousness and also their consciences. When America withdrew from Indochina, tens of thousands of innocent South Vietnamese and millions of Cambodians were murdered by the Communists. The Communist victors reduced the nations they had conquered to impoverished gulags. But these sufferings of the people of Cambodia and Vietnam evoked no response from activists who had once made them the center of their political concerns. The difference was that their oppressors were Communists, not the United States. Today, the aspirations of the Vietnamese themselves are as invisible to American radicals as are the testimonies of the Iraqis freshly liberated from the prisons and torture chambers of Saddam Hussein.

In short, Gitlin's fixation on Vietnam as the symbol of an American essence—and of this essence as evil—is unrelated to any factual reality. It is merely an inverted expression of the utopian idea.

Vietnam was a metaphor for American evil that was required by the radical worldview.[69] It did not create it.

Gitlin is also less than candid in ascribing his own antipatriotic feelings to America's role in the Vietnam War. According to his account, these feelings lasted for more than thirty years, until 9/11. By the same account, his patriotic fervor—if it can be called that—was quite short-lived. A "few weeks" after 9/11, he took down his American flag, because "leaving the flag up was too easy, too easily misunderstood as a triumphalist cliché. It didn't express my patriotic sentiment, which was turning toward political opposition."[70] Patriotism by this tormented logic is associated with opposing one's country rather than supporting it. In other words, precisely the definition of Paul Robeson and Eric Foner.

Gitlin's opposition hardened as the president declared war on America's al Qaeda attackers and identified three states—Iran, North Korea, and Iraq—as an "axis of evil." In Gitlin's words, "By the time George W. Bush declared war without end against an 'axis of evil' that no other nation on earth was willing to recognize as such—indeed, against whomever the president might determine we were at war against. . . . and declared further the unproblematic virtue of pre-emptive attacks, and made it clear that the United States regarded itself as a one-nation tribunal of 'regime change,' I felt again the old estrangement, the old shame and anger at being attached to a nation—*my* nation—ruled by runaway bullies, indifferent to principle, their lives manifesting supreme loyalty to private (though government slathered) interests, quick to lecture dissenters about the merits of patriotism."[71]

Ignoring the particular (and particularly hysterical) claims in this indictment, the statement provokes a question that Gitlin himself has raised but fails to answer: In what way could these particular faults be ascribed not to "wrong-headed policies," but to "some fundamental core of wrongness" in America's constitution? Put another way, why does the fact of Gitlin's turn "toward political opposition" preclude a continued display of the flag—which is to say, an embrace of his nation—particularly when that nation is a democracy that protects opposition and embraces dissent, and is under attack?

Gitlin seems to have learned very little from his brief identification with his country at war. It is certainly possible to love one's country and identify with it even when one regards an individual policy or a series of policies or an entire political administration to be wrong. That is what a democracy is about. The war against terror or the war in Iraq could easily be criticized on many grounds that would be recognized as patriotic and that should not result in alienation from one's flag, or cause one to experience "shame and anger at being attached to a nation."

Perhaps the Iraq war was the wrong war fought at the wrong time. Perhaps the policies pursued were counterproductive and, far from strengthening national security, incurred more risks. Since the policies in question—the decision to go to war and the decision to pursue regime change were ratified by both political parties, they were not the whims of "runaway bullies" and could be changed by pursuing a different electoral result. Gitlin's rejection is much deeper than these considerations and can only have been inspired by hostile assumptions about America itself.

Which is precisely the case. In describing his hatred for America as a sixties radical, Gitlin recalls encounters he had with Communists in Cuba. "Those of us who met with Vietnamese and Cuban Communists in those years were always being told that we had to learn to love our people. In my case, it was a Communist medical student in Cuba who delivered the message in 1967. Love our people! How were we supposed to do that, another SDSer and

I argued back, when our people had committed genocide against the Indians, when the national history was enmeshed in slavery, when this experience of historical original sin ran deeper than any class solidarity, when it was what it meant to *be* an American."

This litany—all too typical for American radicals—is an expression of Gitlin's antipathy for his country rather than a reasonable parsing of observable facts. It is based on a utopian standard with no anchor in any actually existing historical reality. The displacement of America's original inhabitants is a historical tragedy and included many crimes. But there was no such genocide (in any meaningful sense of the word) against the Indians, many of whom fought on the side of the settlers in the frontier wars and more of whom are alive today than were alive when the first Europeans set foot on the continent; moreover, these "exterminated" people now live on vast areas of land that were set up for them and are financially supported by the United States (albeit inadequately), a country in which they also enjoy full citizenship rights.

One may regret the past that led to these events or think more could be done in the present, but to regard America as a genocidal nation because of them is sheer prejudice. There is no nation on earth that was not created through some original aggression. Why should America, which has been more generous to its conquered than other nations, be singled out for such condemnation? The same can be said with regard to Gitlin's rhetorical flourish about the institution of slavery. Historically, America was a more important force in ending slavery than it was in participating in an institution that was embraced by all European, African, Latin American, and Islamic states. The historical record refutes Gitlin's claim that these injustices are somehow the American essence or that they make this country less worthy than, say, Cuba, which, in fact, imported more African slaves than all of England's North American colonies or the United States.[72]

As if to demonstrate the continuity (and rigidity) of his radical views, nearly four decades after his trip to Cuba, Gitlin summarizes the case against a patriotic attachment to America in these terms: "Worst of all, from this point of view, patriotism means obscuring the whole grisly truth of America under a polyurethane mask. It means covering over the Indians in their mass graves.[73] It means covering over slavery. It means overlooking America's many imperial adventures—the Philippine, Cuban, and Nicaraguan occupations, among others, as well as abuses of power by corporations, international banks, and so on. It means disguising American privilege, even when America's good fortune was not directly purchased at the cost of the bad fortune of others, a debatable point. So from this point of view, patriotism betrays the truth."

One could hardly ask for a more typical expression of the utopian view. Is there an actually existing nation that has had *no* war of conquest in its past, embarked on no imperial adventures, experienced no abuses committed by its private institutions, enjoyed no privileged status of one kind or another, and received no good fortune at some other people's expense? There is no such country.

On what grounds, therefore, would this litany persuade one to renounce his native land? Insofar as these claims are justified, they reflect human problems, not particularly American ones. Gitlin's rejection of America can be explained only by the utopian illusions of a worldview that has no anchor in any human reality and whose complaints, therefore, can never be assuaged or redressed.

This contemporary leftist critique and the political alienation it promotes are identical in nature to those of its Communist predecessor, a continuity captured in the designation of both radical generations (by their activists) as "progressive." The term "progressive" aptly describes their common striving toward an unattainable future, whose sole practical effect is to provide a measure by which the present can be condemned.

10

Neo-Communism IV: The Nihilist Left

Noam Chomsky is a cult figure among contemporary radicals and their leading intellectual figure. A *New Yorker* profile has identified him improbably as "one of the greatest minds of the twentieth century," while the left-wing English *Guardian* refers to him as the "conscience of a nation."[74] No individual has done more to shape the anti-American passions of a generation. When Chomsky speaks on university campuses, which he does frequently, he draws ten times the audiences that other intellectuals and legitimate scholars normally do. Abroad he has attracted individual audiences as large as ten thousand. According to the academic indexes that establish such rankings, Chomsky is one of the ten most quoted sources in the humanities, ranking just behind Plato and Freud. His most recent tract on the events of 9/11 sold two hundred thousand copies in America alone, despite the fact that it is not really a book but a series of rambling interviews of pamphlet length.[75] Of the hundred odd "books" on current affairs subjects he has published, all but a handful amount to similar collections of table talk, a further indication of the cultlike nature of his influence.

Chomsky claims to be an anarchist, which frees him from the burden of having to defend any real-world implementation of his ideas. In fact, he does not take his "anarchist" ideas very seriously, either as a program or an intellectual doctrine. His comments on the subject in a political career spanning nearly half a century amount to mere fragments—an article here, an isolated passage there. Moreover, his commitment to anarchist principles, which would presumably entail the rejection of all forms of social hierarchy and coercion, is highly selective. He is more than willing to support "centralized state power" when it is mobilized against private businesses,[76] and defends Marxist dictatorships in Nicaragua, Cuba, Vietnam, and other Third World countries—like Iraq—when they are engaged in conflicts with the United States. Even considered strictly as ideas, Chomsky's anarchist thoughts, if they can be dignified as such, are at base authoritarian and therefore incoherent.[77] The utility of Chomsky's anarchism is to provide an impossibly perfect model of freedom by which to judge the democracies of Western societies as "fascistic" and "oppressive."

The destructive antipathy of radicals like Chomsky toward the existing social order in the West is, as noted, a form of political nihilism. Revolution is a two-sided enterprise. In order to create the revolutionary future, it is necessary first to mobilize massive hatred against the existing world in order to destroy it. Political nihilism is the half of the revolutionary project that has remained intact after the collapse of the Soviet bloc. If no practical model of the revolutionary future exists—and none is possible—then revolution *is* destruction and nothing else.

Nihilism is manifest even in Chomsky's prose style. "To read Chomsky's recent political writing at any length is to feel almost physically damaged," observes *New Yorker* reporter, Larissa Mac-Farquhar. "The effect is difficult to convey in a quotation because it is cumulative. The writing is a catalogue of crimes committed by America, terrible crimes, and many of them; but it is not they that produce the sensation of blows: it is Chomsky's rage as he describes them. His sentences slice and gash, envenomed by a vicious sarcasm.... He uses certain words over and over, atrocity, murder, genocide, massacre, murder, massacre, genocide, atrocity, atrocity, massacre, murder, genocide.... Chomsky's sarcasm is the scowl of a fallen world, the sneer of Hell's veteran to its appalled *naifs*."[78] It is, in fact, a form of literary fascism, attempting to bludgeon the reader into acceptance.

Larissa MacFarquhar's *New Yorker* profile made its appearance just after the successful liberation of Baghdad, and began with three characteristic Chomsky observations. These capture a worldview that is not interested in criticizing particular policies that Americans may have pursued, but in alleging atrocities of such magnitude that America will be condemned in its essence:

> When I look at the arguments for this war, I don't see anything I could even laugh at. You don't undertake violence on the grounds that maybe by some miracle something good will come out of it. Yes sometimes violence does lead to good things. The Japanese bombing of Pearl Harbor led to many very good things.[79]

These comments are noteworthy both for their malice toward America and their misrepresentation of historical events. The interview was conducted before the war, which was concluded in a few weeks, perhaps the swiftest and most bloodless conquest on record. Obviously the military planners of Operation Iraqi Liberation did not count on a "miracle" to achieve a positive result but had reasonable expectations that their objective was both practical and worthwhile.

Any reasonable observer of American policymakers would have assumed this before the war began. The very absurdity of Chomsky's claim underscores the irrational nature of his attack.

The second half of Chomsky's statement is even more perverse, if possible. There are innumerable cases Chomsky might have offered as examples of justifiable violence. The sneak attack on Pearl Harbor is not one of them. Even the Japanese concede that. This makes his point appear preposterous, which is a calculated Chomsky effect. It is his way of setting up an equally typical Chomsky "revelation" for the naifs in hell. Chomsky's choice of Pearl Harbor as an act of noble violence is his attempt to refute the argument for the war on terror in its very core.

Pearl Harbor, as Chomsky is well aware, has been invoked as a historical analogue for 9/11. By using the same parallel, Chomsky intends to reverse the meaning of both events. Like 9/11, Pearl Harbor is an event symbolizing America's shattered innocence and its determination to respond to a malevolent aggressor. Praising the act of infamy is Chomsky's way of assaulting America's will to defend itself. In reversing the meaning of both events, Chomsky expresses the loathing he feels for his own country and provides the Left with a rationale for opposing America's self-defense.

Chomsky's view of Pearl Harbor echoes not only his view of 9/11 but also Osama bin Laden's. Bin Laden claimed that 9/11 was a response to America's "invasion" of the holy lands of Islam. Thus Chomsky explains how Pearl Harbor led to good things: "If you follow the trail, [Pearl Harbor] led to kicking Europeans out of Asia— that saved tens of millions of lives in India alone. Do we celebrate that every year?"

In point of historical fact, Pearl Harbor led to the eventual expulsion of the Japanese empire from Asia, where its brutal rule left behind a trail of atrocities in China, Korea, Malaya, and elsewhere.

But acknowledging these realities would undermine Chomsky's case. His reference to tens of millions of Indian lives saved by independence (which had nothing to do with Pearl Harbor or its effects) is another Chomsky fiction that stands history on its head. One of the recognized achievements of British rule in India was to establish internal peace in place of the intercommunal violence that existed previously and that has recurred ever since. Whatever else may be said of British rule, it *saved* Indian lives that would otherwise have been lost to this violence, a fact epitomized in the communal slaughter that was initiated in the precise moment the British departed. A million Indians were killed in the civil strife that broke out between Hindus and Muslims on the eve of independence, leading to the partition of the country and the creation of a Muslim state in Pakistan.

It is difficult to know if Chomsky believes his own lies. In the very same *New Yorker* profile, Chomsky indicates—without acknowledging any irony or contradiction—that kicking Europeans out of Asia in his view actually led to very bad results. In a comment condemning the Bush family for inviting foreign dictators to Washington, Chomsky names several of the leaders of postwar Asia he despises: "[A gangster] they loved was [Indonesia's] General Suharto. Another they adored was Marcos of the Philippines. In every single one of these cases, the people now in Washington supported them right through their worst atrocities. Are these the people you would ask to bring freedom to Iraqis?" Marcos was actually ousted by the United States. Deputy Secretary of Defense Paul Wolfowitz, one of the planners of Operation Iraqi Freedom, was one of the architects of the new democracy in the Philippines created following Marcos's exit.

Chomsky's twisted history reflects the core belief of anti-American radicals that the United States can do no right. Assailing the victims of Pearl Harbor, for example, is only a small part of Chomsky's distorted account of World War II. To establish a credible picture of American perfidy, he must deny the United States's role in the Allied victory over a global evil. Thus the *New Yorker* profile reports the following Chomsky comment to a college audience: "The United States and Britain fought the war, of course, but not primarily against Nazi Germany. The war against Nazi Germany was fought by the Russians. The German military forces were overwhelmingly on the Eastern Front."

As usual, Chomsky's claim relies on glaring omissions and distortions. To say that larger German military forces were committed on the Eastern front of World War II is correct; to say that "the war against Nazi Germany was fought by the Russians" is absurd. Without massive support from the United States it is doubtful that Russia would have survived at all. The fact that the United States defeated Germany's Axis partners—Italy and Japan—and that Britain vanquished Hitler's African legions was hardly incidental to the Allied victory. And to ignore the fact of the Normandy invasion, the defeat of Hitler's European armies, and the liberation of three-quarters of the German homeland by American arms is grossly dishonest.

Disturbed by the perverse implications of Chomsky's argument, a student in his college audience, objected, "But the world was better off [for America's actions]." Even this was a concession Chomsky was not willing to make. Instead he responded by blaming the Allies for Hitler's victims: "First of all, you have to ask yourself whether the best way of getting rid of Hitler was to kill tens of millions of Russians. Maybe a better way was not supporting him in the first place, as Britain and the United States did." In fact, Britain and the United States did not. American isolationism and British appeasement in the 1930s paled in comparison with the Stalin-Hitler

Pact, which actually launched the war in Poland and was obviously a more instrumental form of "supporting" Hitler than either.

But Chomsky is not content to merely insinuate that Britain and America were Hitler's sponsors and allies. He must make them responsible for the Holocaust as well. "By Stalingrad in 1942, the Russians had turned back the German offensive, and it was pretty clear that Germany wasn't going to win the war. Well, we've learned from the Russian archives that Britain and the U.S. then began supporting armies established by Hitler to hold back the Russian advance. Tens of thousands of Russian troops were killed. Suppose you're sitting in Auschwitz. Do you want the Russian troops to be held back?"

There is no evidence to support Chomsky's claim that America and Britain supported armies established by Hitler to hold back the Russian advance. Some academics puzzled by the bizarre nature of Chomsky's accusation have suggested that he was alluding to Stephan Bandera's Ukrainian nationalists, who had every reason to detest both Hitler and Stalin.[80] But there is no evidence to support Chomsky's contention of allied support for Bandera or any anti-Soviet military forces until 1948, which was during the Cold War and three years after the liberation of Auschwitz. Even the historical premise of Chomsky's claims is a falsification. However important Stalingrad was as a military victory, it was hardly equivalent to winning the war and no one but Chomsky thinks it was—not even the Russians who begged the Allies to open a "second front" to save them from defeat.

These are not mere intellectual lapses for Chomsky but keys to a worldview that is shaped by one overriding imperative—to demonize America as the fount of worldly evil. This agenda entails a revision of history even more ambitious than that of Holocaust deniers, with whom Chomsky has had an unsavory relationship.[81] In a little volume called *What Uncle Sam Really Wants* that has sold over 160,000 copies, Chomsky claims that in postwar Greece—the first battleground of the Cold War—"the United States was picking up where the Nazis had left off."[82] According to Chomsky, America's operations behind the Iron Curtain included "a 'secret army' under U.S.-Nazi auspices that sought to provide agents and military supplies to armies that had been established by Hitler and which were still operating inside the Soviet Union and Eastern Europe through the early 1950s."[83] According to Chomsky, in Latin America during the Cold War, U.S. support for legitimate governments against Communist subversion led to U.S. complicity under John F. Kennedy and Lyndon Johnson, in "the methods of Heinrich Himmler's extermination squads."[84]

Like other Chomsky charges, these claims depend on wildly distorted versions of the facts and in isolating the events from their historical context. Their purpose is not to understand the history in question but to portray America as the satanic principle in a Manichaean world—the Hitler Germany of our times. Chomsky's influence can be detected in the prevalence of this theme among anti-war protesters after 9/11 and during the conflict in Iraq.

Chomsky proffered his view of the 9/11 terrorist attacks the day after they occurred, elaborating it again a few days later. According to Chomsky, although the attacks were counterproductive from a public relations standpoint, they were actually—like Pearl Harbor—a good thing.[85] From a historical perspective, they represented a turning point in the war against American imperialism. "For the first time, the guns have been directed the other way. That is a dramatic change."

As Chomsky observed, 9/11 was the first time the "national territory" had been attacked since the War of 1812. In those years, "the U.S. annihilated the indigenous population (millions of people), conquered half of Mexico, intervened violently in the surrounding region, conquered Hawaii and the Philippines (killing hundreds of thousands of Filipinos), and in the past half century, particularly, extended its resort to force throughout much of the world. The number of victims is colossal."[86]

Anyone accepting Chomsky's words at face value could almost feel the justice of al Qaeda's malignant death package, delivered without warning to the thousands of innocents in the World Trade Center. But this, of course, was their purpose. The premise of Chomsky's argument is that whatever evil is committed against America by others pales in comparison to the evil that America has committed against them. America is the "Great Satan," the power responsible for the oppressions and injustices of the modern world.

But Chomsky's diatribe is no academic exercise. Its purpose is to incite believers to provide aid and comfort to the enemies of the United States. In the same post-9/11 talk Chomsky declared, "The people of the Third World need our sympathetic understanding and, much more than that, they need our help. We can provide them with a margin of survival by internal disruption in the United States. Whether they can succeed against the kind of brutality we impose on them depends in large part on what happens here."

Chomsky revealed just how seriously he meant these words when America finally launched its military response to the 9/11 attacks. On October 18, eleven days after U.S. forces began strikes against the Taliban, Chomsky told an audience at MIT that America was the "greatest terrorist state" and was planning a "silent genocide" against the people of Afghanistan. "Looks like what's happening [in Afghanistan] is some sort of silent genocide" is what Chomsky said.[87] His speech at MIT to two thousand listeners was viewed and heard by millions via Chomsky's impressive media network, the Internet, and a C-SPAN broadcast of the address. His remarks were published as a new Chomsky broadside in pamphlet form.

According to Chomsky, not only was America planning genocide in Afghanistan, but America's cultural elite knew it. And because the targets were Third World people, these privileged Americans were unconcerned. "It also gives a good deal of insight into the elite culture, the culture we are part of. It indicates that whatever, what will happen we don't know, but plans are being made and programs implemented on the assumption that they may lead to the death of several million people in the next few months very casually with no comment, no particular thought about it, that's just kind of normal, here and in a good part of Europe."

As usual, Chomsky's malignant charge was based on a small foundation of fact, a large area of uncertainty (since the future cannot be known), and a readiness to make the most far-fetched assumptions about American motives. It was indeed the case that in Afghanistan the food situation was dire, and that prior to America's intervention a famine was predicted for millions if no help was forthcoming from the West.

But thanks to the determination of the American government, help was already on the way, and the famine was soon averted as a direct result of the massive food transports provided by the American military. This rescue mission was, in fact, already part of the publicly announced White House war plan when Chomsky delivered his address. There was no comment—press or otherwise—on the planned genocide not because of the immoral indifference of Americans and Europeans, as Chomsky suggested, but because there was no factual basis for Chomsky's allegation. As Laura Rozen reported in the online magazine *Salon.com* on November 17, 2001, "Aid experts say that . . . alarms about the impact of the U.S. military campaign against the Taliban have ignored the fact that more food has been reaching Afghanistan since the U.S. bombing began than was before—a lot more."[88]

Given the military uncertainties when the fighting was just getting under way, however, Chomsky's myth could still seem plausible to the uninformed. This was true in Cambridge where he made his initial false charges, and a month later in countries bordering Afghanistan, where he went to spread them to much larger Islamic audiences. He took his campaign of lies against his own country to Delhi and Islamabad, where he made headlines with claims that the United States was the world's "greatest terrorist state" and was planning to conduct one of the largest genocides in history on a neighboring Muslim population.

In Islamabad, the situation was particularly volatile. Pakistan was an unstable "democracy" armed with nuclear weapons and ruled by a military dictatorship whose security forces had set up the Taliban. While the international press discussed the problematic future of the Islamabad regime, and tens of thousands of pro-terrorist demonstrators filled the streets of the capital, the prestigious MIT professor made front-page news in the local press with attacks on his own country as a genocidal threat to Muslims.[89] It was Chomsky's personal effort to "turn the guns around."

11

Neo-Communism V: The Anti-American Cult

Noam Chomsky's demonic views and seditious actions would be of little interest—intellectual or otherwise—but for the fact that they have such wide support in academic circles, the popular culture, and communities abroad, where Chomsky's prominence is even greater than in his homeland.[90] Critics of the Chomsky phenomenon often fail to appreciate that this is not so much the cult of an individual—Chomsky is an impressively boring speaker and middling writer (when he even bothers to write the books he turns out). The Chomsky phenomenon is rather the expression of an *anti-American* cult, for whose primitive hatred Chomsky performs a ventriloquist function. Chomsky did not spring into being *de novo* but is the product of a left-wing culture that had already traveled far down the path of fanaticism and the conviction that a nation conceived in liberty and dedicated to the proposition that all men are created equal is really a Great Satan—an empire built on slavery and dedicated to oppression and imperial conquest.

The scope of this cult is indicated by the proliferation of lesser Chomskys who feed the hungers of movement activists for anti-American litanies and rationales. Most prominent among these is

Chomsky's intellectual twin, the popular historian Howard Zinn. Like Chomsky, Zinn has produced a corpus of work that is a cartoon version of American history in which the nation is pilloried as an evil empire. Zinn has even published a Chomsky-like tract of table talk on 9/11, blaming America and its alleged crimes in the Third World for the terrorist attack and characterizing the victim as a terrorist state.[91]

Less bitter than Chomsky, Zinn is an equally rambling speaker and a pedestrian writer who has attained a celebrity few of his intellectual betters can match. His signature book, *A People's History of the United States*, is a raggedly conceived Marxist caricature that begins with Columbus and ends with George Bush. It has sold over a million copies, greatly exceeding that of any comparable history text. Like Chomsky's rants, Zinn's book has been embedded by leftist academics in the collegiate and secondary schools curricula. The *New York Times Sunday Book Review* gave it this imprimatur: "Historians may well view it as a step toward a coherent new version of American history." The reviewer was Eric Foner.

Like Chomsky, Zinn's readership extends far into the popular culture as well. He was invoked as a "genius" by the lead character in the Academy Award–winning film *Good Will Hunting* (the film's cowriter and star Matt Damon grew up as a Zinn neighbor and enthusiast) and is an intellectual "guru" to movie and music celebrities. Both Chomsky and Zinn have been heavily promoted to rock music audiences by megabands Rage Against The Machine and Pearl Jam even while they are also icons of intellectual journals like the *Boston Review of Books*, which is edited by an MIT professor and Chomsky disciple.[92]

The political agenda of *A People's History of the United States* is already announced in its historical method. In an explanatory coda to his book Zinn explains to the reader that he has no interest in striving for objectivity, and that his intention is to view American history as a conspiracy of rich white men to oppress and exploit "the people."[93] The so-called "people" are Indians and other minorities, especially blacks ("There is not a country in world history in which racism has been more important, for so long a time, as the United States"[94]), women, and the industrial proletariat.

Zinn begins his narrative not with the settling of North America, or the creation of the United States as one might expect, but with a long chapter on Columbus's "genocide" against the native inhabitants, an event that even if it had happened as Zinn describes it—was an act committed by agents of the Spanish empire more than a century before the English settled North America and nearly three centuries before the creation of the United States, which is also geographically well removed from the scene of the crime. It is Zinn's unintended way of announcing the tendentiousness of his entire project, which is really not a "history" of the American people but an indictment of white people and the capitalist system.

The perspective on view in the nearly seven hundred pages of *A People's History* is a plodding Marxism supplemented by the preposterous idea that nation-states are merely a fiction, and only economic classes are "real" social actors:

> Class interest has always been obscured behind an all-encompassing veil called "the national interest." My own war experience [in World War II], and the history of all those military interventions in which the United States was engaged, made me skeptical when I heard people in high political office invoke "the national interest" or "national security" to justify their policies. It was with such justifications that Truman initiated a "police action" in Korea that killed several million people, that Johnson and Nixon carried out a war in Indochina in which perhaps 3 million died, that Reagan

invaded Grenada, Bush attacked Panama and then Iraq, and Clinton bombed Iraq again and again.[95]

This passage illustrates the continuity of left-wing myths in shaping the consciousness of radical generations. A Stalinist in his youth, Zinn retains into his seventies the same ideological blinders he wore as a young man. America's defense of South Korea against a Communist invasion from the North was not initiated by the United States, as the Communist propaganda machine maintained at the time. It was a response to the Communist aggression, initiated by Stalin himself, according to most recent historical accounts.[96]

The war and subsequent American support for the South Koreans resulted in their liberation from both poverty and dictatorship. South Korea was, in 1950, one of the poorest Third World countries, with a per capita income of $250, on a level with Cuba and South Vietnam. Fifty years of American protection, trade, and investment has made South Korea a First World industrial nation with a reasonably stable democracy. By contrast North Korea, which was the industrial heart of the Korean peninsula and which the American armies failed to liberate—thanks to Zinn's political allies at the time—is an impoverished totalitarian state that has starved more than a million of its inhabitants in the last decade, while its Communist dictator hoards scarce funds to build an arsenal of nuclear intercontinental ballistic missiles. The rest of Zinn's examples are equally tendentious and amount to little more than a rehash of Communist propaganda.

Not surprisingly, Zinn describes the founding of the American Republic—the world's most successful democratic experiment—as an exercise in tyrannical control of the many by the few for greed and profit. "The American Revolution . . . was a work of genius, and the Founding Fathers deserve the awed tribute they have received over the centuries. They created the most effective system of national control devised in modern times, and showed future generations of leaders the advantages of combining paternalism with command."[97] In Zinn's reckoning, the Declaration of Independence was not so much a revolutionary statement of rights as a cynical means of manipulating popular groups into overthrowing the King to benefit the rich. The rights it appeared to guarantee were "limited to life, liberty, and happiness for white males"—and actually for wealthy white males—because they excluded black slaves and "ignored the existing inequalities in property"[98] (in other words, they were not socialist). This is an absurd view of the Declaration and of the history of the Republic to which it gave birth, but it is the entrenched belief of the political Left, for whom Zinn is an icon and his tract canonical.

The attack on the American founding is crucial to the outlook shared by Zinn, Chomsky, and the entire spectrum of the Left that has declared its separate war on America. It is central to understanding the Left's animus and the fact that no particular event— least of all a foreign policy event like the war in Iraq—is required to generate the kind of self-hatred evidenced during the Iraq protests. There is nothing original in Zinn's book, nor has he engaged in any serious research other than to connect the dots of Communist clichés.

A People's History of the United States reflects a left-wing culture that despises America in its very roots. As a result of the Left's colonization of the academic social sciences, this anti-American culture is now part of the educational curriculum of America's emerging elites, and as much an element of the cultural mainstream as any other historical tradition. Indeed, it is a dominant element. In 2004, the Organization of American Historians devoted an evening at its annual convention to honor Zinn and his work.

Todd Gitlin, former SDS leader and now professor of sociology and journalism at Columbia University, summed up the Left's academic triumph in these words: "My generation of the New Left—a generation that grew as the [Vietnam] war went on—relinquished any title to patriotism without much sense of loss. . . . The nation congealed into an empire, whose logic was unwarranted power. All that was left to the Left was to unearth righteous traditions and cultivate them in universities. The much-mocked 'political correctness' of the next academic generations was a consolation prize. We lost— we squandered—the politics, but won the textbooks."[99]

Entire fields—"Whiteness Studies," "Cultural Studies," "Women's Studies," "African American Studies," and "American Studies," to mention some—are now principally devoted to this radical assault on American history and society and to the "deconstruction" of the American idea. The study and teaching of American Communism at the university level is now principally in the hands of academics who "openly applaud and apologize for one of the bloodiest ideologies of human history."[100] Even the study of the law has been subverted by political ideologues with ferociously anti-American agendas. Consider the following passage from a legal text on the Fourteenth Amendment, the statute that establishes equal rights for all Americans. Written by a professor at Georgetown Law, one of the nation's most prestigious schools, the text proclaims, "The political history of the United States that culminated and is reflected in the [Constitution] is in large measure a history of almost unthinkable brutality toward slaves, genocidal hatred of Native Americans, racist devaluation of nonwhites and nonwhite cultures, sexist devaluation of women, and a less than admirable attitude of submissiveness to the authority of unworthy leaders in all spheres of government and public life."[101]

These views are replicated in whole libraries of texts written by the academic Left. They present an American reality shaped by the intellectual traditions of Communism and characterized by the crude economic determinism and historical distortion of writers like Chomsky and Zinn. It is hardly surprising, given the orthodoxies of American universities, that hundreds and perhaps even thousands of faculty-led anti-American demonstrations, justifying the attacks of 9/11 and denouncing America as "imperialist" and "racist," were held on campuses during the wars in Afghanistan and Iraq. From this point of view, observes Gitlin, who is himself scorned by the left, "the attacks of September 11, 2001 revealed a symmetry that the hard-bitten Left had long expected. America was condemned by its history. The furies were avenging, chickens were flying home, American detonations were blowing back." The Left had "little hard-headed curiosity to comprehend a fanatical Islamist sect that set no limits to what and whom it would destroy. Whoever was killed in America, Americans must still end up the greatest of Satans."[102]

As a "democratic socialist," Gitlin dissents from the most extreme views articulated by Chomsky, Zinn, and others, but nonetheless shares a disturbingly negative perspective on America's history and world role. "Read history with open eyes and it is hard to overlook the American empire.... You need not subscribe to the Left's grandest claims that America from its birth is essentially genocidal and indebted to slavery for much of its prosperity to acknowledge that white colonists took the land, traded in slaves, and profited immensely thereby; or that the United States later lorded it over Latin America (and other occasional properties, like the Philippines) to guarantee cheap resources and otherwise line American pockets; or that American-led corporations (among others) and financial agencies today systematically overlook or, worse, damage the freedom of others."[103]

This selective memory obscures the other side of the ledger and fundamentally distorts the impact of America's development and the meaning of its history. The glass is not half empty. America is also a nation that was a pioneer in ending slavery and has liberated hundreds of millions of people from totalitarian tyrannies. Its national narrative encompasses expanding spheres of tolerance and inclusion. Its war against terror is being led by a secretary of state and national security adviser who are African American and a postwar military command in Iraq led by an Arab American and a Hispanic American. Its corporate institutions have led the world in technological innovation and its economic order has lifted billions out of poverty, liberating them from unbearable social conditions. Yet the negative myths are constantly being regenerated by the political Left.

This can be illustrated in a postmortem analysis of the Iraq War that appeared in the *New York Review of Books*, written by the celebrated author Norman Mailer. Mailer is a veteran of the "progressive Left," having begun his political life as a prominent literary figure in the Communist-orchestrated Wallace campaign. The political agenda of this campaign was to oppose the Truman Doctrine, America's early Cold War effort to resist Stalin's conquest of Eastern Europe. The Wallace "peace candidacy" was, in fact, a prototype of all the postwar campaigns against America's efforts to resist totalitarian aggression. Twenty years later, Mailer was a leading literary figure in the anti-Vietnam movement of the 1960s, writing a highly praised book, *Armies of the Night*, that celebrated the famous "March on the Pentagon" in 1967—another left-wing campaign to support a totalitarian success.

The New York Review of Books is a magazine of the somewhat moderate Left. Its editors stopped publishing the writings of Noam Chomsky in the 1970s when Chomsky veered too far over the political edge by dismissing early reports of the Communist genocide in Cambodia[104] and defending a Holocaust denier in France.

Nonetheless, the *New York Review* editors were comfortable with Mailer's article, which was acidly titled "The White Man Unburdened,"[105] as though America's war in Iraq were an expression of racial imperialism—and worse.

In its accusatory title, as in its bill of specifics, Mailer's article was actually indistinguishable from the less artfully put-together screeds of Chomsky and Zinn. It illustrated the metaphysical dimension of the anti-American worldview, which enables its adherents to accumulate disinformation with every new event and continually construct demonic images of America's practices and purposes. The fact that on 9/11 America was the victim of an unprovoked attack by religious fanatics is no more discouraging to the anti-American hysterias of these critics than the fact that in April 2003 American forces liberated Iraq from one of the worst tyrannies of the modern world.

Three assumptions underlie the arguments of the anti-American cult: (1) America can do no right; (2) even the rights America appears to do are wrong; (3) these wrongs are monstrous. All of these articles of faith are manifest in Mailer's analysis in the *New York Review of Books*.

Approaching the question of Iraq, Mailer asks, "Why did we go to war?" and sets up his answer by confronting facts that seem to justify the war. Most prominent is the discovery of the mass graves of Saddam's victims. The uncovering of these graves, writes Mailer, appears to show that "we have relieved the world of a monster who killed untold numbers, mega-numbers of victims." But such appearances are mistaken, since (according to Mailer) it is we who are responsible for the corpses:

Nowhere is any emphasis put upon the fact that many of the bodies were of the Shiites of southern Iraq who have been decimated repeatedly in the last twelve years for daring to rebel against Saddam in the immediate aftermath of the Gulf War [of 1991]. Of course, we were the ones who encouraged them to revolt in the first place, and then failed to help them.

Having shifted the blame for Saddam's slaughter to America, Mailer explains why Washington failed to help Iraq's Shi'ites in a way that compounds its culpability. A successful Shi'ite rebellion, he writes, "could result in a host of Iraqi imams who might make common cause with the Iranian ayatollahs. Shiites joining with Shiites!" Racists and imperialists, of course, would want none of that. But this is a highly selective, not to say distorted, view of why America might have feared an alliance between Shi'ites in Iraq and Iran. The Iranian revolution of 1979 spawned a revival of radical Islam and began with the seizing of the American embassy by Iranian revolutionaries a million strong chanting, "Death to America." To support its hatred of America and the imperial ambitions of radical Islam, the Iranian regime developed long-range missiles and probably nuclear warheads to tip them with. It became sponsor and host to Hizbollah, the largest terrorist army in the world, which in 1983 blew up a U.S. marine barracks in Lebanon, killing 245 servicemen. If the Iraqi Shi'ites had overthrown the regime of Saddam Hussein in 1991 and forged a radical alliance with Iran, this would certainly have posed a threat to American interests that had nothing to do with racist paranoia.

There was another consideration behind America's decision not to overthrow Saddam in 1991. The Bush administration did not want to proceed without U.N. authorization or without authorization from its Arab coalition partners (who were unanimously opposed to toppling Saddam). It may be argued that the first Bush should have ignored these considerations and proceeded unilaterally, but not by someone like Norman Mailer who opposed the second Bush's war in Iraq on exactly those grounds.

In his analysis Mailer also forgets the opposition of the Democratic majority in Congress to the Gulf War, and thus to any regime change in Iraq. Although the first Bush formed the Gulf War coalition in faultless multilateral fashion, his war policy was still opposed by the majority of Democratic legislators and he was barely able to secure the congressional authorization required to reverse Iraq's conquest of Kuwait. Although he assembled an international coalition of forty nations, only ten Democratic senators finally voted to authorize the use of force—even for the limited goal of liberating Kuwait. Moreover, three of those senators, Al Gore among them, did so reluctantly and at the last minute. In other words, Norman Mailer and the political Left he represents were opposed to the very war that he now complains did not go far enough and lead to the removal of Saddam.

What is Mailer's own accountability—or the accountability of those who share his politics—for positions that led to Saddam's massacre of the Iraqi Shi'ites? He concedes none. The ironies of his past oppositions don't even occur to him. This is because his intent is not to understand the war but to make America—the Great Satan—responsible for Saddam Hussein's killing fields: "Today [the Shi'ites] . . . may look upon the graves that we congratulate ourselves for having liberated as sepulchral voices calling out from their tombs—asking us to take a share of the blame. Which of course we will not." In other words, in addition to being mass murderers, we are hypocrites too.

"Yes, our guilt for a great part of those bodies remains a large subtext and Saddam was creating mass graves all through the 1970s and 1980s. He killed Communists *en masse* in the 1970s, which didn't bother us a bit." This Mailer accusation is not only tendentious, it is downright puzzling. What other nation, it could be asked, would be held accountable for not rescuing its own enemies? The events Mailer is referring to were a series of power struggles between Fascists and Communists who both wanted Americans dead and America destroyed. What is Mailer suggesting with his accusations? That America should have intervened in a Soviet sphere of influence and risked nuclear war to rescue the foot soldiers of the Communist bloc?

Mailer next accuses America of "supporting" Saddam in his war with Iran in the 1980s, a common charge of the anti-war Left. But this is to confuse realpolitik with affection. " [Saddam] slaughtered tens of thousands of Iraqis during the war with Iran—a time when we supported him." The latter verb is a deception. "Support" implies approval. What we actually did was to tilt to Saddam's side—supplying him with weapons—when it looked as if he would be defeated by the fanatical, anti-American Shi'ite regime in Iran. We did not want to see a totalitarian Iran with three times the population of Iraq dominating the Middle East. If Iran had prevailed in the war, the ayatollahs would have come into control of the majority of the world's oil reserves and the empire of radical Islam. With its terrorist armies operating in Europe and elsewhere, Iran would have become a global force. To prevent this by aiding Saddam was realism, not "support."

The military equipment America supplied to Iraq in the war was designed to balance the arms Iran received from the Soviet empire, still a going concern at the time. The Soviets also would have benefited handsomely from an Iranian victory. What would Mailer have had American planners do? If they had failed to take any action at all, Mailer would have blamed America for the deaths Iran inflicted in Iraq, and for the disastrous consequences that would ensue from its victory. Instead, American arms contributed to a military stalemate and a peace that saved hundreds of thousands of lives. But these are things Mailer chooses to ignore.

When it comes to adding up the balance sheet of America's efforts in Iraq, Mailer does it with steely disdain: "A horde of those newly discovered [Shiite] graves go back to that period [of the Iran-Iraq war]. Of course, real killers never look back." Real killers. In other words, Americans. America can do no right. Even the right America does is wrong, and the wrongs America is responsible for are monstrous. This syllogism encompasses the entire logic of the anti-American mind.

12

Neo-Communism VI: The Great Satan

A crucial element in the worldview of American radicals is the belief in American omnipotence—the ability of America's leaders to control the circumstances of their international policies without regard to the interests of allies or the threats of adversary powers or the constraints imposed by domestic political forces. Radicals never see America as reacting to a threat that cannot either be subdued or ignored, or to a set of circumstances in which it cannot determine the outcome. A typical expression of this assumption is a statement made by James Weinstein in his recent book *The Long Detour*, about the reemergence of the American Left. A Communist in the 1940s, and the founder of the New Left in the 1960s, and of the socialist newspaper *In These Times*, he advocates that socialists should work within the Democratic Party to achieve their ends. In Weinstein's book, which was published two years after 9/11, he writes, "The realistic military threat to the United States from any other nation, of course, is near zero."[106]

A corollary of the view that America is the master of world events is the idea that America has no worthy enemies, only rebellious subjects. America's perceived adversaries are actually only reacting to America's own aggressions. In an interview on March 31, 2003, as the U.S. military entered Iraq, Noam Chomsky put a rhetorical question to himself, "Has Saddam ever posed a threat to the U.S.?" and answered it: "The idea verges on absurdity."[107] Three months before the Iraq war, Daniel Ellsberg, leaker of the Pentagon Papers on Vietnam and a protester against the impending conflict, had been asked, "What threat does Iraq now pose or could pose in the future to essential U.S. objectives in the Middle East or globally?" Ellsberg's answer: "No threat at all, so long as Saddam is not faced with overthrow or death by attack or invasion."[108] In other words, Iraq posed no dangers to American security that America itself did not provoke. This is the perfectly circular and self-validating logic of the anti-American cause.

Even a backward and impoverished nation like Afghanistan under the Taliban had shown it could pose a serious threat to American security through its support of terrorists. Estimates of the economic damage caused by 9/11 range as high as $600 billion; whole industries—airlines and travel in particular—were threatened with bankruptcy. If 9/11 had been followed by similar terrorist attacks in the United States and Europe, the possibility of global economic instability with attendant civil and political disruption was a real and daunting prospect.

The assumption of America's omnipotence, unanchored in fact, is a function of the religious element in the radical worldview. It is as evident in the Left's understanding of the Cold War with the Soviet bloc as it is in the war with Iraq. A favored reference of activists opposed to the Iraq war is the book *Rogue State* by William Blum, a former State Department employee and a featured speaker at university "teach-ins" against the War on Terror after 9/11.

The "rogue state" in Blum's title, as in his campus presentations, is the United States. The book itself is subtitled "A Guide to the

World's Only Superpower," and comes with encomiums from authors as disparate as Gore Vidal and Noam Chomsky on the one hand, and Thomas Powers and former *New York Times* bureau chief A. J. Langguth on the other. This is the way Blum opens his text: "This book could be entitled *Serial Chainsaw Baby Killers and the Women Who Love Them.*"[109] In the author's view the chainsaw baby-killers are American officials and their agents, and the women who love them are supporters of American foreign policy.

In partial fairness to Powers and Langguth, their praise for Blum was based on a volume published prior to *Rogue State* called *Killing Hope: U.S. Military and CIA Interventions Since World War II.* But while the tone of this book is more dispassionate, the irrational animus toward the United States remains the same in both. Blum begins his introduction to the 1995 edition of *Killing Hope* with these words: "In 1993, I came across a review of a book about people who deny that the Nazi Holocaust actually occurred. I wrote to the author, a university professor, telling her that her book made me wonder whether she knew that an American holocaust had taken place, and that the denial of it put the denial of the Nazi one to shame.... Yet, a few million people have died in the American holocaust and many more millions have been condemned to lives of misery and torture as a result of U.S. interventions extending from China and Greece in the 1940s to Afghanistan and Iraq in the 1990s."[110] In other words, America is worse than Nazi Germany.

From its opening image, *Rogue State* proceeds to dismiss the idea that the Cold War was a conflict between nuclear superpowers or a contest between totalitarianism and freedom. Instead *Rogue State* presents the Cold War as the concoction of a single omnipotent power—a power whose ends are predatory and evil—able to manipulate events in order to establish its global rule:

For 79 years the United States convinced much of the world that there was an international conspiracy out there. An *International Communist Conspiracy* [italics in original] seeking no less than control over the entire planet for purposes which had no socially redeeming values. And the world was made to believe that it somehow needed the United States to save it from communist darkness. "Just buy our weapons," said Washington, "let our military and our corporations roam freely across your land, and give us veto power over whom [sic] your leaders will be, and we'll protect you."[111]

There is no discernible difference between this view of America's role in the Cold War and the crudest Communist caricature manufactured in the Kremlin at its height; between the Stalinism of a Herbert Aptheker and the "anarchism" of a Noam Chomsky, the "progressivism" of a Howard Zinn, or the views expressed on scores of Internet websites like Indymedia.org, commondreams.org, counter-punch.org, and zmag.org, which serve as the organizing venues of the "anti-war" Left.[112] When it comes to the perception of American policy and its purposes, these views are substantively the same: American policy and purpose are controlled by a corporate ruling class whose guiding interest is profit and plunder. External enemies are "mythical"; they serve merely as a smokescreen for suppressing revolts against the empire. Thus, in *What Uncle Sam Really Wants*, Chomsky writes, "[After World War II] U.S. planners recognized that the 'threat' in Europe was not Soviet aggression . . . but rather the worker- and peasant-based antifascist resistance with its radical democratic ideals, and the political power and appeal of the local Communist parties."[113]

Chomsky's allusion to resistance movements is to those of France and Greece, which were dominated by Communists. Their "radical democratic ideas" were to establish Soviet satellites and totalitarian states. The views of Chomsky, Zinn, and Blum, which accurately reflect the political culture of the organizers of the movement against the war in Iraq,[114] reprise the Stalinist propaganda during the Cold War and are based on long-discredited Marxist analyses of the democratic West. These views demonize America as a satanic force in the modern world, the linchpin of a global order of hierarchy and privilege that is responsible for the misery of the world's impoverished masses.

As long as America continues to maintain the will and ability to protect what radicals regard as the global order of "social injustice," all reforms and social advances within the existing structures of American democracy will be illusory. This is the meaning of Nicholas De Genova's claim that all progressives should wish for the defeat of American power in Iraq and elsewhere, because America can have no place in a world that is at peace and just.

PART THREE:
UNHOLY ALLIANCE

*There is the beginning of a permanent global war to
cement the domination of the U.S. Government and its
allies. . . . Islam is being demonized, while racism and xenophobia are deliberately propagated. . . . Opposition to the
war is at the heart of our movement.*

—SOCIAL MOVEMENTS' MANIFESTO
WORLD SOCIAL FORUM, 2000

13

Islamic Revolution

The survival of a Neo-Communist Left explains the otherwise inexplicable alliances that self-described progressives have made with Arab fascists and Islamic fanatics in their war against America and the West. Except for the generally informal character of these alliances, there is nothing new in this updated version of the Nazi-Soviet entente. During the 1930s and after, Arab nationalism in Palestine, Syria, and Iraq modeled itself on Italian and German fascism. In the 1950s Arab nationalists forged military and diplomatic alliances with the Communist bloc and incorporated the Marxist indictments of the West in their own. In doing so, they became part of the international Communist coalition and eventually its post-Communist successor.

The accommodation of Islamic fundamentalists came later on. In its inception Islamic radicalism was hostile to Communism and to its Western sources, but in the 1950s it began assimilating ideological influences with anti-American and anti-Western agendas.[1] Sayyid Qutb, the author of a seminal text called *Social Justice in Islam,*[2] was the leading theoretician of the Egypt-based Muslim Brotherhood, founded by Hassan al-Banna in the 1920s, a forerunner of al Qaeda.³ The writings of Qutb have been described as the "main ideological influence" on the emerging radical Islamic movement, including its principal leaders, the Ayatollah Khomeini and Osama bin Laden, and its principal terrorist organizations— Hizbollah, Hamas, and al Qaeda.

The agenda of the Islamic radicals was to impose Islamic law— sharia—on the entire world as the necessary condition of its purifi- cation and redemption. In his writings, Qutb describes sharia as "a universal declaration of the freedom of man from servitude to other men and from servitude to his own desires, which is also a form of human servitude; it is a declaration that sovereignty belongs to God alone."⁴ The puritanical idea of humanity's need for liberation from its own desires differentiates Islamic radicalism only in part from the radicalisms of the West. Despite the libertine inclinations of some factions of the political Left, Western radicals' efforts to purify their tainted souls of "racism, sexism, and homophobia" reflect parallel inclinations. In any case, the moralistic fervor of Islamic fanatics has not proved an obstacle to collaboration. Both movements are total- itarian in their desire to extend the revolutionary law into the sphere of private life, and both are exacting in the justice they administer and the loyalty they demand.⁵

In an insightful essay exploring the incipient alliance between Western radicalism and Islamic jihad, the socialist author Paul Berman suggests that in Sayyid Qutb's writings about social justice he was inspired by the "Universal Declaration of Human Rights." Qutb stopped short, however, of incorporating the Marxist idea of class conflict into his doctrines. But a decade after Qutb's execution, Iran's Ayatollah Ruhollah Khomeini did take this step transforming Shi'ia Islam into a revolutionary force.

It was under the influence of the Paris-based Marxist translator of Frantz Fanon's *Wretched of the Earth* that Khomeini introduced into radical Islamic thought the pivotal Marxist concept of a world divided into oppressors and oppressed. To accomplish this, he employed the moral terms of Islam—*mostakbirine* (the "arrogant") and *mostadafine* (the "weakened").[6] In 1979 Khomeini overthrew the shah of Iran and instituted a radical Islamic state, launching the global Islamic movement and its anti-Western jihad in a single stroke. After Iranian students seized the American embassy, Khomeini introduced the terms "Great Satan" and "Little Satan" into the vocabulary of radical Islam to describe the United States and its Israeli ally, and aligned his revolution with the political left:

> Once in power, the onetime opponent of land reform and women's suffrage [Khomeini] became a 'progressivist,' launching a massive program of nationalization and expropriation and recruiting women for campaigns of revolutionary propaganda and mobilization. The Leninist characteristics of his rule—his policy of terror, his revolutionary tribunals and his militias, his administrative purges, his cultural revolution, and his accommodating attitude toward the U.S.S.R.... gained him the active support of the Moscow-aligned Iranian Communist Party.... [7]

The goals of radical jihad are purification and social justice, both of which are to be achieved through the institution of Islamic law in the states conquered by Islamic arms.[8] The tactic of suicidal terror viewed as a redemptive martyrdom fuses the political and religious dimensions of the cause. Since the religious goal can be achieved only through the conquest of worldly power, the holders of that power necessarily personify evil. As the world's only superpower—secular and liberal at that—the United States stands in the path of the revolution and earthly redemption. It is the Great Satan. This fact—not any particular act or crime the United States may be said to have committed—is the primary source of the anti-American fury of radical Islam.

By portraying his movement as a revolution of the oppressed, the cleric Khomeini was able to rally the support of the political Left in Iran and abroad. Consequently, at its inception the Islamo-fascist regime was supported by both the Iranian Communist Party and the international "progressive" Left. "In this way," observes Berman, "Islamism, treading a path that Ba'ath Socialism had already taken, acquired what Mussolini had pioneered long ago—the revolutionary mixture of extreme Left and extreme right."[9]

This mixture congealed in the perception of a common enemy. In 1948, the Egyptian Ministry of Education sent Sayyid Qutb on a study mission to the United States, which he came to regard as the embodiment of worldly decadence, the antithesis of the purified Islamic state clerical radicals like himself were seeking to achieve.[10] This view of America came to be shared by Islamic radicals generally. In the words of Middle East expert Bernard Lewis, "the sinfulness and also the degeneracy of America and its consequent threat to Islam and the Muslim peoples became articles of faith in Muslim fundamentalist circles."[11]

In *The Crisis of Islam*, Lewis summarizes the radical Islamic indictment of America and its sins in terms that are not dissimilar from Gitlin's, Chomsky's, and Zinn's:

> By now there is an almost standardized litany of American offenses recited in the lands of Islam, in the media, pamphlets, in sermons, and in public speeches.... The crime sheet goes back to the original settlement in North America, and what is described as the expropriation and extermination of the previous inhabitants and the sustained ill treatment of the

survivors among them.[12] It continues with the condemnation
of the enslavement, importation, and exploitation of blacks
(an especially inappropriate accusation, coming from this particular source[13]) and of immigrants in the United States. It
includes war crimes against Japan at Hiroshima and
Nagasaki, as well as in Korea, Vietnam, Somalia, and elsewhere. Noteworthy among these crimes of imperialist aggression are American actions in Lebanon, Khartoum, Libya,
Iraq, and of course helping Israel against the Palestinians.
More broadly, the charge sheet includes support for Middle
Eastern and other tyrants, such as the Shah of Iran and Haile
Selassie of Ethiopia . . . [14]

These indictments are easily embraced by Western leftists. Less
comprehensible is their support for the Islamic movements themselves, which represent so many values seemingly antithetic to their
progressive creeds. But as previously noted, the history of the Western left shows that these are not the insurmountable obstacles they
may seem. Radicalism is a cause whose utopian agendas result in an
ethic where the ends outweigh and ultimately justify any means.
Like the salvationist agendas of jihad, the Left's apocalyptic goal of
"social justice" is the equivalent of an earthly redemption. A planet
saved, a world without poverty, racism, inequality, or war—what
means would not be justified to achieve such millennial ends? By
way of contrast, less ambitious reform movements are able to weigh
gains against probable costs, and avoid the kind of excesses and
atrocities endemic to radical causes.

In his reflections in *Terror and Liberalism*, Paul Berman—himself a Second International socialist—draws attention to a crisis in
Western radical circles precipitated by the wave of suicide bombings
that characterized the second Palestinian intifada. These attacks

were launched after the Palestinian Authority rejected a peace agreement that would have granted their demands for a Palestinian state
and 97 percent of the land to which they had laid claim in the same
negotiations. These suicide bombings were acts of Islamic martyrdom in which the targets were innocent families, including women,
old people, and small children, and for which the perpetrators were
promised a heavenly reward and officially hailed by the Palestinian
authority as national heroes. Public opinion polls revealed that the
overwhelming majority of Palestinians supported the suicide bombings.[15]

According to Berman, the suicide bombings provoked a crisis
among secular radicals, "whose fundamental beliefs would not be
able to acknowledge the existence of pathological mass political
movements."[16] What Berman meant was that socialists and progressives whose outlook had been shaped by the rationalism of the
Enlightenment would not be able to grasp the pathological nature
of Palestinian and Islamic fascism,[17] but would rationalize it as the
product of "root causes." This had many precedents in Western radicalism, as for example in the evolution of Italian Fascism from its
Marxist antecedents (Mussolini had begun his political career as a
left-wing socialist), in the collaboration of German Communists
with the Nazis in overthrowing the Weimar democracy, and in the
subsequent failure of French socialists to appreciate the Nazi threat.

Berman was himself shocked by the 2002 meeting of the Socialist Scholars Conference, whose participants were his political comrades and at which he had been a featured speaker. "At the 2002
event," he recalled, "a substantial crowd listened to an Egyptian novelist defend a young Palestinian woman who had just committed
suicide and murder—and having heard the defense, the crowd broke
into applause."[18] Previously Berman had witnessed anti-globalization
marchers in Washington, D.C., stalwarts of the Left who were by

no means predominantly Muslims—chanting "Martyrs not murderers," as though the cold-blooded killing of innocent families
could conceivably be termed a religious act. These episodes, wrote
Berman, "typified a hundred other events all over the United States,
and even more in Europe, not to mention Latin America and other
places."[19]

Berman is mystified that progressive utopians could join such a
united front and embrace movements that were in their nature so
pathological. He attributes this to a naiveté endemic to the liberal
attitudes of nineteenth-century progressives—"an unyielding faith
in universal rationality,"[20] a belief that even people who blow themselves and little children up in the expectation of a place in heaven,
and seventy-two virgins besides, must ultimately be inspired by real-
world grievances.

But there is another dimension to this political empathy, created
by the common utopian expectations that underlie both: The Greek
scientist Archimedes said, "Give me a lever and a place to stand on
and I will move the world." This is an archetype of the radical outlook, both secular and religious, which believes it has identified an
institution and an agency that will move the world. The radical
Islamist believes that by conquering nations and instituting sharia,
he can redeem the world for Allah. The socialist's faith is in using
state power and violent means to eliminate private property and
thereby usher in the millennium.

Belief in this transformation is the reason the secular radical does
not take the religious pathology of radical Islam seriously. The secular radical believes that religion itself is merely an expression of
real-world misery, for which capitalist property is ultimately responsible. "Religious suffering," Marx famously wrote, "is at one and the
same time the expression of real suffering and a protest against real
suffering. Religion is the sigh of the oppressed creature, the heart of

a heartless world, and the soul of a soulless condition. It is the opium of the oppressed."[21] In other words, religious belief is a response to the suffering caused by private property, and a mask that obscures its practical causes. The revolution that removes the cause of this suffering will also remove the religious beliefs it inspires. Thus, the liberation of mankind from private property—the defeat of America and Western capitalism—will liberate Islamic fanatics from the need to be Islamic and fanatic.[22] This is the real source of the radical "naiveté" that Berman observed.

The problem presented in accommodating radical ideals to the realities of Islamic jihad is really no different from the problem faced by New Leftists in the 1960s when they accommodated their New Left radicalism to Communist movements and regimes. When the leaders of Soviet Communism acknowledged the crimes of the Soviet state and thus the totalitarian nature of the cause progressives had supported, the exposure did not prompt them to leave the radical faith. Instead, radicals proclaimed themselves "anti-anti-Communists" and thus on the same side of history the Communists had claimed as their own. In this way New Leftists were able to maintain their connection to Communist movements, focusing their attention on what they believed to be the more attractive proxies of the cause, the regimes in Cuba and Vietnam. Because Cuba and Vietnam belonged to the Third World, whose inhabitants were "of color," leftists could imagine their Communist rulers to be persecuted Davids, racially oppressed and struggling for self-determination against the white, rich Goliath of the north.

Such sentiments were accurately expressed in an article titled "One-and-a-Half (Strangled) Cheers for the USSR"[23] that appeared in 1980 after the Soviet invasion of Afghanistan. It was written by a noted New Left author, Andrew Kopkind, who put forward the same defense of the Soviet state as Eric Hobsbawm:

that whatever atrocities the Soviets had committed or miseries they had caused, the Soviet state was nonetheless a defender of revolutionary hopes and an obstacle to the predations of the democratic West.

"The real world as it has evolved since World War II is convulsed in a crisis of revolution and reaction," wrote Kopkind. "For reasons neither pure nor simple, the Soviet Union has almost invariably sided with the revolutionaries, the liberationists, the insurgents. The United States, with equal consistency, has supported the enemies of rebellion." To substantiate this claim, Kopkind provided a list of insurgencies that the Soviet Union had supported and the United States opposed. The list included Zimbabwe (where a Marxist revolution in fact produced the racist police state of dictator Robert Mugabe), Iran (where the insurgents were Islamic radicals who instituted the fascist theocracy of the Ayatollah Khomeini), and Ethiopia (where the so-called liberationists established the Stalinist *Derg* of Mengistu Haile Mariam, who instituted a "Red Terror" and precipitated a devastating famine), as well as Communist Cuba, North Vietnam, North Korea, and China—totalitarian tyrannies all. What these revolutions had in common that made them appealing to Kopkind and the Left (and has kept subsequent generations of that Left from being impressed by the damage they did) was that each took place in a Third World country, had a Marxist agenda, and was a self-declared enemy of the United States and the West.

In other words, the condition under which the Western Left could join an international coalition with Islamic jihadists was the existence of a "liberation" struggle backed by Islamic regimes (however brutal) that were opposed to some degree by the United States. This condition was met in the Arab war against Israel, which in the last decade of the twentieth century became the fusion point of western radicalism and Islamic jihad.

14

The Palestinian Fusion

While the elements necessary for an alliance between American and Islamic radicals were present to some degree at the outset of the Middle East conflict, it was a confluence of events occurring in the last quarter of the century that allowed them to reach critical mass. These events included Iran's Islamic revolution, the creation of an Islamic jihad in Afghanistan in 1979, and the subsequent transformation of the Palestinian struggle from a secular movement inspired by fascism and Communism into a full-fledged Islamic holy war. The Islamic transformation of the Palestinian cause was completed during the second Intifada, when Yasser Arafat created the Al-Aqsa Martyr's Brigade and began the suicide attacks of September 2000.

The significance of these developments is often overlooked when the Middle East war is misperceived as a conflict peripheral to the War on Terror, a provocation to Arab resentments rather than the focus of Arab agendas. The jihads of Palestinian terrorist groups are then seen as the desperate reactions of victims rather than as extensions of the general holy war that radical Islam has declared on the West.

It is a historical misunderstanding of the Arab-Israeli wars to regard them as a dispute over conflicting desires for self-determination and land. It would be difficult to explain how a desire of the Jews to establish a state on 1 percent of Arab lands or 10 percent of the Palestine Mandate should lead to more than fifty years of bloodshed and war.

The Arab-Israeli wars were initiated as a result of the rejection by the Arab League of a United Nations partition plan to create Israeli and Palestinian states on 20 percent of the Palestine Mandate, a territory that had been ruled by the Turkish Empire for the preceding four hundred years. The remaining 80 percent of the mandate had previously been ceded to Jordan—a state with a Palestinian Arab majority—accompanied by a ban against any Jew settling on the land. Thus the exclusion of the Jews was already an established principle prior to the creation of the Jewish state.

If the U.N. partition plan had been accepted, it would have created a Palestinian state on what is now the contested West Bank, and thus would have given the Palestinians everything they still claim to desire. The reason for the rejection of the plan was in the first instance the intolerance of Arab nationalism infused with a fascist political ideology, and in the second, the fact that the Arab leaders were Muslims and could not tolerate an independent, secular democracy in their midst.

Like its Arab neighbors (Jordan, Lebanon, Syria, and Iraq), Israel was created on land that belonged to the Ottoman Turks[24] and was not part of any nation in any meaningful sense of the term. It was not created by Jewish conquest but by the edict of the victorious powers in World War II who shifted national boundaries and also large populations in Europe to create a new order when the war was over. As allies of the defeated Axis, the Arabs were in a weak position to oppose the change, but they massed armies that had once served Rommel to attack the newly created state of Israel with the explicit intent of achieving its destruction.

The history of the Middle East refutes the myth that this conflict is about a Palestinian state or about land for the Palestinian Arabs. Both land and a state were offered at the outset of the dispute and fifty years later in the Oslo proposals, and were rejected twice. Moreover, from the Arab side it is only Jews who are regarded as an obstacle to Palestinian aspirations. The disenfranchisement of the majority Palestinian population in Jordan by its Hashemite rulers evokes no protest at all from the Arab world or the Palestinians. There could not be clearer evidence that other agendas prevail.

The war launched by the Arabs in 1948 to destroy the state of Israel has continued without formal interruption for more than half a century. In the intervening years, Jordan and Egypt signed peace agreements with Jerusalem, demonstrating that such agreements are feasible and their rejection is one-sided. The military occupation of the West Bank by Israel is a result of three Arab wars of aggression and the failure of other Arab states to negotiate, let alone sign, such agreements. As a result of Arab aggressions using the West Bank as an attack corridor, the disputed terrain of the conflict is a security matter for Israel, which can only be resolved by a peace treaty that would allow the withdrawal of Israeli troops.

A Palestine Liberation Organization expressing the "national" aspiration of Palestinian Arabs was not established until 1964, fifteen years after the creation of the state of Israel. Even then it was not created by Palestinian Arabs but by the Egyptian dictator Gamal Abdel Nasser, architect of the 1967 war against Israel, whose explicit agenda was the destruction of the Israeli state.[25] This was also the attitude of its eventual leader Yasser Arafat, who in 1970 rejected the idea of a Palestinian state in Palestinian Jordan, explaining, "We shall oppose the establishment of this state to the last member of the

Palestinian people, for if ever such a state is established it will spell the end of the whole Palestinian cause."[26] That cause was the destruction of Israel and the creation of a Palestinian state "from the Jordan to the sea."

At the time of the PLO's creation, the now disputed territories in the West Bank and Gaza did not exist as independent entities. They had been annexed by Jordan and Egypt in 1949 after the Arab war of aggression. These annexations elicited no protest from the Arab world, including the Palestinians. The reason for this silence was that the goal of most Arab nationalists at the time—including most Palestinians—was the creation not of individual nation-states but of a United Arab Nation, which would include all the artificial states created by British and French imperialism.[27] Not only was there no Arab protest of the annexations of Gaza and the West Bank by Jordan and Egypt, no objection was raised in the charter of the new Palestine Liberation Organization either. Instead the PLO charter referred to Palestinians as part of the "Arab nation," declared any partition of the Palestine Mandate to be fraudulent and illegitimate, and declared that "the Jews are not one people with an independent personality because they are citizens of the countries to which they belong."[28] In other words, Palestinian nationalism called for the destruction of the Jewish state. This goal expressed the agendas of both secular Arab nationalism and imperial Islam, and has not changed since.

After the Second World War, there were two democratic non-Islamic states in the Middle East: Israel and Lebanon. Lebanon was a democracy with a Christian majority. In the course of the postwar jihads, this non-Islamic, multireligious democracy was destroyed by Syria and the PLO. The charter of the PLO refers to the creation of Israel as the *Naqba* or the "catastrophe." All the Arab states and the Palestinians refer officially to the creation of Israel by this term.

Arafat has even created a formal "Naqba Day" for Palestinians to mourn Israel's birth.[29] In other words, in the eyes of the Arab world and the Palestinians, the very creation of Israel is regarded as a disaster. To the Islamic and nationalist Middle East, the existence of a non-Islamic, non-Arab state in its midst is unacceptable. This is the meaning of Nasser's famous statement, "Israel's existence is itself an aggression,"[30] and the true source of the Middle East conflict. Israel is a non-Arab, infidel state, part of the Dar al Harb, the Islamic "House of War." The Middle East conflict is an extension of the conflict of radical Islam with the non-Muslim West.

15

One Jihad

The Palestine Liberation Organization was initially defined by its secular Marxism and pan-Arab nationalism. Four years after its creation, Yasser Arafat became its leader. Arafat was born and educated in Egypt well before the creation of the State of Israel. He was trained by the Muslim Brotherhood and was inspired by Islamic models. For example, he self-consciously employed Muslim rhetoric in his pronouncements and took his alias in the Palestinian underground from an Islamic hero, whom he described as Islam's "first martyr" and someone whose name had become "the symbol of total fidelity to one's faith and beliefs in the Arab world."[31]

Until the 1979 Islamic revolution in Iran, Arafat led the Palestinian cause within the framework of pan-Arab nationalism established by its sponsors. The Palestinian cause was drawn into the Islamic fold by the Islamic jihad ignited by the Iranian revolution and the mujahideen resistance in Afghanistan, in which Palestinian figures played a leading role. This development was further abetted by the creation of Hizbollah, an Islamic terrorist force sponsored by Iran, which collaborated with the PLO and the Syrians in destroying Lebanon's multireligious democracy. Hizbollah also opened a new front against Israel from its Lebanon base.

Among the Palestinians inspired by the events in Iran was a medical doctor named Fathi Shqaqi, who wrote a widely influential book called *Khomeini: The Islamic Alternative*. Shqaqi dedicated his work jointly to Khomeini and Hassan al-Banni, the founder of the Muslim Brotherhood. In his tract, he criticized both the secular nationalism of the Palestinian movement and the religious passivity of the Brotherhood. In Shqaqi's view, the Khomeini victory "demonstrated that even against an enemy as powerful as the Shah, a jihad of determined militants could overcome all obstacles." Shqaqi put his creed into practice by creating Palestine Islamic Jihad, a terrorist organization that began to escalate the violence against Israel in the 1980s.[32]

One of the three founders of Palestine Islamic Jihad and its chief organizer in the United States was Sami al-Arian, a professor based at the University of South Florida. Al-Arian was a well known and widely respected figure in the American Left, and through his activities Palestine Islamic Jihad exerted a powerful influence within the Left, linking its anti-Americanism with the forces of the jihad in the Middle East.[33]

The armed resistance to the Soviet invasion in Afghanistan had an immediate impact on the Islamic jihad in the West Bank. The cause attracted Islamic militants from many countries including the Arab Middle East. Among them was the Saudi Osama bin Laden, who had been converted to radical Islam by the Muslim Brotherhood and whose al Qaeda terror network was essentially created in the crucible of this war.

Abdallah Azzam, a Palestinian professor and Muslim Brother, was a central figure among the Arabs joining the Afghan resistance. Together with bin Laden he established the Sidda training camp for

the Arab mujahideen who came to Peshawar to fight the Russians.
While in Peshawar, Azzam met with Sheik Abdel Omar Rahman,[34]
the Egyptian leader of the Islamic terrorist group responsible for the
first World Trade Center bombing in 1993. Azzam founded a magazine called *Al Jihad* and wrote a pamphlet called *Defending the Land
of the Muslims Is Each Man's Most Important Duty.* "This duty," he
wrote, "shall not lapse with victory in Afghanistan, and the jihad will
remain an obligation until all other lands which formerly were Muslim come back to us and Islam reigns within them once again. Before
us lie Palestine, Bukhara, Lebanon, Chad, Eritrea, Somalia, the
Philippines, Burma, South Yemen, Tashkent, Andalusia . . . "[35] This
Islamic radical vision is the political faith that drives the terrorist war.

In July 2000, the Palestinians openly joined that war when Arafat
walked out of the Oslo peace talks at Camp David and unconditionally rejected a plan that would have established a Palestinian
state. The plan proposed by President Clinton and Israeli president
Ehud Barak offered the Palestinians an independent state with its
capital in Jerusalem and 97 percent[36] of the land they had demanded,
with the other 3 percent to be made up by cessions from Israel.[37] The
rejection of the Oslo settlement—even as a framework for further
negotiations—revealed the maximalist goals of the Palestinian cause,
which could no longer be confused with a plan for co-existence with
a non-Islamic, non-Arab state in the Middle East.

After walking out of the Oslo talks, Arafat returned from Camp
David and began planning the second Intifada as an explicit extension of the Islamic jihad. Two months later he launched a new war
against Israel. The vehicle he created for the war, which began September 28,[38] was the Al-Aqsa Martyrs Brigade, named after one of
Islam's holiest mosques on the Temple Mount.[39]

Days before the full-scale eruption of Arafat's Palestinian jihad,
four leaders of the general Islamic campaign issued a manifesto

calling on all Muslims "to expel the Jews and Christians from the holy places, and to endeavor to release our *ulema* from the United States." The call was issued by Osama bin Laden; his right-hand, Alyman al-Zawahiri, the Egyptian Islamist leader Rifi Amad Taha; and the son of Sheik Omar Abdel Rahman, mastermind of the first World Trade Center bombing. The statements were part of a short video filmed when the four met in Afghanistan and broadcast over several days during the week before the Palestinian attack at the Al-Aqsa Mosque. In the words of one history of the breakdown of the Oslo peace process, "This brief videotape, particularly given bin Laden's personal appearance, brought the Islamist call to jihad to the forefront of the Arab world's attention. In retrospect, it served to mobilize the eruption of violence that was soon to come."[40]

The Palestinian jihad, or second Intifada, began with a week of suicide attacks that killed sixty Palestinians and five Israelis. Over the next two years, one hundred eighty Israelis were murdered in "martyrdom" homicides. The martyrdoms were an Islamic tradition going to back to the fifteenth-century "assassins," whose honor was invested in sacrificing their own lives in service to the faith.[41] Their reward for martyrdom, according to the Islamic doctrines that justified their jihad, was seventy-two virgins and eternal life in Allah's garden. However, the original assassins targeted powerful individuals—kings and caliphs—who had allegedly betrayed the Islamic cause. Under Arafat and his lieutenants, the targets were the powerless and the innocent, including women, children, and the old. For blowing up the defenseless, the Palestinian "martyrs" were anointed national heroes by Arafat and the Palestinian Authority, while their families were paid $25,000 for each atrocity, courtesy of the government of Saudi Arabia and Iraq's dictator Saddam Hussein. Saddam had begun his political career as a traditional Ba'ath fascist, but like

Arafat he now embraced Islamic jihad in his war with the United States.[42]

In 2002, after Palestinian terrorists assassinated an Israeli cabinet minister and a wave of suicide attacks killed one hundred thirty civilians, Israeli Defense Forces moved into the West Bank and the town of Ramallah, where Arafat was headquartered. The beleaguered Arafat claimed the Israelis were attempting to assassinate him, and from his bunker ranted on Al Jazeera TV: "The Israelis want me as a captive, an exile or dead. But I will be a martyr, martyr, martyr. . . . We ask Allah to grant us martyrdom, to grant us martyrdom. To Jerusalem we march—martyrs by the millions! To Jerusalem we march—martyrs by the millions!"[43] The Palestinian cause was now an integral part of the Islamic jihad.

The revival of the martyrdom tradition of the assassins had begun during Iran's war with Iraq, when the Ayatollah Khomeini deliberately sent hundreds of thousands of Iranian youths to their deaths in human waves to be sacrifices for the cause. Virtually the entire political generation that had supported Khomeini was wiped out in this fashion.[44] Another stage of its revival occurred in Lebanon, when the Iranian-sponsored Islamic terrorist organization Hizbollah carried out a suicide bombing on a U.S. barracks that killed 243 U.S. Marines in Beirut. The subsequent withdrawal of the Marines without retaliation inspired Osama bin Laden to regard America as a weak adversary. In a 1998 interview, bin Laden told ABC news reporter John Miller, "We have seen in the last decade the decline of the American government and the weakness of the American soldier, who is prepared to fight cold wars and unprepared to fight long wars. This was proven in Beirut when the Marines fled after two explosions. It also proves they can run in less than twenty-four hours, and this was also repeated in Somalia [in 1993]."[45]

In the Islamic war against the West, Israel is like the canary in the mine. It is targeted not only as a non-Islamic state, but also as the Middle East outpost of the chief infidel power, the United States. "Our primary assumption in our fight against Israel states that the Zionist entity is aggressive from its inception, and built on lands wrested from their owners, at the expense of the rights of the Muslim people [sic]. Therefore our struggle will end only when this entity is obliterated."[46]

In the 1990s, the rising tide of radicalism in the Arab world led Egypt's Muslim Brotherhood to sponsor a new terrorist organization, Hamas, whose Palestinian arm became a leading force in the jihad against Israel. On September 11, 2001, Hamas issued an "Open Letter to America," justifying the attacks as retribution for America's sins:

> You will face the mirror of your history for a long time to come. Thus you will be able to see exactly how much you have oppressed, how corrupt you are, how you have sinned— how many entities you have destroyed, how many kingdoms you have demolished! America, Oh sword of oppression, arrogance and sin.... Do you remember how the blacks lived under your wing?.... Your white son bound their necks with the fetters of slavery, after hunting them in the jungles and on the coasts of Africa... Have you asked yourself about your actions against your "original" inhabitants, the Indians, the Apaches? Your white feet crushed them and then used their name, Apache, for a helicopter bearing death, demolition, and destruction for anyone with rights who dared to whisper in his own ear that he has those rights....
>
> Why do you pour this continuing oppression on the head of Baghdad as you do on the head of Jerusalem, on the head of

Jenin ...? Every time Dick Cheney and his girlfriend Condoleeza Rice admonish us, [and] gloat at our misfortune, they incite to more [violence against us]!! We stand in line and beg Allah to give you to drink from the cup of humiliation—and behold, heaven has answered.[47]

This is an indictment with which Western radicals could—and did—readily agree. It reprised their litany of American crimes. They had already embraced the Palestinian movement in the 1960s, when Arafat, backed by the Soviet bloc, created modern terrorism. They did so because Soviet Communism and Palestinian terrorism presented themselves as enemies of the American Satan. With the help of the Castro dictatorship, which the American Left embraced for similar reasons, Arafat established the first terrorist training camps and launched the first international campaign of airline hijackings and hostage-takings. The attack of 9/11—whose weapon of choice was hijacked airliners loaded with hostages and whose targets were Wall Street and the Pentagon, the very symbols of American empire—was thus the juncture at which the two jihads finally met.

16

The New Radicalism

Ten days before the 9/11 attacks, a conference was held in Durban, South Africa. It became the first expression of the new global coalition. The ostensible purpose of the U.N. World Conference Against Racism, Racial Discrimination, Xenophobia and Related Intolerance, was to combat intolerance, but its real agenda was to orchestrate an international assault on the democracies of the West, and more specifically against the United States, Britain, and Israel. These three nations—and these alone—were condemned in speeches and resolutions for their alleged racism, historical involvement in slavery, and colonialism. European slavery and colonialism were in turn alleged to be the principal sources of racism in the world, despite the fact that America and Britain had led the world in combating racism by introducing the idea of racial equality as a basic human right two hundred years earlier and by taking the lead in ending slavery, an institution that had been universally accepted for three thousand years. The attack on European colonialism made little sense as well, since Europe's colonies had been granted independence nearly half a century before.

Not only was slavery still practiced by Muslim regimes in Africa (which went unmentioned at the U.N. conference) but the largest ethnic genocide since World War II had occurred in Rwanda ten years earlier and was a legacy neither of colonialism nor of slavery but a tribal affair.[48] Moreover, the U.N. itself had ignored the Rwandans' appeals for intervention to prevent the genocide—an intervention that could have avoided the slaughter of one million Africans.

The dictators and tyrants whose governments set the U.N. agenda and whose regimes were characterized by the very crimes decried, and who were present as delegates to the conference itself, included Yasser Arafat, Fidel Castro, and spokesmen for the governments of Iran, Iraq, and the League of Arab States. The conference agenda had been arranged nine months earlier at a formal gathering in Tehran, the capital of a xenophobic Islamic theocracy, whose regime barred Jews, members of the Baha'i faith, and American citizens from attending the proceedings as unfit by nationality and religion from entry into the Islamic state.

The U.N. conference was convened on September 1, 2001. Fidel Castro and other dictators were the keynote speakers during the opening-day proceedings, assailing the United States and Israel— and these two nations alone—as racist, aggressive, and imperialist predators. The speakers demanded reparations from America for Africans enslaved two hundred years earlier, and retribution from Israel for the alleged "crimes against humanity" it had committed since 1948—that is, since its very creation. They referred to the birth of Israel (created by an act of the U.N.) as the Naqba.

An unofficial resolution submitted by the six thousand "non-governmental organizations" in attendance went even further, attempting to revive a slander the U.N. had already withdrawn by condemning Zionism—the Jewish national liberation movement— as "racism," and calling on the U.N. to convene a "war crimes tribunal" that would put Israel's elected leaders in the dock. The proposal precipitated a walkout and boycott of the proceedings by the governments of the United States and Israel three days after the conference began.[49]

By all reports, the atmosphere of the conference was as rife with Jew-hatred as a Nuremberg rally in the 1930s. The Arab Lawyers Association, attending the event as a "nongovernmental organization," even displayed posters of Hitler to complete the Nazi symbolism. Conference participants demonstrated in the streets distributing flyers that portrayed Jews "with fangs dripping blood and wearing helmets inscribed with Nazi swastikas," a display of ethnic hatred described by one reporter as "a venomous carnival of incitement." A yarmulke-wearing bystander was confronted by Arab and South African demonstrators chanting "Kill the Jews."[50] Lord Greville Janner, a British MP, characterized the events in Durban, including the official proceedings, as "the worst example of anti-Semitism that I have ever seen."[51]

Although the American government, led by Secretary of State Colin Powell, withdrew from the conference in protest over its anti-Semitic and anti-American extremism, members of American nongovernmental organizations (NGOs) chose to stay and join in the attacks on America's withdrawal. The American nongovernmental delegation, funded by the Ford Foundation, included the American Civil Liberties Union, the NAACP, the Mexican American Legal Defense and Educational Fund, the National Lawyers Guild (an old Communist Party front) and the pro-Castro Center for Constitutional Rights, whose executive, director Ron Daniels was present to explain that "to talk about fighting against racism is to talk about revolution."[52]

The fifty American NGOs called on the UN "to hold the United States accountable for the intractable and persistent problem of discrimination,"[53] although the United States as a democracy had means for addressing such problems that the majority of the U.N. member states who were attacking it did not, and had recently achieved the most dramatic advances in racial equality on record.[54] Jesse Jackson and NAACP chairman, Julian Bond, were also part of the American delegation, who, along with ten members of the Congressional Black Caucus, demanded trillions of dollars from the United States government in "reparations" for the slave system that the same government had abolished nearly a century and a half before.[55]

The political nature of these attacks was underscored by the absence of reparations demands against any other states, including the African states whose predecessor kingdoms had been involved in the slave trade for a thousand years before Europeans or Americans set foot on the continent. Their resolutions against racism failed to mention the regime in Sudan, whose Islamic government had enslaved hundreds of thousands of black Africans and slaughtered more than a million black Christians during the previous decade. Cuba, an island that had imported more slaves than the entire North American continent,[56] spoke for the *plaintiffs* on reparations, as did the League of Arab States, whose ancestors had enslaved black Africans since the seventh century and traded in more black African chattel than all the European powers and the North American colonies combined.[57]

In a parallel vein, America and Israel qualified as "racist" at the conference but the slave-holding Sudan and Zimbabwe (which was conducting a race war against its white population) and Iraq (a regime that had gassed its minorities) did not. Israel—a country whose Arab citizens enjoyed more rights than the citizens of any Arab country in the Middle East—was ritually denounced as an "apartheid state," while Arab states that denied their own citizens the vote and their women basic rights and refused to even permit Jews on their soil were the accusers and portrayed themselves as victims.

The relentless double standard in the U.N. resolutions was the expression of the new radical worldview, which had been refashioned as a result of the Communist fall, and which framed its indictments in terms of gender and racial oppression. Traditionally, Marxists had condemned the Western democracies as "class dictatorships." But in the wake of the Communist debacle, these rhetorical formulas were less effective in their political impact than the charge of "racism." The same logic inspired radicals to introduce the term "globalization" to replace "international capitalism" as a description of the oppressor system and to use the term "social justice" as a code for socialist and totalitarian agendas.[58]

In leftist theory, the tripartite model of class-race-gender oppression assigns each element an equal weight. But in the political war that requires a moral indictment of entire social systems, race inevitably assumes the dominant role, trumping other factors. Thus Arab regimes that oppress women and rule tyrannically over impoverished multitudes can be excused by progressives because they occupy a low rung of the international hierarchy and are not white.

In the new radical worldview, racism is redefined in order that it may be integrated with traditional Communist theories. Racism is no longer regarded as a social attitude or philosophical belief, but is the objective expression of an inequality of power that is pervasive and outside individual control. In this analysis, an individual does not have to be prejudiced to participate in racial oppression but merely to occupy a "privileged" position in an alleged hierarchy of groups and classes. (In Western democracies characterized by upward mobility, the very concept of hierarchy is, of course, a fictional construct.)

In the radical view, racism is alleged to be "systemic," or "institutional" that is, built into the very structure of capitalist societies. In its most vulgar form this idea is expressed in the proposition that "only whites can be racist." This is because whites are allegedly a cohesive group that monopolizes power. Since America and Europe can be said to include the most prosperous and powerful societies, radicals allege that the same hierarchy of class and race exists globally. Hence the global system and the "globalization" process that express this hierarchy are also "racist."

Like traditional Marxism, this new radical paradigm is a totalitarian perspective in which no individual escapes the control of a system that is described as "institutionally racist" and is targeted for destruction. Because the hierarchy and "oppression" are alleged to be systemic, no escape from racism is possible without a systemic remedy, which is the politically enforced creation of a Communist economic and social order.[59] This radical view is now the academic doctrine of American university faculties, where race-gender-class hierarchies are a staple of the academic curriculum. A typical formulation can be found in *Racist America*, written by Joe Faegin, a former president of the American Sociological Association and author of forty academic texts: "Systemic racism includes the complex array of anti-black practices, the unjustly gained political-economic power of whites, the continuing economic and other resource inequalities along racial lines ... Like a hologram, each major part of U.S. society—the economy, politics, education, religion, the family—reflects the fundamental reality of systemic racism."[60] In sum: "One can accurately describe the United States as a 'total racist society' in which every major aspect of life is shaped to some degree by racist realities."[61]

Viewed through this totalitarian lens, the racist attitudes manifested by minorities themselves or among Third World elites can be dismissed as mere by-products of the "divide and conquer" strategies of the dominant white race, whose position of privilege and power is secured by the global "system." This is why anti-black racism in

Sudan—a Third World dependency ruled by people of color and victims of "Islamophobia"—can be ignored, while discrimination in America is a "crime against humanity."

With this ideological framework in place, in the hands of the Left racism becomes a morally powerful code for condemning the capitalist democracies of the West and their international influence, or "globalization." In a typical declaration at the U.N. proceedings in Tehran, the Asian delegations of NGO radicals explained:

> Globalization describes the ever-increasing integration of human society at economic, social, cultural and political levels. It historically derives from the process of colonial integration of the world. Globalization is therefore an iniquitous structure, one that is based on unequal power relations. It has promoted an institutional racism at both the national and the international level.[62]

In other parts of this U.N. document, racism is defined not as race hatred or prejudice but as "an ideological construct that assigns a certain global power over others on the basis of a notion of superiority, dominance and purity." The source of this ideological construct is the hegemony of the "metropolitan" powers. (The term "metropolitan" itself is of Marxist origin and refers to the assumption that the world is an integrated system in which the success of the industrial centers comes at the expense of the impoverished "colonial" periphery.)

> This global hegemony by the metropolitan powers has resulted in the continuing domination of the European-originated cultures and the marginalization of other world civilizations. The current strategies of the global big powers contribute to create

a pervasive culture of racism, one example being Islamophobia. Xenophobia and intolerance is sharply reflected in the global mass media for example, in its racist bias in the reporting of the Palestinian problem and its coverage of the aggression against Iraq.

Thus the familiar themes of the Communist Left are resurrected under the banner of racial "tolerance" to defend Islamic jihad, Palestinian terrorism, and the fascist regime of Saddam Hussein. In this ideological framework, opposition to Marxist radicalism and its anti-Western agendas becomes by definition a form of racism, while the Western democracies are assaulted in the name of the very ideals—racial tolerance and equality—that they first invented and then established as civil rights.

17

The New International

The anti-American, anti-Israel conference in Durban in September 2001 brought together Islamo-fascists from Iran, Iraq, Syria, Libya, and Palestine with an array of American leftist organizations who promoted their radical agendas under the banner of "human rights." Months later the same international coalition would reemerge as a global movement against America's War on Terror.[63]

The western actors in this "anti-war" coalition had become an international network in the previous decades through the activities of self-described "social justice" and "solidarity" movements. These movements were the product of the Cold War, and in the case of the Committees in Solidarity with Nicaragua and El Salvador were in fact created by the intelligence agencies of Communist states.[64] They were now focused on the Palestinian and Iraqi causes.

Joining with environmental and labor radicals, the solidarity and social justice movements began, in the 1990s, to target meetings of institutions symbolizing the international system they regarded as their ideological enemy. These included the International Monetary Fund, the World Bank, and the World Economic

Forum, a gathering of heads of state and corporate leaders that met periodically in Davos, Switzerland. On the surface the "antiglobal" protests involved seemingly disparate issues, but in the eyes of the activists they were all related by a common anticorporate theme and by a shared perspective in which private property and the capitalist system were the root cause of social evils.

Thus a Cold War Stalinist and anti-Iraq-war radical, Alex Cockburn, explained to his peers how environmental concerns could lead directly to an agenda for destroying the World Bank: "One issue flows into another, as the Berkeley-based International Rivers Network discovered years ago. As the ... Network battled dams around the world, it found that dams mostly had one thing in common: financial backing from the World Bank. So the International Rivers Network founded the enormously effective '50 Years Is Enough' campaign against the bank."[65] Influenced by this kind of conspiratorial logic, radical activists from all over the world began gathering in protests at meetings of the World Bank and similar institutions. In the process they formed an international coalition even without the guidance of an overarching global organization such as the Communist parties and the Socialist Internationals had once provided.

Two years prior to the U.N.'s Durban conference, this "antiglobalist" movement reached a critical mass as radicals gathered in Seattle to protest the annual meeting of the World Trade Organization.[66] Five thousand delegates and dignitaries from 134 nations, including President Clinton, had come to Seattle for the proceedings.[67] On November 30, 1999, fifty thousand activists descended on the streets of Seattle with the intention of obstructing the conference. The protesters included not only radical environmentalists, anarchists, and Communists, but trade unionists as well, including the heads of the two left-wing government unions (and huge contributors to the Democratic Party), the Service Employees International Union

(SEIU) and the American Federation of State, County, and Municipal Employees (AFSCME). As was widely noted, it was the first time since the heyday of the Communist movement that organized labor and radicals had joined forces in political protests of such magnitude.

In a speech to the protesters, AFSCME union leader Gerald McEntee—soon to be a key player in the presidential candidacy of Vice President Al Gore—invoked a famous phrase from the 1960s, declaring, "We have to name the system, and that system is corporate capitalism."[68] Naomi Klein, author of *No Logo*, one of the hallmark tracts of the "antiglobalization" protests, agreed: "If this new movement is anti-anything, it is anti-corporate."[69]

During several days of protests, the demonstrators blocked streets, firebombed businesses, and provoked mass arrests, producing a chaos that so overwhelmed the available security forces that conference conveners were compelled to terminate their proceedings prematurely and failed to open a new round of trade talks. The size of the demonstrations—unseen for a generation, and particularly over such radical agendas—inspired activists to envision a new radical age, galvanizing the political Left worldwide.[70]

In an account of the demonstrations by two veterans of the Left, Seattle is even celebrated as *Five Days That Shook the World*, evoking John Reed's famous characterization of the Bolshevik Revolution.[71] "Among American activists," another radical commented, "Seattle has become a watershed, much as Chicago '68 was for the previous generation." It was "the most important and exciting social movement since the 1960s."[72] Medea Benjamin, head of an innocuous sounding anticapitalist group called Global Exchange and one of the principal organizers of the demonstrations, described Seattle as being a "kind of battle cry; we now know we can mobilize hundreds of thousands of people."[73]

Leftists followed the Seattle protest with large disruptive demonstrations at the World Trade Organization's subsequent meetings in Prague, Quebec, and Genoa. Seattle immediately became an inspiration not only to escalate the level of activism but also to create a framework where activists could meet and discuss common strategies and programs. A year later (and one year before 9/11), radicals organized a "World Social Forum" in Porto Alegre, Brazil, a name adopted as a mirror of the World Economic Forum in Davos, where radicals seemed to imagine that the executive committee of the world ruling class assembled to plan the global future. The new World Social Forum was scheduled to coincide with the Davos meetings and to fill a crucial gap in the fragmented radical international. "The failure of Seattle," explained Christophe Aguiton, one of the French organizers, "was the inability to come up with a common agenda, a global alliance at the world level to fight against globalization."[74]

The World Social Forum was the brainchild of a French group advocating taxation of all investment transactions, a socialist scheme proposed in the United States by Green Party leader Ralph Nader. The forum itself was sponsored by the socialist Brazilian Workers Party, the governing political force in Porto Alegre and shortly afterward in Brazil itself. The pro-Castro presidents of both Brazil and Venezuela spoke at the first forum events. Funding was provided by the Ford Foundation, which had also underwritten the anti-American and anti-Israel protests in Durban.[75]

About ten thousand radicals from 120 countries, representing a thousand organizations, attended the opening of the first World Social Forum in January 2001.[76] The political tone of the event was set by the presence of Colombia's terrorist organization, the Revolutionary Armed Forces of Colombia, or FARC (also present on platforms of the anti-Iraq "peace" rallies), and the warm embrace of

Castro's police state: "Every night the conference adjourned to an outdoor amphitheater where musicians from around the world performed, including the Cuarteto Patria, one of the Cuban bands made famous by Wim Wenders's documentary, *The Buena Vista Social Club*. Cuban anything was big here. Speakers had only to mention the existence of the island nation for the room to break out in chants of Cuba! Cuba! Cuba!"[77]

The first World Forum was a success beyond the expectations of its planners. The second session, held in January 2002, attracted five times as many participants. This dramatic growth prompted Noam Chomsky, one of its keynote speakers, to describe the forum somewhat grandiosely as a "second superpower," and as "[providing] at least the seeds of the first authentic international, the dream of the Left."[78] The third annual World Social Forum convocation took place in January 2003 during the lead-up to the war with Iraq and drew one hundred thousand activists, who made a point of cheering the Iraqi delegation. Kevin Danaher, a leader of Global Exchange (and husband of Medea Benjamin), reminded the audience that the American Left had supported Communists and other leftists abroad for decades, and concluded, "Now we need you to stand in solidarity with us, as we stand up to a dictatorial government bent on war."[79]

Among the five hundred American delegates attending, several were selected to be members of the forum's "international council." These included a representative from Ralph Nader's Public Citizen organization, Medea Benjamin and Linda Chavez-Thompson, executive vice president of the AFL-CIO. The Ford Foundation rewarded the Forum's success by raising its funding level to $500,000 for the next event.[80]

Unlike the Communist International that preceded it, the World Social Forum was not a tightly run or centrally directed organization.

In describing its formation, its semi-official historians acknowledge the role played by the collapse of the Soviet bloc in shaping its organizational framework: "Because of the failures of the Soviet project and the politics of difference[81] ... progressives are wary of any group playing a vanguard in defining the society that the overall global movement should pursue." Therefore, "a contemporary counter-hegemony has to embrace a respect for difference without precluding a capacity to articulate a common vision."[82]

The World Social Forum was a self-conscious effort to develop specifics for an alternative future that the fragmented factions could jointly support. But the results of this effort were meager. When it came time to describe the common vision that had emerged from their meetings, the forum organizers chose the phrase "reinventing democracy."

Reinventing democracy was explained as "the radical transformation of the existing class, gender and racialized relations of power that prohibit the full functioning of democracy."[83] In other words the agenda was the imposition of equality at every level of society through political power—precisely the agenda of the Communist movements of the past. But the radicals who came to the World Social Forum were no closer to agreeing on the specifics of this transformation or how their utopia would be practically organized than they had been since the collapse of the Soviet empire—or, indeed, since the beginning of the "new" Left, more than forty years before.

Journalist Nancy Klein perfectly captured this vacuousness concerning the revolutionary future in her report of the forum's opening meeting: "'We are here to show the world that another world is possible!' the man on stage said, and a crowd of more than 10,000 roared its approval. What was strange was that we weren't cheering for a specific other world, just the possibility of one. We were cheering for the idea that another world could, in theory exist."[84]

In fact, the only practical thread binding the disparate "social justice movements" that had gathered in Porto Alegre was the anticapitalist nihilism that had inspired radicals since the collapse of the Soviet experiment. This nihilism, their only commonly shared vision, was lucidly expressed in a brief "Social Movements' Manifesto,"[85] which summarized the unifying themes of the forum: "We are building a large alliance from our struggles and resistance against a system based on sexism, racism and violence, which privileges the interests of capitalism and patriarchy over the needs and aspirations of the people."[86] The manifesto endorsed the claim for reparations against the United States and included the statement that "an urgent task of our movement is to mobilize solidarity for the Palestinian people and their struggle for self-determination as they face brutal occupation by the Israeli state."

PART FOUR:
THE WAR AT HOME

"We have in Washington a poisonous government that spreads its venom to the body politic in all corners of the globe. We now resume . . . our quests . . . like David going forth to meet Goliath, like Beowulf the dragon slayer, . . . like Sir Galahad seeking the holy grail. And modern heroes, dare I mention? Ho and Mao and Lenin, Fidel and Nelson Mandela and John Brown, Che Guevara who reminds us, 'At the risk of seeming ridiculous, let me say that the true revolutionary is guided by a great feeling of love.'"

—LYNNE STEWART, NATIONAL LAWYERS GUILD ATTORNEY FOR SHEIK OMAR ABDEL RAHMAN, MASTERMIND OF THE WORLD TRADE CENTER BOMBING IN 1993

18

Anti-war Protests

I n retrospect, the anti-war movement to oppose American policy in Iraq had actually been launched on an international scale within weeks of the attack on 9/11, long before the lead-up to the Iraq war itself. This anti-war movement was a product of the same forces and organizations that had assembled to riot against the World Trade Organization in Seattle and against the World Bank in Prague, and to promote the anticapitalist agendas of the World Social Forum in Porto Alegre.[1] It was spurred not so much by the actual events—either the attacks of 9/11 or the war against Saddam Hussein, as by the opportunities these events afforded to a radical movement whose permanent agenda was war against America and its perceived global "domination."

Its agenda was summarized by the leading intellectual of the movement, Noam Chomsky, in a book titled *Hegemony or Survival*. The title was itself a calculated echo of Rosa Luxemburg's apocalyptic claim that the world faced a choice between "socialism or barbarism," which had been issued almost a century earlier. Chomsky's book was an attempt to make the identical case in contemporary terms.

America's preeminent global position, Chomsky argued, is a threat to world survival. This is because America supported a doctrine of aggressive war, wanted to extrude weapons into space, had obstructed the international control of weapons of mass destruction, and had undermined the Kyoto protocol, which was the "world's" effort to protect itself from extinction through global warming.

Against this "nightmare" future, Chomsky went on, a world "rights" movement had arisen. "The solidarity movements that developed in mainstream America in the 1980s, concerning Central America in particular, broke new ground in the history of imperialism; never before had substantial numbers of people from the imperial society gone to live with the victims of vicious attack to help them and offer them some measure of protection.[2] The international solidarity organizations that evolved from these roots now function very effectively in many parts of the world."[3]

What Chomsky was describing in these passages was a twenty-first century version of the "international civil war" between capitalists and socialists that Marx and Lenin had proclaimed in an earlier epoch: "One can discern two trajectories in current history: one aiming toward hegemony, acting rationally within a lunatic doctrinal framework as it threatens survival; the other dedicated to the belief that 'another world is possible,' in the words that animate the World Social Forum"[4] This was the real vision that inspired the anti-war movement that developed between 9/11 and the invasion of Iraq.

After the attacks of 9/11, the first protest of America's security policies was held in the nation's capital on September 29, 2001, and was described by its organizers as a response to "a frenzied war drive emanating from the White House."[5] The reference was to the president's September 20 speech to Congress in which he declared, "Our War on Terror... will not end until every terrorist group of global reach has been found, stopped, and defeated."

Medea Benjamin and other organizers of the anti-globalization movement had planned protests in Washington for September 29 to coincide with meetings of the World Bank and the International Monetary Fund. Because of the proximity to the 9/11 attacks on the World Trade Center and the national grieving that followed, the organizers decided that to proceed with their plans was tactically unwise and that disruptions in the nation's capital so shortly after the tragedy might produce an adverse public reaction. Consequently, they withdrew their plans. A more radical faction wanted to go forward however. On September 19, one of the original groups participating in the antiglobalist protest put in a request to obtain new permits for a demonstration against the war. The group was called International ANSWER (Act Now to Stop War and End Racism) and the official theme of the demonstration it planned was, "Say No To Racism, Aggression, Xenophobia."[6]

International ANSWER, which would go on to sponsor almost all the "national" anti-war demonstrations over the next year, was ostensibly a "coalition" of radical groups. But the components of this coalition were actually fronts for the Worker's World Party, a Marxist-Leninist vanguard that was aligned with North Korea's Communist regime and with the International Action Center that had been formed by a veteran opponent of American policies, former U.S. Attorney Ramsey Clark. Clark had a long history of acting as advocate and legal counsel for self-declared enemies of the United States. His clients included Communist North Vietnam, the ayatollahs' regime in Iran, the Communist dictatorship in North Korea, the war criminal Slobodan Milosevic, and the regime of Saddam Hussein.[7]

For a year following 9/11, the ANSWER coalition's demonstrations remained relatively small. When America launched its military campaign to remove the Taliban regime in Afghanistan, there were significant protests in Europe and Asia, but domestic opposition to the War on Terror was still muted, except on college campuses, where a hard-core Left entrenched in university faculties and funded by university programs, held teach-ins and aired familiar attacks on American society and its policies.

This pattern began to change in the fall of 2002, when International ANSWER sponsored a series of demonstrations timed for the anniversary of its first post-9/11 protests. The demonstrations, which began on September 27 and also targeted the International Monetary Fund and the World Bank, were kicked off by an "Anti-Capitalist Greed" march, featuring large banners declaring "No More Capitalist Wars." The purpose of the demonstrations was further described by the organizers as a commemoration of the second year of the Al Aqsa Intifada, the campaign of suicide bombings that the Palestine Authority had launched after walking out on the Oslo peace talks. There were 649 arrests, and estimates of the demonstration's size ranged from five thousand to twenty thousand.[8]

This event was followed by a demonstration in New York's Central Park on October 6, which attracted twenty thousand protesters. It was organized by a group calling itself "Not In Our Name," which was a front created by the Revolutionary Communist Party, a Marxist-Leninist sect aligned with Communist China.[9] Like ANSWER and Ramsey Clark's group, the Not In Our Name organizers not only opposed America's policy toward Iraq, but also openly defended the Saddam regime.

Other leftists were not happy with the openly pro-Saddam aspect of these demonstrations, but the energy of protest was proving contagious, and on October 26, more than a hundred thousand protesters responded to International ANSWER's call and showed up for anti-war rallies in Washington, D.C., and other American cities. It was the biggest anti-war protest in America since the Vietnam War.

The high visibility of the demonstrations continued to trouble seasoned activists who feared that the vulgar Communism on display would prevent the anti-war movement from winning popular support. The announcement of the impending International ANSWER demonstration of October 26 prompted these critics to go public and take steps to challenge the control of the "peace" movement by the Marxist-Leninist sects. A lead article in the left-wing online magazine *Salon.com* by Michelle Goldberg described the organizers of the October 26 event as "Peace Kooks" and warned, "The new anti-war movement is in danger of being hijacked by bizarre extremist groups—and most protesters don't even know it."[10] The statement was technically true but it was a stretch to suggest that attendees of the demonstrations would be significantly offended by such politics since the speakers at the protests were all selected by International ANSWER, routinely denounced Washington as the "Axis of Evil," called for revolution in the United States, and led the crowd in chants of "*Allahu Akhbar.*"[11]

Notwithstanding their politics, the NION and ANSWER groups (as the *Salon* article recognized) "remain[ed] the two most prominent ones organizing large-scale anti-war protests." *Salon* quoted Todd Gitlin, who warned, somewhat melodramatically, that the scheduled October 26 ANSWER demonstration would be "a gigantic ruination for the anti-war movement," because of its identification with such primitive elements of the Left. Since mainstream media, including the *New York Times* and the *Washington Post*, were more than sympathetic to the demonstrators and had not previously shown any inclination to expose the bizarre politics of the protest organizers, Gitlin's fears were probably overstated.[12]

Nonetheless, leading figures in the Left now concluded that despite the residue feelings from 9/11, an anti-war movement might have political potential. This potential would be severely limited if control of the demonstrations remained in the hands of paleo-Communists like NION and ANSWER. In the words of *Salon*: "[These] aren't just extremists in the service of a good cause—they're cheerleaders for some of the most sinister regimes and insurgencies on the planet. Once people realize this, it could easily discredit any nascent anti-war movement, unless a more rational group moves to the forefront."

Accordingly, steps were taken to produce "a more rational group." On October 25, the day preceding the scheduled Washington event, a meeting was held in the offices of People for the American Way with the express purpose of creating an umbrella organization for future protests that would be more prudent in its political rhetoric and that would attempt to create a more palatable image for the anti-war protests.[13] This tactical refurbishing was familiar to veterans of the anti-Vietnam War movement forty years earlier. At that time, the two principal umbrella groups for the national protests against the war were controlled, respectively, by the Trotskyist Socialist Workers Party and by the Communist Party.[14] The Trotskyist "radicals" wanted to wave Communist flags and march behind the slogan "Bring the War Home." The Communist Party "moderates" preferred to wave American flags and promote the more saleable slogan "Bring the Troops Home." The softer formulation allowed the demonstration organizers to recruit supporters who did not share their radical agendas. The substantive politics, however—to force an American withdrawal that would secure a Communist victory—remained the same. No group of activists, of course, was excluded from either coalition.

A similar strategy was now adopted by the activists opposing the war in Iraq. The newly created group was named Coalition United for Peace and Justice, and had the support of the National Council of Churches. But its steering committee had room for the American Communist Party and no group was excluded from its demonstrations, including supporters of the most radical forces in the Middle East, like Al-Awda, the Palestine Right of Return Coalition. The Palestinian flag itself was still prominent, although, as in the Vietnam demonstrations forty years before, the American flag became more prominent.[15] This particular change was taking place before United for Peace and Justice was able to mobilize its first demonstration in February. After an International ANSWER–sponsored protest in Washington, D.C., on January 18, which attracted as many as 30,000 demonstrators, *Salon*'s Michelle Goldberg filed a report titled "Peace Goes Mainstream":

> American flags outnumbered Palestinian and Iraqi ones at Saturday's anti-war march in Washington. Though the enormous protest was called by ANSWER, a front group for the Stalinist Workers World Party, the National Mall next to the Capitol building was flooded by ordinary, outraged citizens. They completely overwhelmed the Spartacus Leaguers, the Maoists and other assorted wackos who turn out to support anything opposed to the U.S. government. Sure, there were still plenty of signs featuring George Bush with a Hitler mustache or declaring "CIA=Al-Qaeda," but they were more than matched with placards saying, "Peace Is Patriotic" and "Don't Assume I Support Hussein."

This report was somewhat disingenuous since the tenor of the demonstration and of all its ANSWER-vetted speeches was rancid denunciation of the United States and its allegedly imperialist agendas. The rational protesters present were apparently less concerned about their totalitarian allies than about the menace of their own government.

The newly appointed "national coordinator" for the Coalition United for Peace and Justice was Leslie Cagan, a veteran of nearly forty years of the Communist Left and the New Left, and the Vietnam-era Coalition for Peace and Justice. Cagan understood the dynamics of building a radical movement behind a "liberal" cause—whether it was designated a cause for "peace" or "human rights." She had helped to organize the anti-war protests of the 1960s, the pro-Castro Venceremos brigades and "anti-racism" struggles of the 1970s, the Communist "solidarity" movements of the 1980s, early "solidarity"efforts with the Palestinians, a "lesbian-feminist" group, and the radical effort to oppose the Gulf War in 1991. When interviewed by a *New York Times* reporter, Cagan explained that to be effective the peace movement would have to "include the people who could be described as mainstream—but that doesn't exclude the people who are sometimes thought of as the fringes."[16]

In conjunction with the meeting that created United for Peace and Justice, a phalanx of ancillary anti-war organizations were also set up. These included the celebrity-focused Win Without War and Code Pink organizations. The latter was billed as a "grassroots" organization of women opposed to the war. In fact, Code Pink was a wholly owned subsidiary of Medea Benjamin's anti-corporate group, Global Exchange.[17] The efforts of the United for Peace and Justice radicals resulted in massive demonstrations on February 15, when half a million people turned out in New York and San Francisco, and other American cities, and—through the auspices of the global network that Medea Benjamin had helped to organize as part of the antiglobalization protests—an estimated 10 million protesters worldwide.

"The most exciting aspect of the anti-war organizing has been its global reach," observed Benjamin. "While in the anticorporate globalization movement we had already formed impressive ties with grassroots movements overseas, anti-war organizing has given us the opportunity to expand geographically to areas such as the Middle East, where we had less-developed contacts; to multiply our ranks with a dazzling array of new sectors, from city councils to women's and civil rights organizations such as NOW and the NAACP; and, most important, to merge the peace movement with the movement to fight corporate-dominated globalization."[18]

Benjamin was the principal organizer of the San Francisco anti-war demonstration and, like Cagan, was a veteran of the Communist Left and particularly its "solidarity" campaigns in support of Marxist guerrilla wars in Central America. She had spent ten years working for a U.N. agency and in the 1980s settled in Cuba and married a Cuban national. Interviewed about her life in Castro's police state by the *San Francisco Chronicle* she remarked that compared with America, her years in Cuba "made it seem like I died and went to heaven."[19]

Benjamin's tactical choices reflected her Communist roots. As an organizer of the Seattle demonstrations, she was a "moderate" opposed to the anarchist rioting that she felt would discourage recruitment.[20] In 2000, she ran as the Green Party senatorial candidate in California (but in 2004 abandoned the party to support the Democrat nominee "in order to beat Bush"). Her view of 9/11 was that Washington "[had] responded to the violent attack of 9/11 with the notion of perpetual war." After America's victory in Afghanistan, she took four relatives of World Trade Center victims—members of a leftist group called Peaceful Tomorrows—to Afghanistan to meet with victims of America's War on Terror. "We must insist that governments stop taking innocent lives in the name of seeking justice for the loss of other innocent lives," she said at a press conference, asserting a moral equivalency between terror and self-defense.[21]

A little over a week after American forces entered Baghdad, Medea Benjamin was telling left-wing audiences, "Here at home, our greatest challenge is to make sure that our anti-war coalitions don't fall apart after the immediate crisis ends.... Let's channel the bursting anti-American sentiment overseas into targeted boycotts against corporations profiting from the war.... Let's start a Bring All the Troops Home campaign"[22] For Benjamin and Cagan and their followers, the wars in Afghanistan and Iraq were expressions of America's sinister global hegemony and the system of corporate oppression that accompanied it. Consequently, when American troops were liberating Baghdad and had begun the task of rebuilding Iraq, Cagan and Benjamin were launching a joint attack on the American peace efforts.

To facilitate this offensive they formed a new organization called Occupation Watch, cosponsored by Cagan's United for Peace and Justice and Benjamin's Code Pink. They established an Occupation Watch Center in Baghdad and a website, whose multiple agendas were encouraging American soldiers to defect (by declaring themselves "conscientious objectors"); exposing the machinations of American companies involved in the rebuilding effort (which Benjamin referred to as "the corporate invasion of Iraq"); publicizing American casualties with the hope of discouraging home-front support; and reporting alleged "civil liberties abuses" by American authorities as a way of undermining their credibility and weakening the American presence.

The negative reports on the American presence in Iraq that flowed relentlessly from the Occupation Watch Center were publicized not only on its own website but through a formidable network of similar sites,[23] both domestically and internationally, and regular news organizations in which the anti-war Left and its sympathizers had a large and sympathetic representation. To run the Occupation

Watch Center in Iraq, Benjamin recruited a Left-wing Iraqi named Nerween al-Mufti, who for twenty years had been a journalist in the Saddam-controlled press and a willing tool of the regime. Al-Mufti told an American radio audience, "As an Iraqi, I hate the occupation."[24]

The Left's goal of forming a permanent international coalition against America's War on Terror was realized on the first anniversary of Iraq's liberation, barely a week after al Qaeda terrorists had detonated three packs of bombs in Madrid, killing more than two hundred people, tipping an election against the conservative government that had joined America's coalition in Iraq. The new socialist prime minister promptly announced that he would withdraw the Spanish troops. In this political climate, demonstrations across the United States (coordinated with demonstrations throughout the world) were held on March 20, 2004, under the joint auspices of the "moderate" United for Peace and Justice, and the radical Not In Our Name and International ANSWER coalition.[25]

The popular front established by the organizers made their ideological differences irrelevant to their primary agenda, which was to undermine America's efforts to secure a stable regime in Iraq and to conduct a defensive war against the terrorists. The moderate partner in the front, United for Peace and Justice, called for "an end to the occupation of Iraq and Bush's militaristic foreign policies," and also "opposition to the so-called Patriot Act."[26] Its radical partner International ANSWER demanded: "Bring the troops home now! End colonial occupation from Iraq to Palestine and everywhere!" and "Overturn the USA Patriot Act."[27]

The inclusive nature of the international protest meant that opponents of American "militarism" and "imperialism," appeasers of al Qaeda, opponents of the Patriot Act, supporters of terrorist organizations like Hamas and Hizbollah and of Islamic jihad, supporters of Saddam Hussein and of Communist dictatorships in North Korea, Cuba, and China, would march arm in arm in the name of "peace" and of putting an end to "American hegemony."

19

Homeland Security

In January 2004, two months before the global protest, President Bush delivered his annual State of the Union address. He reviewed the victories of the past two years in Afghanistan and Iraq, and assessed the war tasks ahead. "As we gather tonight, hundreds of thousands of American servicemen and women are deployed across the world in the War on Terror. By bringing hope to the oppressed and delivering justice to the violent, they are making America more secure." Homeland security was prominent in the president's agenda: "Each day, law enforcement personnel and intelligence officers are tracking terrorist threats; analysts are examining airline passenger lists; the men and women of our new Homeland Security Department are patrolling our coasts and borders. And their vigilance is protecting America."

The cornerstone of this domestic security program was the Patriot Act, which Congress had passed in 2001 just after the World Trade Center attack. When the president came to the point in his address where he intended to ask legislators to renew the act, however, there was an unscripted moment in the proceedings. "Key provisions of the Patriot Act are set to expire next year," he said. The

Democrat side of the chamber broke out in applause. The president paused to look in the direction of his opponents, and then, with emphasis on each word that followed, he said, "The terrorist threat will not expire on that schedule." Now the Republican side applauded. "Our law enforcement needs this vital legislation to protect our citizens. You need to renew the Patriot Act."

Just six days after the president's speech, a federal judge in Los Angeles struck down one of the Patriot Act's key provisions "aimed at blocking support for foreign terrorist groups."[28] The provision prohibited citizens from providing material support to foreign terrorist organizations by giving them "expert advice or assistance." This provision had been incorporated from the Anti-Terrorism and Effective Death Penalty Act, signed into law by President Clinton in 1996 after the bombing of the Oklahoma federal building.

It was a Clinton appointee, Judge Audrey Collins, who decided in favor of the plaintiffs in the Los Angeles case, agreeing with their lawyers that the Patriot Act provision—which prohibited technical and personnel assistance to designated terrorist organizations— would violate the First Amendment. The governments' lawyers defended the provision, arguing that the law "made clear that Americans are threatened as much by the person who teaches a terrorist to build a bomb as by the one who pushes the button."[29] The judge's rejection of this argument was summarized by a *Wall Street Journal* reporter as "a setback for government anti-terrorism policies."[30]

The Los Angeles lawsuit—*Humanitarian Law Project et al v. Reno et al.*—was brought by the radical Center for Constitutional Rights, which had been challenging the law on behalf of the same defendants—the Kurdish Workers Party, of Turkey, and the Tamil Tigers,[31] of Sri Lanka—since 1996.[32] The center was one of a group of legal organizations—the fraternally related National Lawyers Guild was another—with a long history of legal campaigns against federal internal security measures and an equally long history of political agitation on behalf of radical and terrorist groups accused of violating them. Both organizations were core constituents of the "legal Left" and its protest movements against American national security policies and against American policy generally.[33]

The Center for Constitutional Rights was founded in 1966 by William Kunstler, Arthur Kinoy, and Morton Stavis, attorneys who were either members of the Communist Party or politically allied with the radical agendas of the "new left."[34] Michael Ratner, long-time president of the center, has also been president of the National Lawyers Guild,[35] which began as a Soviet front and has continued to embrace the Communist political heritage. The center and the guild are integral parts of the radical Left and see themselves as the legal arm of a movement against American "imperialism." Each has a long history of obstructing the American government's efforts against Communism in the Cold War with Russia and in Vietnam and other fields of conflict. Ratner and Ramsey Clark—the central figure in the International ANSWER coalition—for example, were among the founders of the Lawyers Committee Against U.S. Intervention in Central America in the 1980s.[36]

Since the attorneys themselves are activists in these movements, they see themselves as supporters of radicals who are declared enemies of the capitalist system and are there to help them when they get themselves into trouble. In an interview with George Packer for the *New York Times*, Kunstler law partner Ron Kuby, a member of both groups, was candidly introspective in talking about a colleague who had been indicted for aiding and abetting a terrorist: "Lawyers are cowards, Kuby told me. . . . They live vicariously through their clients. 'Movement' lawyers, especially, identify with the people they represent. . . . In the best of cases we identify with their determination, with their courage, and we see the people that maybe we could have been had we the courage to do what they did. And as a result, if you're a good lawyer, you spend a lot of time doing gut checks. And because it's a profession that is so cowardly, enjoying the aura of being those people without ever taking the risks of being those people, it's easy to say: this is the right thing to do, I'm not hurting anyone, this is morally justified."[37]

While embracing the agendas of their clients, the radical legal groups assumed deceptive names like the Center for Constitutional Rights and passed themselves off as "civil liberties" organizations. Their terrorist clients, on the other hand, frequently presented themselves as "humanitarian groups." This was the case with the plaintiffs in Los Angeles. The court obligingly accepted their self-description at face value and referred to them as such, a practice adopted by the news media covering their legal proceedings.[38] In the Los Angeles case, the plaintiffs bore names like the "Tamil Human Rights and Welfare Committee," although this was in a fact a front group for a Marxist terrorist organization, the Liberation Tigers of Tamil Eelam.

The two terrorist organizations involved in the Patriot case—the Kurdish Workers Party was the other—were among the largest in the world, responsible for hundreds of suicide bombings and more than 100,000 deaths between them. Both had been officially designated terrorist groups by Secretary of State Madeleine Albright during the Clinton administration.[39] In arguing their case, the lawyers for the Center for Constitutional Rights contended that the designation of groups as "terrorist" was itself unconstitutional—a position maintained by the legal Left generally. But in Los Angeles, Judge Audrey Collins ruled against the plaintiffs, affirming that such governmental designations were valid.

The lead plaintiff in the case was an American organization, the Humanitarian Law Project. This was a radical organization with a record of years of service providing legal counsel and promotional help to the Kurdish Workers Party, the Liberation Tigers of Tamil Eelam and the Zapatistas, a Marxist guerrilla group in Mexico. The Humanitarian Law Project is part of a network of radical organizations funded by the Anagnos Peace Foundation and housed rent-free in the Anagnos Peace Center that includes the National Lawyers Guild and the Coalition for World Peace, an equally radical group. One of the member organizations in the coalition is the Committees of Correspondence for Democracy and Socialism, a Communist Party faction cochaired by Leslie Cagan. The directors of the Humanitarian Law Project are well-known leftists and veterans of the "solidarity" campaigns in behalf of the Communist movements in Central America in the 1980s.[40]

In making its case, the Humanitarian Law Project claimed that the "expert advice" it provided to the terrorists was in the area of "international law and the art of peace-making and negotiation," and that its free speech in these areas would be infringed by the Patriot Act. The government's lawyer countered that advice in these areas "was not even arguably expert."[41]

Acting as lead counsel for the plaintiffs and the Center for Constitutional Rights was Georgetown Law Professor David Cole, himself a radical and one of the advisory board members of the anti-war organization and Maoist front group, Not In Our Name. In court, Cole maintained that the provisions of the antiterrorism law that designated "material support" for terrorists a criminal act were unconstitutional. His argument was that they "do not require proof that an individual intended to further terrorist activity, and that the law, therefore, imposes guilt by association, rather than on the basis of one's acts."[42]

The same argument was being used at the time by Palestinian nongovernmental organizations who were refusing to accept U.S.

foreign AID "rather than sign a pledge promising that the money would not be used to support terrorism." James Zogby, head of the radical Arab American Institute, defended the Palestinian organizations saying that their refusal to sign the pledge "should not be seen as support for terrorism," and that the very "idea of providing non 'material support' is such a broad brush stroke, it compromises the ability of the humanitarian organizations to function."[43]

Both Zogby's and Cole's legal arguments ignored the fact that "accessory to a crime" and "conspiracy to commit murder" are features of established law.[44] Their argument would make Saddam Hussein innocent of complicity in suicide bombings in Israel if the $25,000 donations he made to the families of "martyrs" were paid through a charitable organization. But as terrorism expert Michael Radu has observed, "In a globalized world of mass communications, travel and instant financial transactions, [terrorist organizations like] the Kurdish Workers Party and the Liberation Tigers of Tamil Eelam cannot survive without international help. The same can be said of al Qaeda, Hamas, the Philippines's New People's Army, the Basque ETA, and many other violent groups. As Clausewitz put it, war is the continuation of politics by other means. Giving 'political and humanitarian' aid to terrorists is paying for murder."[45]

The "material support" provision of the Patriot Act had become an important instrument in the battle against terrorism, because terrorist organizations depended so heavily on political and charitable fronts for financial and legal help and to recruit members and advance their agendas. This was as true of the Irish Republican Army, whose political arm was Sinn Fein, as it was of Islamic terrorist groups like Hizbollah, Hamas, and al Qaeda. Millions of dollars had been raised through charitable fronts in the United States to fund global Islamic terror.[46]

Charitable and political nonprofits were not incidental to the terrorist threat but central. A prime counterterrorism effort of the federal government, for example, was to pressure the Saudis not to fund *madrassas* or religious schools, which were the principal recruiting centers for al Qaeda. As terrorism expert Steven Emerson summed it up, "By far the most important tactic utilized by terrorist groups in America has been to use non-profit organizations to establish a zone of legitimacy within which fund-raising, recruitment, and even outright planning can occur."[47]

An underappreciated fact about the War on Terror is that America itself is a primary base of Islamic terrorist operations. America has functioned as a prime organizing site for international terrorism because the liberties provided by the American legal system allow terrorists to travel freely, raise money, propagandize, recruit, and move men and money across international borders. Terrorist organizers, including the leaders of al Qaeda, Hamas, and the Muslim Brotherhood have all traveled extensively in the United States, raised funds, recruited soldiers and sent emissaries back and forth across America's borders. This makes control of borders and other immigration issues a crucial front in the anti-terrorist war.

Not surprisingly, the National Lawyers Guild, the Center for Constitutional Rights, the American Civil Liberties Union (ACLU), and associated legal experts like David Cole are also fierce opponents of border control and immigration security. They are leaders of the movement to open America's borders and to establish rights for illegal immigrants that would blur the distinction between citizens and noncitizens and extend the protections of the Constitution to the latter. Since 9/11, this movement, which includes dozens of radical organizations, has targeted every effort by the Homeland Security Department under the Patriot Act to strengthen America's borders.[48]

The principal financier of the open-borders movement is the Ford Foundation which was also the financier of the hate-fest in Durban and the World Social Forum. Its $11 billion in assets makes it the largest dispenser of "philanthropic" dollars in the world. On the second anniversary of the 9/11 attacks, the Ford Foundation published a newsletter interview with David Cole about his new book (also Ford-funded) *Enemy Aliens: Double Standards and Constitutional Freedoms in the War on Terrorism*. The Ford grant to underwrite Cole's book was intended to "safeguard human rights and civil liberties of non–U.S. citizens and to inform policy makers and the public about these issues." The Ford newsletter warned that "Cole's fight has taken on new urgency, as the government has detained thousands of Arab-American and Muslim men, held hundreds of 'enemy combatants' without trial, charges or access to legal representation, and endorsed racial profiling in terrorism cases."

In the interview Cole denounced "the criminalization of what the government calls *material support for terrorist organizations* [emphasis added]. This is a practice that was introduced, again through the immigration law, against foreign nationals, but has now become part of the criminal law, and applies to both U.S. citizens and foreign nationals. It criminalizes any support of any blacklisted terrorist organization without regard to whether one's support actually had any connection whatsoever to terrorist activity that the group undertakes."[49] As already noted, however, making a member or supporter of a criminal group accountable for its crimes is an established legal concept. Funding a suicide bomber or the organization that supports suicide bombers obviously makes the crimes themselves possible.

The reforms introduced by the Anti-Terrorism and Effective Death Penalty Act of 1996 and the Patriot Act of 2001 were inspired by the fact that the existing framework of legal protections had made America a primary organizing base for global terrorism, and in particular for terrorism directed against the United States. Before embarking on their fatal mission on 9/11, all of the terrorists had lived, operated, and trained within the United States. The terrorist organizations Hamas and Palestine Islamic Jihad had actually been created in the United States and were able to coordinate their worldwide terror with the aid of existing American laws.[50]

Among the architects of the terrorist jihad who had taken advantage of the situation existing prior to the enactment of the antiterrorism legislation was the Palestinian radical Abdullah Azzam, the mentor of Osama bin Laden himself. A university professor and member of the Muslim Brotherhood, Azzam founded the Alkifah Center in Peshawar in the early 1980s, where he had gone following the Soviet invasion of Afghanistan. Starting with only a storefront, he revived the concept of armed jihad among Muslims with the best-selling tract *Defending the Land of the Muslims Is Each Man's Most Important Duty.* In 1985, Azzam recruited a young Osama bin Laden to be the financier of the holy war he had launched against Israel and the United States.[51]

As Steven Emerson reports, "It was in the United States that Azzam was able to raise much of his money, enlist new fighters, and—most important—enjoy the political freedom to coordinate with other radical Islamic movements. From 1985 to 1989, Azzam and his top aide, Palestinian Sheikh Tamim al-Adnani, visited dozens of American cities, exhorting new recruits to pick up the sword against the enemies of Islam. They raised tens of thousands of dollars and enlisted hundreds and hundreds of fighters and believers." Thus, the First Conference of Jihad was held by Azzam not in Peshawar or Riyadh or Damascus, but in Brooklyn, at the Al-Farook Mosque on Atlantic Avenue. There, in 1988, Azzam exhorted the nearly two hundred Islamic militants who attended the conference with the following words:

Every Muslim on earth should unsheathe his sword and fight to liberate Palestine. The jihad is not limited to Afghanistan.... You must fight in any place you can get.... Whenever jihad is mentioned in the Holy Book, it means the obligation to fight. It does not mean to fight with the pen or to write books or articles in the press or to fight by holding lectures.[52]

The terrorist centers created by Azzam were embedded in mosques and Islamic community centers across the United States. He opened branches of Alkifah in Atlanta, Boston, Chicago, Brooklyn, Jersey City, Pittsburgh, Tucson, and thirty other American cities, as well as in Europe and the Middle East. He published a magazine called *Al-Jihad* with inflammatory articles directed against the United States, Christians, and Jews, exposing their alleged crimes against Islam. "*Al-Jihad* called for Muslims to pick up the gun and wage jihad to kill the infidels and 'all enemies of Islam.'"[53]

According to Emerson, these Alkifah centers shipped bombs, timers, and explosives to Hamas in Gaza, counterfeited money to purchase weapons, and forged passports to enable Islamic militants to visit the United States and the jihad battle fronts. Azzam's Tucson Alkifah Center was a base for Wadih el-Hage, Osama bin Laden's personal secretary, who was convicted of the bombing of the U.S. embassies in Africa. When Azzam was assassinated in Pakistan in 1989, a power struggle ensued to control his organization. The center of this struggle was not in Pakistan, but in the Brooklyn Alkifah Center.

The victor in this struggle (his rival was also assassinated) was the blind sheik Omar Abdel Rahman, leader of a terrorist organization called the Islamic Group, and of the terrorist cell that bombed the World Trade Center in 1993 in an attempt to kill

250,000 people.[54] (The group also intended to blow up the Lincoln and Holland Tunnels when they were filled with rush-hour traffic, but the plots were thwarted.) When he was arrested for the Trade Center bombing, the blind sheik was represented by Lynne Stewart, a Center for Constitutional Rights attorney and a member of the National Lawyers Guild. In direct defiance of a Justice Department order, Stewart used her role as the sheik's counsel to enable him to communicate with his terrorist followers in Egypt, specifically to break a truce between violent factions. The Justice Department promptly indicted Stewart for providing material support to terrorist organizations.

Stewart's attitude toward her terrorist client (and he was not the first) was described by her Center for Constitutional Law colleague Ron Kuby this way: "When the lawyer is as loving and committed as Stewart, [Kuby] said, and the client as charismatic as Sheik Omar Abdel Rahman, the identification becomes passionate."[55] Stewart described her own view of "Muslim fundamentalists" to the radical magazine *Monthly Review*: "They are basically forces of national liberation. And I think that we, as persons who are committed to the liberation of oppressed people, should fasten on the need for self-determination.... My own sense is that, were the Islamists to be empowered, there would be movements within their own countries... to liberate."[56]

When asked about her attitude toward terror by the *New York Times*, Ms. Stewart suggested that violence and revolution were sometimes necessary to right the economic and racial wrongs of America's capitalist system. Stewart elaborated: "I don't believe in anarchistic violence, but in directed violence. That would be violence directed at the institutions which perpetuate capitalism, racism, and sexism, and the people who are the appointed guardians of those institutions, and accompanied by popular support."[57] This was a solid basis for what Kuby described as the "passionate...identification" between radical attorneys like Stewart and their terrorist clients.

Stewart's comradely attitude towards Islamic terrorists was hardly unique in the American Left. One of the most sophisticated terrorist leaders based in America was able to insert himself into the very heart of this Left and become one of its best-known Muslim figures. Osama (Sami) al-Arian was a Palestinian professor of engineering who operated out of the University of South Florida. Al-Arian created two nonprofit organizations, a think tank associated with the university called the World Islamic Studies Enterprise (WISE) and the Islamic Committee for Palestine, which raised funds and recruited soldiers for Islamic jihad. Al-Arian's Islamic Committee had featured the blind sheik, Omar Abdel Rahman, as a guest speaker while Tarik Hamdi, a board member of WISE, was known by authorities to have personally delivered a satellite telephone and battery pack to Osama bin Laden in Afghanistan in May 1998.[58]

Sami al-Arian was, in fact, the North American head of Palestinian Islamic Jihad, one of the principal terrorist organizations in the Middle East, responsible for suicide bombings that took the lives of more than a hundred people, including two Americans, aged sixteen and twenty, before he was arrested in February 2003. An FBI surveillance video of al-Arian's fundraising tour of American mosques shows al-Arian being introduced as "the president of the Islamic Committee for Palestine.... The active arm of the Islamic Jihad Movement." While others in the video praise the killing of Jews and Christians, al-Arian states, "Let us damn America...Let us damn [her] allies until death." In another speech al-Arian said, "We assemble today to pay respects to the march of the martyrs and to the river of blood that gushes forth and does not extinguish, from butchery to butchery, and from martyrdom to martyrdom, from jihad to jihad."[59]

In 1997, al-Arian created another organization, the National Coalition to Protect Political Freedom. He appointed Kit Gage, a member of the National Lawyers Guild and a veteran of the anti-Vietnam Left to be its executive director. The specific purpose of the National Coalition to Protect Political Freedom was to oppose the Anti-Terrorism and Effective Death Penalty Act—the predecessor to the Patriot Act—which had been passed in 1996 following the bombing of the federal building in Oklahoma City, a terrorist atrocity that killed 175 innocent people. Pursuant to the act, Palestinian Islamic Jihad was declared a terrorist organization. The act made "material support" for terrorist organizations illegal and authorized the use of secret evidence in terrorist cases. Sami al-Arian's brother-in-law, Mazen al-Najjar, was arrested under its terms, held for three and a half years, and eventually deported after 9/11. His attorney was David Cole, the Center for Constitutional Rights counsel in the Los Angeles Patriot Act case and the Ford Foundation's legal scholar and advocate against post-9/11 immigration controls.

Among the organizations supporting al-Arian's "civil liberties" crusade against the terrorist legislation along with the National Lawyers Guild, the Center for Constitutional Rights, and the ACLU, were the American Muslim Council (AMC) and the Council on American-Islamic Relations (CAIR), two radical Islamic groups that also pretended to be civil liberties organizations. CAIR is an offshoot of the Hamas-created Islamic Association for Palestine, and several of its leaders have been arrested as terrorists. The American Muslim Council is the "founder, corporate parent and supporter of several militant Islamic groups, while its leaders have openly championed Hamas terrorists, defended Middle Eastern terrorist regimes, [and] issued anti-Semitic and anti-American statements."[60]

The 120-page indictment of al-Arian issued by the Ashcroft Justice Department was based on a seven-year investigation, including extensive wiretaps of al-Arian's conversations with Hamas terrorists in Syria and the Middle East. Among the two hundred specific acts connecting al-Arian to the terrorist organization listed in the indictment were a fax sent "to Saudi Arabia, [that] inquired about obtaining palletized urea fertilizer [a chemical compound used in explosives] in fifty kilogram bags suitable for ocean transportation,"[61] and telephone calls arranging payments to the families of suicide bombers, which was one of al-Arian's responsibilities as financial head of the terrorist organization.[62]

Sami al-Arian was arrested for his terrorist activities in February 2003. He had been under investigation by the FBI since 1996 and had long been publicly identified as a terrorist by close observers of the Islamic jihad movement like Steven Emerson. The basis for their suspicion was fairly transparent. For example, one board member of al-Arian's think tank (WISE), a Palestinian academic named Khalil Shiqaqi, was the brother of Fathi Shiqaqi the well-known founder of Palestinian Islamic Jihad. When Fathi Shiqaqi was assassinated, he was replaced as head of the terrorist organization by Ramadan Abdullah Shallah, who was the director of al-Arian's think tank and a board member of WISE himself. At the same time, al-Arian's nonprofit—the Islamic Committee for Palestine—was involved in raising money and recruiting at public events across America to "sponsor" Palestinian martyrs and featuring appeals by fundraisers "who begged for $500 to kill a Jew."[63]

When Emerson began warning the public about al-Arian's terrorist recruitment efforts and his connections to Palestinian Islamic Jihad, he was ferociously attacked for "Muslim-bashing" and "McCarthyism" by prominent figures in the political Left, among whom al-Arian was by now a familiar colleague. On September 26, 2001, al-Arian made the mistake of appearing on the FOX News Channel's *O'Reilly Factor*. The host confronted al-Arian with his public calls for "Death to Israel" and declared, "If I was the CIA, I'd follow you wherever you went." The ensuing public uproar produced enough embarrassment to University of South Florida officials that they finally suspended al-Arian from his professorship, albeit with pay.

Al-Arian immediately adopted the posture of the victim: "I'm a minority," he said. "I'm an Arab. I'm a Palestinian. I'm a Muslim. That's not a popular thing to be these days. Do I have rights, or don't I have rights?"[64] The American Left sprang to al-Arian's defense. Their efforts included articles in *The Nation* and *Salon.com*, whose reporter Eric Boehlert called it "The Prime Time Smearing of Sami al-Arian" and explained, "By pandering to anti-Arab hysteria, NBC, FOX News, Media General and Clear Channel radio disgraced themselves—and ruined an innocent professor's life."[65] Others who joined the al-Arian defense chorus included the ACLU, the Center for Constitutional Rights, the University of South Florida faculty union, and the American Association of University Professors.[66] The leftist head of Georgetown's Middle East studies program, John Esposito, expressed concern that al-Arian not be a "victim of... anti-Arab and anti-Muslim bigotry," and Ellen Schrecker, the foremost academic expert on the McCarthy era (who regards American Communists as well-meaning social reformers and innocent victims of government persecution), called al-Arian's suspension "political repression."[67]

After the *O'Reilly* show and just before al-Arian's indictment, Duke University held a symposium called "National Security and Civil Liberties." Al-Arian was the featured (and university-sponsored) speaker. After his arrest, a report on his appearance at Duke was posted on the leftist website CommonDreams.org. It was written by Sarah Shields, a professor of Middle Eastern Studies at the University of North Carolina:

Professor Sami al-Arian made an impassioned plea for free speech. An immigrant, a professor, a leader of his Muslim community, al-Arian had campaigned against the use of secret evidence in court, embracing the democratic guarantees of a constitution designed to protect the innocent. Professor al-Arian had seen first hand the triumph of our most valued principles. At a time when Americans needed the information about the growing number of Muslims in this country, he helped found a think tank [WISE] devoted to the study of Islam in this country.... Sami al-Arian has spent the past decade arguing passionately for the freedom of conscience, for the protections against arbitrary imprisonment that form the very foundations of our civilization. Now he is locked up, unable to appear in court in his own defense, awaiting trial under conditions uncommon for even the worst convicted criminals.... When I was in preschool, I heard fairy tales about all-powerful kings who arbitrarily threw people into dungeons. When I was in Hebrew school, I learned how Jews were rounded up by rulers during times of instability.... And today I wonder: was there a warning in those fairy tales, those stories about bad kings, evil advisors, and their dungeons?"[68]

Sami al-Arian was arrested five months after the O'Reilly episode. The arrest took place seven years after the FBI investigation began, and was made possible only by provisions adopted in the Patriot Act. The reason for the long delay was the existence of a government rule that created a wall between criminal and intelligence investigations, and barred the FBI and intelligence agencies from communicating with each other. It was this rule that had prevented FBI agents in Minneapolis from breaking into the computer of Zacarias Moussaoui—the so-called twentieth hijacker—a month before 9/11. Had the FBI agents been given permission to search Moussaoui's computer, two of the 9/11 hijackers would have been identified along with the Hamburg cell that planned the attack, and it is possible that the 9/11 tragedy would have been averted.[69]

The rule erecting a barrier between intelligence and criminal investigations had been put in place by Attorney General Janet Reno in July 1995.[70] Referred to as "the wall," it caused a breakdown in the collaboration between investigators that national security officials had long realized was a danger to public safety. In the words of Mary Jo White, a Clinton-appointed U.S. attorney who was the most seasoned al Qaeda prosecutor before 9/11, "The walls are the single greatest danger we have blocking our ability to obtain and act on [terrorist] information."[71] One of the important innovations of the Patriot Act was to eliminate these walls. This made possible the collaboration between intelligence agencies and the FBI and led directly to the arrest of Sami al-Arian and his associates.

Another post-9/11 security reform was removing the so-called "Levi" guidelines implemented by the Ford administration, which barred the FBI from conducting surveillance on radical organizations unless they could be shown to have committed (or be planning to commit) specific criminal acts. Under these guidelines, a terrorist organization—such as Abdullah Azzam's Alkifah or Sami al-Arian's Islamic Crusade for Palestine—could recruit soldiers and funds for a holy war against the United States and be insulated from FBI scrutiny unless it could be tied to an actual criminal act. In the new age of terror, this could mean an act as destructive as 9/11 itself.

Yet it was precisely these provisions of the Patriot Act to which the Left objected and against which it mounted a ferocious national campaign. For more than half a century the Left had defended revolutionaries and agents of revolutionary states who had broken American laws. Radical legal organizations like the National

Lawyers Guild and the Center for Constitutional Rights, as well as Sami al-Arian's National Coalition to Protect Political Freedom, had been created for the express purpose of doing so. They supplied the lead counsels for violent radicals and terrorist suspects both before and after 9/11 and were themselves vocal antagonists of America's wars and its national security defenses.

It was the idea of terrorism itself that radicals found problematic. In a lengthy statement of its position, the Center for Constitutional Rights complained, "the [Patriot] Act creates a new category of crime, domestic terrorism, which blurs the line between speech and criminal activity. Section 802 of the Act defines domestic terrorism as, 'acts dangerous to human life that are a violation of criminal laws [that] appear to be intended to influence the policy of a government by intimidation or coercion.' This definition is so vague that acts of civil disobedience may be construed to violate the law.... Thus, a spontaneous demonstration that blocks the path of an ambulance might invite charges of domestic terrorism under the new law."[72]

In fact, exactly this kind of civil disobedience that served terrorist agendas was close to what American radicals had actually planned for the opening stages of the war in Iraq. As the left-wing magazine *Salon.com* reported, "If bombs start falling on Iraq, peace activists say, expect insurgency at home."[73] On the eve of America's engagement, *Salon* explained, a radical group called the Military Globalization Project announced plans to march on the Vandenberg Air Force base in California, which was coordinating military operations in Iraq via satellite. The radicals identified the base as "the electronic nerve center of the global-surveillance-targeting, weapons-guidance and military-command satellites that will largely direct the war." Their express purpose was to disrupt the war effort. Fortunately, this particular plan for "civil disobedience" was discouraged when the base commander warned that trespassers would be shot on sight.[74]

American radicals were not ready yet to actually die for Saddam Hussein.

Other radical groups, however, did stage civil disobedience demonstrations that were calculated to block busy downtown hubs in major cities across the nation, and timed for the outbreak of hostilities. In Los Angeles, one-tenth of the entire police force—900 officers —who might otherwise have been engaged in homeland defense efforts were tied up handling these "civil disobedience" protests.[75] If al Qaeda or some other foreign terrorist organization had been able to mount attacks in these cities coinciding with the outbreak of the war, the activities of domestic radicals could have obstructed ambulances and other Homeland Security defense services. It was this kind of political support for terror that the legal radicals were determined to protect.

Any legislation as comprehensive and complex as the Patriot Act inevitably has gray areas over which legal jurists might reasonably disagree when striking an appropriate balance between security requirements and civil liberty needs. The principal organizations opposed to the Patriot Act, however, were not "civil libertarians" in a primary sense. They were radical activists whose agendas went well beyond their expressed concerns about constitutional issues, and whose concern for constitutional issues was subordinate to the "higher" goals of their radical agendas. These ulterior agendas were the inspiration for their blanket condemnation of the Patriot Act and the near hysteria with which they expressed their objections to its specific provisions.

When it had been put to a congressional vote, the Patriot Act was passed overwhelmingly by both parties in Congress with only one dissenting vote in the Senate and only sixty-six in the House. Its terms were far milder than measures that had been adopted in America's previous wars by revered historical figures like Lincoln, who suspended *habeas corpus,* and by Franklin Roosevelt who relocated and interned Japanese aliens and Japanese Americans away from coastal areas as a security measure during World War II.[76] The Patriot Act stayed well within the parameters of established law. Its enforcement provisions, including extraordinary searches, were made subject to judicial review and required judicial writs and warrants to authorize them. Yet the attacks on the Act described it in extreme terms as "unpatriotic" and a "war on our freedoms," misrepresenting it as "arguably the most far-reaching and invasive legislation passed since the espionage act of 1917 and the sedition act of 1918."[77]

Directed by organizations like the ACLU, the National Lawyers Guild, the Center for Constitutional Rights, the Bill of Rights Defense Committee, and People for the American Way, radicals mobilized legislators in local and state governments to obstruct the enforcement of the law. As of June 2004, 320 cities, towns, and counties, as well as four states had adopted resolutions condemning the Patriot Act, many refusing to cooperate with Homeland Security officials in the enforcement of its security measures.[78] The ACLU's model resolution—posted on its website and designed for municipalities to copy—came close to incitement to sedition:

> Therefore, be it resolved that the council of the city of
> _____ ... directs the Police Department of the City of
> _____ to:
>
> (a) refrain from participating in the enforcement of federal immigration laws;
>
> (b) seek adequate written assurances from federal authorities that residents of the City of _____who are placed in federal custody will not be subjected to military detention;

secret detention; secret immigration proceedings; or detention without access to counsel, and refrain from assisting federal authorities to obtain custody of such individuals absent such assurances.

(c) refrain, whether acting alone or with federal or state law enforcement officers, from collecting or maintaining information about the political, religious or social views, associations or activities of any individual, group, association, organization, corporation, business or partnership unless such information directly relates to an investigation of criminal activities, and there are reasonable grounds to suspect the subject of the information is or may be involved in criminal conduct;

(d) refrain from the practice of stopping drivers or pedestrians for the purpose of scrutinizing their identification documents without particularized suspicion of criminal activity... [79]

No opposition to the Patriot Act was more revealing than the determination of the leftist legal groups to prevent security officials from scrutinizing radical Islamic religious groups and political organizations aligned with radical Islam and its terrorist jihad. Their zeal in this matter revealed how the legal battle was really a front line of the War on Terror itself. During the 1970s, there had been more than a thousand domestic bombings connected with the protests against the Vietnam War. One terrorist cult, the Weather Underground, had collaborated with adversary governments in Cuba and North Vietnam and carried out dozens of bombings of targets that included the Pentagon and the U.S. Capitol. Moreover, they had been able to do so with relative impunity. Despite the fact that the Weather leaders had declared "war" on the United States in official "communiqués" and law enforcement knew their identities, the FBI was never able to arrest their leadership or interdict its operations. In part this was because of the support and protection these terrorists received from American leftists and in part because the FBI was hamstrung in its investigations by restrictions on its activities in the name of civil liberties. If the Weather bombers had been in league with Islamic radicals and their arsenal had included biological and chemical weapons, the consequences of their violence might have been catastrophic.[80]

Such considerations carried no weight with the radical legal organizations opposing the Patriot Act for the simple reason that they and their members identified with the political movement that spawned the terrorist group. Indeed, the principal (and unrepentant) leader of the Weather Underground (America's first terrorist cult) is now a prominent member of the legal left and its opposition to the Patriot Act. Bernardine Dohrn is a law professor at Northwestern University, a prominent figure in the American Bar Association,[81] and a vocal defender of the terror she pursued in the Vietnam era. In an article written in the spring of 2003 for the Marxist periodical *Monthly Review* ("Homeland Imperialism: Fear and Resistance"), Dohrn characterizes the "war at home" as a "resistance" to U.S. imperialism, and describes counterterrorism efforts as a McCarthy witch hunt and "the USA Patriot Act and now the bill creating the Homeland Security Department as . . . the actual tools of repression."[82] According to Dohrn, "Prosecutions are underway that are reminiscent of the indictments of the early-fifties McCarthy period and the conspiracy indictments of the early seventies pre-Watergate Mitchell Department of Justice, the two most recent periods of overtly political repression. For example, [Attorney General] John Ashcroft has orchestrated a series of high profile indictments against Islamic charities, including the Holy Land Foundation in Texas."

In fact, the indictment against the Holy Land Foundation and other "charities" had nothing to do with their political advocacy or Islamic identity. The Holy Land Foundation had been launched with seed money provided by Moussa Abu Marzouk, the leader of the terrorist organization Hamas. Marzouk had been arrested in the United States in 1995 with documents that established his Hamas position and detailed "a $10 million commercial and non-profit empire in the United States, which he controlled allegedly to finance Hamas operations."[83] Like those of other Islamic radicals, Marzouk's defense was provided by the Center for Constitutional Rights and one of its lead lawyers, Stanley Cohen, who was an attorney and an advocate for both Hamas and the Syrian government. Marzouk was eventually deported and wound up in Syria as head of Hamas's terrorist operations there.[84]

As with al-Arian, when the Holy Land Foundation was raided, the legal left rallied to its defense. They were joined in their protests by the radical Muslim "civil liberties" fronts, the Council on American-Islamic Relations (CAIR) and the American Muslim Council, which claimed the raid was part of "an anti-Muslim witch-hunt promoted by the pro-Israel lobby in America."[85] Documents seized in the raid revealed that the Holy Land Foundation was part of a large network of organizations that Hamas had created through Marzouk's efforts, and that linked the Islamic Association for Palestine, CAIR, the Muslim Students Association, and al Qaeda.[86]

The common political agendas of the legal left and their terrorist clients are exemplified by Lynne Stewart, the attorney for the "blind sheik," Omar Abdel Rahman. Since her indictment by the Ashcroft Justice Department, Stewart has become their martyr and icon.

Lynne Stewart is a protégé of William Kunstler and Ramsey Clark, who had originally suggested that Stewart sign on as attorney for the blind sheik.[87] Following her indictment for providing material support for the sheik's terrorist activities, Stewart—like Sami al-Arian before her—received full support from her political comrades on the left. Her decision to aid and abet her terrorist client was defended as a civil liberties matter by the ACLU, the American Bar Association, the National Lawyers Guild, and the Center for Constitutional Rights. She was invited by radical law professors to speak at law schools across the country including Stanford, Seattle, and William Mitchell in St. Paul where she addressed a "Social Justice Dinner" sponsored by the National Lawyers Guild. These accolades encouraged leftist law students at the City University of New York to attempt to present her with the school's Public Interest Lawyer of the Year Award at graduation ceremonies in 2003. A petition including seventy-three names— more than half the law school graduating class—was sent to administrators. But after the award was leaked to the press, CUNY law school dean Kristin Booth Glen informed students via e-mail that Stewart would not be honored. The reason given was not that she had betrayed her country or broken the law, but that the award "could lead to consequences that could be damaging."[88]

Stewart was a speaker at the Socialist Scholars Conference, an annual gathering of the intellectual Left, where she shared a panel with Columbia professor Todd Gitlin and others. She was a featured speaker at the anti-war demonstration sponsored by United for Peace and Justice on February 15, 2003. The sentiments she expressed on these occasions were the banal and vulgar clichés of the anti-American and Communist Left. As the final keynote speaker at the National Lawyers Guild National Convention in 2003, Stewart described the enemy—corporate capitalism—as "a consummate

evil that unleashes its dogs of war on the helpless; an enemy motivated only by insatiable greed... In this enemy there is no love of the
land or the creatures that live there, no compassion for the people.
This enemy will destroy the air we breathe and the water we drink
as long as the dollars keep filling up their money boxes."[89] The
enemy was the Great Satan, the same enemy that motivated Stewart's client to plot the destruction of the World Trade Center and
the Lincoln and Holland tunnels.

Lynne Stewart's rant reflects not only the shared anti-American
agendas of Islamic jihadists and the radical Left, but also the
hypocrisy the Left displays in its complaint against the Patriot Act—
that it violates First Amendment rights. In her *Monthly Review*
interview, Stewart was asked to imagine that she was part of a revolutionary government that had "liberated" its people from the horrors of capitalism. If Stewart herself were to become part of such a
government, the interviewer wanted to know, was there a point at
which she would think that monitoring and controlling the counterrevolutionary adversaries of that government was acceptable? Her
answer: "I don't have any problem with Mao or Stalin or the Vietnamese leaders or certainly Fidel locking up people they see as dangerous. Because so often, dissidence has been used by the greater
powers to undermine a people's revolution." [90] In other words, totalitarian repression—complete with firing squads and gulags—is fine
for Communist states, as far as Stewart is concerned but criminalizing acts that aid and abet terrorists in a democracy is not.

In their defense of America's terrorist enemies, the organizations
of the legal left are reminiscent of Communist Party fronts of the
Cold War era. One of these was the National Lawyers Guild itself.
Another was the American Committee for the Protection of the
Foreign Born, which was created by the Communist Party to defend
its leaders and organizers—many of whom were immigrants—from

being deported because of their activities in behalf of the Soviet empire. Even though the Communist Party was a totalitarian organization whose goal was the establishment of a political dictatorship in the United States, it was able to recruit many prominent liberals to sit on the board of the American Committee for the Protection of the Foreign Born and to argue that in defending the internal enemies of American democracy, the organization was actually defending the Constitution itself.[91]

In a symposium on homeland security measures that appeared in the *Boston Review of Books*, a group of left-wing legal experts commented on a paper by Georgetown law professor David Cole. The Cole paper was an assault on the Patriot Act, as were most of the commentaries. These included essays by Harvard constitutional law professor Laurence Tribe and Juliette Kayyem, a former Clinton Justice Department official.[92]

Among the participants in the symposium was another Georgetown law professor, Mari Matsuda, an advisory board member of the ACLU. This is of particular note since Mari Matsuda is one of the legal architects of the notorious "speech codes" that were imposed by college administrations in the 1980s and 1990s to suppress words that were designated "insensitive" or "hate speech." Matsuda is a coauthor of *Words That Wound*, the primary text defending what is now generally recognized as blatant censorship and the most serious infringement of First Amendment rights in half a century. Yet the ACLU, on whose board Matsuda sits, wants the public (and the courts) to believe that its primary concern in opposing the concept of material support for terrorism is its desire to protect free speech.

Cole's symposium paper was titled "Their Liberties, Our Security," and his charge was that Americans were sacrificing the liberties of aliens and immigrants in the name of their own security. Matsuda's contribution, "A Dangerous Place," began with an epigraph from the 1940 annual report of the long-defunct American Committee for the Protection of the Foreign Born: "Attacks on the rights of non-citizens are disguised attacks on the rights of all Americans, native and foreign born."

In a self-revealing explanation to her readers, Matsuda wrote, "The American Committee for the Protection of the Foreign Born was a progressive civil liberties organization or a Communist front, or both, depending upon which side of history you choose." Only a delusional member of the Communist Left could make a statement like this—someone who believed that Communists were on the "right side" of history, as well as someone uninterested in the facts, since there is not a scintilla of doubt that the American Committee for the Protection of the Foreign Born was a Communist Party front, which subordinated any civil liberties concerns to the Party's agendas.[93] Thus, one year after the committee statement quoted by Matsuda, claiming that an attack on the foreign-born is an attack on all Americans, the American Committee for the Protection of the Foreign Born actively *supported* the internment of Japanese Americans during World War II[94]—which Matsuda regards as an enormously significant injustice in her article. The American Committee for the Protection of the Foreign Born betrayed Japanese immigrants because it saw their internment as a necessary measure to win the war, and it wanted to win the war because its ideological motherland, the Soviet Union, had been attacked by the Axis forces.

Matsuda's claim that facts depend on which side of history you are on is an expression of the totalitarian mentality of the radical Left and explains how this Left maintains its institutional loyalties and political attitudes across generations and is thus able to forge alliances of convenience with Nazis in one era and Islamic terrorists and their anti-American jihads in another. It also shows the acuity of President Bush's remarks to Congress following the 9/11 attacks, in which he declared, "We have seen their kind before. They are the heirs of all the murderous ideologies of the twentieth century. By sacrificing human life to serve their radical visions, by abandoning every value except the will to power, they follow in the path of fascism, Nazism and totalitarianism."

PART FIVE:
A NATION DIVIDED

"The most important thing is we should focus on what's the best way to build Iraq as a democracy. ...We should be pulling for America on this. We should be pulling for the people of Iraq. We can have honest disagreements about where we go from here, and we have space now to discuss that in what I hope will be a nonpartisan and open way."

—BILL CLINTON, JULY 22, 2003

"He betrayed us. He took America on an ill-conceived foreign adventure, dangerous to our troops that was preordained and planned before 9/11."

—AL GORE, AUGUST 7, 2003

"There was no imminent threat. This was made up in Texas, announced in January to the Republican leadership that the war is going to take place and was going to be good politically. This whole thing was a fraud."

—TED KENNEDY, SEPTEMBER 18, 2003
"REGIME CHANGE BEGINS AT HOME"
MOVEON.ORG

20

Loyal Opposition

The Bush administration's decision to respond to the attacks of 9/11 by declaring war on global terrorists and the nations who provided them safe harbors was a sharp departure from the politics of the previous Democratic administration. Beginning with the first World Trade Center bombing in 1993 and throughout the Clinton decade, Americans had been the target of attacks by Islamic radicals. But the previous administration had dealt with these attacks as criminal activities committed by individuals and made no attempt to hold the regimes who harbored and encouraged them accountable.

Although a number of congressional Democrats had voiced opposition to the president's war metaphor, the shock of the 9/11 attacks was so vivid and the national mood so overwhelmingly favored a military response that the opposition remained marginal, and a majority of the Congressional Democrats voted in favor of an American land war for the first time since Vietnam. But this bipartisan unity started to crack when the Bush administration began to act on the presidential pledge to take on regimes that provided support for terrorists and were developing weapons whose only purpose was terror.

From the moment the Taliban regime was toppled in December 2001, the Bush administration made it clear that the first of these regimes would be Iraq. In particular, the administration was going to hold the Iraq regime to the terms of the truce it had signed to end the Gulf War in 1991, which left its government in place.

Iraq was the unfinished business of the Clinton administration. In the beginning of 1998 Saddam had expelled the U.N. weapons inspectors required by the Gulf War truce to prevent him from proceeding with his chemical, biological, and nuclear weapons programs. For ten years Saddam Hussein had forced the United States and Britain to engage in a permanent low-level military conflict in the airspace over Northern Iraq to protect the Kurdish minority from another gas attack. Saddam had provided safe harbor for the terrorists Abu Abbas and Abu Nidal and financed suicide bombings in Israel. In an attempt to dissuade the dictator from his confrontational course, Clinton had fired 415 cruise missiles into Iraq with no practical effect.

"One way or the other," Clinton warned, "we are determined to deny Iraq the capacity to develop weapons of mass destruction and the missiles to deliver them. That is our bottom line."[1] Convinced that Saddam could not be persuaded to adhere to the U.N. resolutions or to desist from future aggressions, Clinton submitted a use-of-force resolution against Iraq and a call for "regime change." The resolution passed both Houses of Congress without significant dissent. The Clinton administration then launched air and missile strikes against targets in Iraq, but no invasion was contemplated and the regime remained.

One month after the liberation of Afghanistan, President Bush laid down the first marker that the unfinished business with Iraq was his agenda. Appearing before Congress to deliver his State of the Union Address,[2] he said America had "two great objectives." The first was to "shut down terrorist camps, disrupt terrorist plans and bring terrorists to justice." The second was to prevent "regimes who seek chemical, biological and nuclear weapons from threatening the United States and the world." America, he warned, was not prepared to "wait on events while dangers gather." If America was threatened, America would strike first. Singling out Iraq as one of three states that constituted an "Axis of Evil," he said, "This is a regime that has already used poison gas to murder thousands of its own citizens, leaving the bodies of mothers huddled over their own children. . . . If Saddam Hussein does not fully disarm, for the safety of our people and for the peace of the world, we will lead a coalition to disarm him."

More than a year later, when the war with Iraq was concluded, *New York Times* correspondent Todd S. Purdum commented, "No presidential oratory had been more bellicose" in the forty-one years since John F. Kennedy's Inaugural Address in 1960. The "hard words" of the president, he observed, "implied a big new idea: America could no longer wait to be roused to action by attacks on its shores or its interests. It would act first."[3] But at the time there was no such sense of a radical departure from the foreign policy consensus. Two weeks after the State of the Union address, former Vice President Al Gore appeared before the Council on Foreign Relations to speak on foreign policy issues for the first time since 9/11.

At the time, Gore was still the titular head of the Democratic Party and his speech reflected the bipartisan unity that still prevailed as he endorsed both the president's "bellicosity" and the policy of preemption he had announced in the State of the Union address. "President Bush deserves tremendous credit for the way he has led the nation in a highly successful opening counterattack in the war against terror," Gore said. "I also support the president's stated goals in the next phases of the war against terrorism as he laid them out in the State of the Union."

Gore specifically endorsed Bush's use of the phrase "Axis of Evil," which had been the object of some negative comment from the president's opponents:

> Since the State of the Union there has been much discussion of whether Iraq, Iran and North Korea truly constitute an "Axis of Evil." As far as I'm concerned, there really is something to be said for occasionally putting diplomacy aside and laying one's cards on the table. There is value in calling evil by its name.[4]

On the subject of Iraq itself, Gore could not have more wholeheartedly embraced the proposed confrontation, including, if necessary the impending war:

> In 1991, I crossed party lines and supported the use of force against Saddam Hussein, but he was allowed to survive his defeat as the result of a calculation we all had reason to deeply regret for the ensuing decade. And we still do. So this time, if we resort to force, we must absolutely get it right. It must be an action set up carefully and on the basis of the most realistic concepts. Failure cannot be an option, which means that *we must be prepared to go the limit*. (emphasis added)

The consensus behind the president, his War on Terror and his impending confrontation with Iraq could hardly have been stronger. In the face of the prevailing patriotic mood, even the anti-war Left, was relatively cautious. The main skepticism about White House policy came from European allies and U.N. officials. It took a Republican with unquestionable security credentials to break the domestic silence and launch the first serious attack on the administration's strategy.

This came from General Brent Scowcroft, national security adviser to President Gerald Ford and to the first President Bush during the Gulf War. On August 4, Scowcroft told the CBS news program *Face the Nation* that an invasion of Iraq "could turn the whole region into a cauldron, and thus destroy the war on terrorism." He followed his statement eleven days later with an op-ed in the *Wall Street Journal* bluntly titled "Don't Attack Saddam."[5]

In the article, Scowcroft made two salient arguments that were to become themes of the brewing Democratic opposition: "The central point is that any campaign against Iraq, whatever the strategy, cost and risks, is certain to divert us for some indefinite period from our war on terrorism. Worse, there is a virtual consensus in the world against an attack on Iraq at this time. So long as that sentiment persists, it would require the U.S. to pursue a virtual go-it-alone strategy against Iraq, making any military operations correspondingly more difficult and expensive."[6]

Pressure for a multilateral approach to the crisis was also forming inside the administration. Responding to international sentiments, the State Department urged the White House to seek United Nations support. On September 12, President Bush went before the United Nations General Assembly and appealed to the organization to enforce its own resolutions respecting Iraq. "The conduct of the Iraqi regime is a threat to the authority of the United Nations," the president told the delegates, "and a threat to peace. Iraq has answered a decade of U.N. demands with a decade of defiance. All the world now faces a test, and the United Nations a difficult and defining moment. Are Security Council resolutions to be honored and enforced, or cast aside without consequence? Will the United Nations serve the purpose of its founding, or will it be irrelevant?"

Despite some grumbling over the bluntness of the ultimatum, the response to it was overwhelmingly favorable. Faced with the president's strong words and a steady American buildup of military forces in the Gulf, Saddam agreed to readmit the U.N. inspectors he had ejected four years previously. Thus began a new phase of the tactics that he had used to thwart the Security Council resolutions for more than a decade.

In America and elsewhere, the new political opening had an immediate catalyzing effect on the anti-war movement, which now found itself with what seemed like reasonable options to support— more time for inspectors, and more negotiations rather than a military confrontation. Key elements of the anti-war movement, moreover, were core constituencies of the Democratic Party. These included trade union activists, virtually all groups involved in the so-called "rights coalitions," and liberal party funders including many entertainment industry celebrities. Consequently, inside the Democratic Party the political dynamic also began to change in ways that would impact the coming test of wills.

On September 19, one week after the president's U.N. address, the *New York Times* published an ad attacking the entire War on Terror under the banner headline "Not In Our Name." The text began, "Let it not be said that people in the United States did nothing when their government declared a war without limit and instituted stark new measures of repression." Among its 65,000 signers were such Democratic constituency leaders as Al Sharpton, Jesse Jackson, and Gloria Steinem, and dozens of well-known Hollywood figures.[7] From this juncture, the Democratic Party would be confronted by powerful forces in its own ranks urging its leaders to move to the left and oppose the impending conflict, thus weakening the pressure on the Iraq regime to comply with the U.N. resolutions.

In the presidential campaign of 2000, Al Gore had run a "populist" campaign that appealed strongly to the Party's political Left. On September 23, 2002, he made a foreign policy speech before the

Commonwealth Club of San Francisco. Like his appearance seven months earlier, in which he endorsed the president's designation of Iraq as part of the "Axis of Evil," his words received national media attention. But this time Gore departed sharply from the bipartisan track, as he launched a frontal assault on the administration's national security agendas.[8] Unlike the president's State of the Union address, Gore's speech was truly radical. It was the first break in the bipartisan unity on a fundamental issue of national security by a leader of either party since the McGovern campaign of 1972. That campaign was itself driven by a radical anti-war movement and was the only such departure from the bipartisan foreign policy that had been supported by both parties since the end of World War II.

In his Commonwealth Club address Gore revisited the 1991 war as he had done seven months earlier, but now the edges were sharp, the tone belligerent, and his differences with the administration dramatic. In his February speech, Gore had discreetly referred to the way Saddam Hussein "was allowed to survive his defeat," attributing it to "a calculation we all had reason to deeply regret." Now, however, he referred to the same event by saying, "I felt *betrayed* by the first Bush administration's hasty departure from the battlefield" (emphasis added). In addition to its emotional overtones, the statement itself was suspect, since he had made no mention of such feelings at the end of the Gulf War, while his own party had overwhelmingly opposed the war itself.

While continuing to acknowledge that "Saddam does pose a serious threat to the stability of the Persian Gulf," Gore no longer referred to Iraq as part of an axis of evil or as one of the "next phases of the war against terrorism as [the president] laid them out in the State of the Union." Instead Gore described the agendas in Iraq as conflicting with the War on Terror, pointing out that while "we know that [Saddam] has stored secret supplies of biological and chemical weapons throughout his country...we have no evidence...that he has shared any of those weapons with a terrorist group." It was apparently no longer necessary to "go to the limit" in dealing with Saddam Hussein.

In revisiting the first Gulf war, Gore sought to distinguish it from the impending conflict. In the first place, he observed, Saddam had not sent any armies across international borders as he had before. In the second place, there was no international coalition for the war this time. (Not exactly the case, since more than thirty nations had signed on.) Third, there was no U.N. resolution sanctioning the war. (This was also a questionable assertion, since Saddam was in violation of sixteen resolutions, which effectively stipulated that their violation would provide a justification for the unfinished war to be resumed.) Fourth, since there was no international coalition, the United States would have to pay all the costs of the conflict. And fifth, unlike his father, who had waited until after the midterm congressional elections to put the war resolution up for a vote, President Bush was now demanding a vote before them. Gore interpreted this as an effort by the president to make the war a partisan issue. But as the rest of Gore's speech showed, the war in his mind was already partisan.

In January, he had endorsed the presidential doctrine of preemption in regard to Iraq. Now he attacked it, making an invidious equivalence between what the president proposed and the 1979 Soviet invasion of Afghanistan—a country that presented no military threat to Moscow or any other state. The Soviets's "preemptive war" (which is the way Gore described it) was in fact a naked aggression. Gore dismissed the president's doctrine of pre-emption out of hand as "not needed in order to give the United States the means to act in its own defense against terrorism in general or Iraq in particular." He characterized the conflict with Iraq as a "distraction" from the War on Terror.

Taking up the domestic theme of the anti-war Left, he decried "the administration's attack on fundamental constitutional rights," specifically referring to the White House's decision to jail al Qaeda soldiers captured during the war in Afghanistan and hold them as prisoners of war, instead of as accused individuals subject to the judicial process. "That this can be done on the say-so of the president, or those acting in his name," Gore declared, "is beyond the pale." Strong words for the leader of a national political party in a time of war.

Finally, in his San Francisco speech, Gore assailed the administration's "unilateral" approach to the current crisis, even though the president had gone to the U.N. to seek a Security Council resolution just two weeks previously. At the same time, and in the same remarks, Gore himself pointed out that a new U.N. resolution was unnecessary from a legal standpoint, since Iraq was already in violation of the U.N. resolutions adopted in 1991 to terminate the Gulf War. The reason for seeking a new resolution, Gore acknowledged, was simply to build an "international consensus" behind any policy that might lead to war.[9] Evidently, the president's unilateralism lay not in his approach to the policy but in the reluctance of Saddam's European allies—France and Russia—to support it.

On the same day as Gore's partisan assault on the president's policy, President Jimmy Carter weighed in with his own attack. In a speech in Virginia, Carter warned of the "great danger" in conducting a war with Iraq that was not sanctioned by a vote of the U.N. Security Council. The timing was odd, since the president's appearance at the U.N. was an obvious appeal for such a vote. Instead of acknowledging this, Carter described the current administration policy as "a radical departure from the traditions that have shaped our nation's policies under Democratic and Republican presidents for the last fifty or more years in dealing with the Middle East, in dealing with the United Nations, in honoring our international agreements that we ourselves have helped to forge and supporting a common commitment through the United Nations and marshaling allies before we take military action. I think we should not do anything with Iraq until the United Nations Security Council prescribes a means and a time schedule in which we act."[10]

Carter did not attempt to explain how the Clinton administration's missile strikes against Sudan, Afghanistan, and Iraq or the war in Kosovo—all conducted without consulting the U.N., let alone following Security Council timetables—fell within the parameters and traditions he specified. Like Gore, he also avoided addressing the potential consequences of the U.N.'s failure to enforce its resolutions against Iraq.

On October 11, a week after both houses of Congress had passed the use-of-force resolution requested by President Bush, the international Left awarded the Nobel Peace Prize to Carter. In announcing the prize, the presenters cited Carter's decades of work seeking "peaceful solutions" and "promoting social and economic justice."[11] Asked whether the prize had been given as a criticism of Bush, the head of the Nobel Committee told the press, "With the position Carter has taken on this, it can and must also be seen as criticism of the line the current U.S. administration has taken on Iraq."[12]

One month later, on November 8, the U.N. Security Council passed Resolution 1441, declaring Iraq to be in "material breach" of all sixteen previous U.N. resolutions and providing the regime with a final opportunity to comply. It called for the destruction of Iraq's aggressive weapons and weapons programs and for "immediate, unimpeded, unconditional and unrestricted access" for inspectors to determine whether it had complied. Iraq was given thirty days, or until December 7, to comply with these terms "or face serious consequences." The Security Council vote was unanimous.

When the deadline arrived, the Iraq regime provided a report that was generally conceded not to have met the terms of the ultimatum. U.N. chief inspector Hans Blix summarized the Iraqi submission: "The chemical area of the text was an updated version of a declaration submitted in 1996. The missile part also had largely the same content as a declaration of 1996, with updates added. I reported to the Council that our preliminary examination of the declaration had not provided material or evidence that solved any of the unresolved disarmament issues."[13] These included the fact that "8,500 liters of anthrax, 2,100 kilograms of bacterial growth media, 1.5 metric tons of VX nerve agent and 6,500 chemical bombs" that the U.N. inspectors had ascertained were at one time in Saddam's possession were unaccounted for.[14] Resolution 1441 had called on Saddam Hussein to document their destruction. Even the French ambassador noted that "there was no new information in the declaration"[15] Afterward Blix wrote of the declaration, "My gut feelings, which I kept to myself, suggested to me that Iraq still engaged in prohibited activities and retained prohibited items, and that it had the documents to prove it."[16]

Iraq's failure to meet the deadline meant that the moment of decision had finally arrived. Yet three veto-wielding members of the Security Council—France, Russia, and China—balked. These were all powers that had supplied Saddam Hussein's regime with weapons and were invested in Iraqi oil. Documents seized when the war was over showed that France alone stood to gain tens of billions in Iraqi oil contracts. They also revealed that Saddam had used part of the $10 billion stolen with the help of U.N. officials from the oil-for-food program to bribe French, Russian and British public figures to oppose the war.[17] During the decade leading up to the war, the same three powers had lobbied for lifting sanctions against Saddam when he was in proven violation of U.N. resolutions, and, they in general had been helpful to Iraq in evading U.N. demands.

On December 19, two weeks after the deadline had passed, President Bush and Prime Minister Tony Blair formally declared Iraq to be "in material breach" of the Security Council resolution.[18] In private, U.N. chief weapons inspector Hans Blix, agreed though he equivocated in public because he was opposed to the use of force on principle.[19] "Material breach" was a diplomatic phrase designed to trigger the "serious consequences" that the ultimatum had called for. But America and Britain were the only Security Council members to take this step.

Meanwhile, the very effort to force the Iraq regime to the decision point had already changed the dynamics of the political situation. The United States had begun massing hundreds of thousands of troops in the Gulf region. To maintain the force indefinitely while Saddam and his Security Council friends maneuvered would be impractical. To withdraw the allied forces without a positive result would be a dangerous show of weakness. Even if Iraq had destroyed its stockpiles of weapons of mass destruction, it could rebuild them in a matter of months after the United States and British troops had left. The withdrawal itself would send a powerful message to other terrorist states like Syria, North Korea, and Iran that resolutions of the U.N. could be ignored and the United States defied without consequences. Barring a catastrophic event, like 9/11, it would be extraordinarily difficult for the president to assemble such a military force soon again. This would provide the Iraqi regime—which was already attempting to negotiate a weapons deal with North Korea—plenty of time to develop precisely the arsenal that the U.N. resolution was designed to prevent.

On the other hand, the very steps that had been taken to reach the point of confrontation and accountability—the congressional vote in October, the Security Council resolution in November, and the mobilization of military force in the Gulf—aroused the anti-war

Left, bringing a new actor into the unfolding drama. Two days before the congressional vote on the war, the AFL-CIO's left-wing President John Sweeney sent a letter to members of Congress stressing that the United States must "deal with Hussein's lawlessness in a manner that reinforces international law" and "respects the United Nations." In the months that followed, union after union adopted resolutions against the war. Many of these resolutions were modeled on a statement prepared by two radical anti-war organizations— Win Without War and Keep America Safe—specifically rejecting the administration's position that America would strike first to defend itself.

In October there were tens of thousands of demonstrators. By February, 10 million anti-war protesters had been mobilized worldwide, half a million of them in the United States.[20] These mobilizations exerted a direct influence on the diplomatic process. In Iraq the growing internal divisions in the allied coalition stiffened Saddam's resistance. As subsequently became clear in interviews with his lieutenants, Saddam never fully believed the allies would invade his country and take down his regime, a miscalculation that accounted for the weak resistance his military put up in the actual conflict. A factor in his calculation would certainly have been that popular pressures in Europe and the United States against the use of force might eventually sap the military resolve of the coalition leaders.

But this assumption was close to the actual events taking place. In England, Prime Minister Tony Blair, the staunchest supporter of Washington's Iraq policy, came under heavy attack from the political Left, climaxed by an anti-war demonstration in Hyde Park with 750,000 protesters, a proportion the equivalent of several million in the United States. Tony Benn, a veteran leader of the Labour Party Left, went to Iraq to conduct a friendly interview with Saddam and came back to declare, "President Bush and Mr. Blair are planning to tear up the charter of the United Nations to make a war which would be an aggressive war and to kill people, which would be a war crime, and to do it in a way that would endanger world peace over a long period and set the Middle East aflame."[21] The *Daily Mirror*— a Labour Party paper and the largest daily in England—filled its front-page with a picture of the prime minister with bloodstained hands. The feature article advertised on the cover was a two-page screed by *Mirror* journalist and Noam Chomsky acolyte John Pilger, who wrote that the Bush administration was "the Third Reich of our times," and that Blair himself was a "liar" and a "coward."[22]

To appease the anti-war faction in the Labour Party, Blair appealed directly to his American partner to seek an additional U.N. resolution authorizing the war. From a legal point of view, such a resolution was entirely unnecessary, as Al Gore had pointed out. Resolution 1441 had specifically given Iraq a "final opportunity" to comply. An additional resolution would in itself weaken the credibility of U.N. resolutions and thus the force of international law. The motivation for seeking yet another resolution was entirely political— to neutralize the opposition from the Labour Party Left.

On March 6, after weeks of diplomatic efforts by Bush and Blair to secure another resolution, the French declared that they would unconditionally oppose the measure. Foreign Minister Dominique de Villepin told U.S. Secretary of State Colin Powell directly that France would veto any resolution authorizing war.[23] Four days later, Prime Minister Jacques Chirac went on television to declare that his government would veto a war resolution under any circumstances— *quelles que soient les circonstances.*[24]

Responding to the French declaration, Blair underscored the irony of France's position. The very nation that was demanding that the U.N. be the agency for enforcing the peace was denying the U.N. the ability to enforce it. "This is such a foolish thing to do at this moment in the world's history," Blair lamented. "The very people who should be strengthening the international institutions are undermining [them]."[25] Under the circumstances the French had created by their unconditional opposition to the use of force, there would never be a reason for Saddam Hussein to disarm or to give up his destructive plans.

Three days later, former president and newly minted Nobel laureate Jimmy Carter blasted the Bush administration for what he claimed were violations of the most fundamental principles of morality and law:

> Profound changes have been taking place in American foreign policy, reversing consistent bipartisan commitments that for more than two centuries have earned our nation greatness. These commitments have been predicated on basic religious principles, respect for international law, and alliances that resulted in wise decisions and mutual restraint. Our apparent determination to launch a war against Iraq, without international support, is a violation of these premises.[26]

Carter's claims were preposterous, but they accurately reflected the political mood of the opposition.

The president, was undeterred. In his January State of the Union message, he had made the United States position inescapably clear: "We will consult. But... if Saddam Hussein does not fully disarm, for the safety of our people and for the peace of the world, we will lead a coalition to disarm him." Two months later, on March 17, 2003, one week after the French pronouncement, the president went on television to give Saddam and his sons a 48-hour ultimatum to leave the country or face the consequences.

The president's ultimatum drew an immediate response from Senate Minority Leader Tom Daschle. Appearing before the American Federation of State, County, and Municipal Employees (AFSCME), a major force in Democratic Party politics and a leader of its political Left, Daschle launched the most partisan attack on the administration's national security strategy to date. Questioning the very premise of the impending conflict, he attacked the judgment of its commander in chief: "I'm saddened, saddened that this president failed so miserably at diplomacy that we're now forced to war."[27] Daschle didn't even attempt to explain how he—or anyone else—would have been able to persuade France, Russia, and China, Saddam's business partners and allies, to reverse their positions, or why he thought any president of the United States should allow these powers to have a veto over American security interests.

Two days later the president's deadline passed and the war began.

21

Anti-war Democrats

On April 10, 2003, the day after American forces liberated Baghdad and helped to pull down the monument to its defeated dictator, House Minority Leader Nancy Pelosi held a press conference. "I have absolutely no regret about my vote [against] this war," she told reporters. The cost of the war in terms of lives and capital, she said, was too high. "The cost to our budget [was] probably $100 billion. We could have probably brought down that statue [of Saddam Hussein] for a lot less."[28]

Her remarks were just the beginning of a Democratic offensive against the war's commander in chief, which would be pursued relentlessly and without letup for the next year, becoming the focus of the presidential campaign. The Democrats went on the attack without pausing to savor America's swift victory or consider the potentially destructive impact of their attacks on the War on Terror. Instead, they prosecuted a political war against the president even while the military battles to consolidate the victory in Iraq were still raging and while the administration was engaged in a daunting effort to create a stable postwar regime.

Initially, the Democrats picked up Daschle's argument that Bush had conducted an unnecessary and unilateral war. They repeated the complaints that the White House had alienated allies like Russia and France, while never explaining how it would have been possible to remove Saddam without doing so. Nor did they explain why this war, which was sanctioned by U.N. resolution 1441, was nonetheless different from Clinton's war in Kosovo, which lacked such U.N. sanction or even authorization by Congress. The Democrats criticized the president for not better anticipating the problems of the peace when looting occurred in Iraqi government buildings and antiquity museums. And they repeated the charge the war was a distraction from the war on al Qaeda, even though by the end of the fighting two-thirds of al Qaeda's leaders had been killed or disabled and Iraq had become a center of the War on Terror.[29]

Because it was difficult to attack a war that had so few casualties and had liberated 25 million people, the Democrats focused attacks on the war's rationale. On July 10, the Democratic National Committee released a television ad, which they titled "Read His Lips: President Bush Deceives the American People."[30] The subject of the ad—and of weeks of unrelenting Democratic attacks—was a sentence containing sixteen words from the president's State of the Union address of January 28. The words referred to an alleged attempt by the Iraqi government to purchase "yellow cake" uranium in the African state of Niger: "The British government has learned that Saddam Hussein recently sought significant quantities of uranium from Africa." The ad included a clip of the president uttering the second half of the statement, but omitting the fact that he was citing a British intelligence report. The DNC text continued, "But now we find out that it wasn't true. Far worse, the administration knew it wasn't true. A year earlier, that claim was already proven to be false. The CIA knew it. The State Department knew it. The

White House knew it. But he told us anyway." In other words, the commander in chief was a liar, and his deceptions had taken America to a war that was needless and that cost America lives.

Democrats were certainly aware of the seriousness of their attacks on the integrity of the president, not to mention the possible ramifications for national security. Presidential candidate John Edwards told a *New York Times* reporter, "The most important attribute that any president has is his credibility—his credibility with the American people, with its allies and with the world. When the president's own statements are called into question, it's a very serious matter."[31] The fact that the accusations were being made over such a flimsy claim was thus particularly troubling. The British government continued to stand by its report, making the presidential statement literally true. Moreover, the ad's insinuations in regard to the CIA and the State Department were misleading, since both had vetted and approved the president's speech.[32] Neither of these considerations served to restrain the Democrats' attacks.

A year later, when major damage to the commander-in-chief's credibility had already been done, a bi-partisan Senate committee investigating intelligence failures leading up to the war exonerated him: "We conclude also that the Statement in President Bush's State of the Union Address of 28 January 2003 that 'The British Government has learned that Saddam Hussein recently sought significant quantities of uranium from Africa' was well-founded."[33]

The charges and the rhetoric escalated through the summer and fall. According to the Democrats, an aggressive and imperial-minded "neoconservative" cabal had driven the administration's policy toward Iraq. It had misled the world about the imminence of the Iraqi threat and in its claims that the Iraqi regime had stockpiled weapons of mass destruction. These had not been discovered by the coalition forces that now controlled Iraq. They pointed to passing remarks by administration officials and to the case Colin Powell had presented to the U.N. as evidence of the false claims. They further charged the president with misleading the American people into thinking Saddam Hussein was involved in the World Trade Center attacks and that his regime had links with al Qaeda. In sum, according to the Democrats, the rationale for the war presented by the administration was that Saddam Hussein confronted America with an "imminent" threat linked to the War on Terror, and there was no such threat and no such link. And the administration knew it.

In fact, the administration had made no such claims, and in particular that Saddam Hussein had presented an imminent threat. If there *had* been an imminent threat, "the president would not have taken 18 months to act to protect the nation," as Washington journalist Stephen Hayes pointed out. "In fact, the case for war was built largely on the *opposite* assumption: that waiting until Iraq presented an imminent threat was too risky"[34] (emphasis added). The president had made this clear in presenting his case for war in the State of the Union address on January 28, 2003,[35] less than two months before the opening of hostilities:

> Before September 11th, many in the world believed that Saddam Hussein could be contained. But chemical agents, lethal viruses and shadowy terrorist networks are not easily contained. Imagine those 19 hijackers with other weapons and other plans—this time armed by Saddam Hussein. It would take one vial, one canister, one crate slipped into this country to bring a day of horror like none we have ever known. We will do everything in our power to make sure that day never comes.

The president then turned to the issue of imminence: "Some have said we must not act until the threat is imminent. Since when have terrorists and tyrants announced their intentions, politely putting us on notice before they strike? If this threat is permitted to fully and suddenly emerge, all actions, all words, and all recriminations would come too late. Trusting in the sanity and restraint of Saddam Hussein is not a strategy, and it is not an option."

As the British writer William Shawcross explained, the distinction critics failed to grasp was between the imminence—or immediacy—of the Iraq threat and its inevitability.[36] When Saddam Hussein expelled the U.N. weapons inspectors in 1998, President Clinton requested a congressional authorization for the use of force and justified it this way: "If we fail to respond today, Saddam and all those who would follow in his footsteps will be emboldened tomorrow by the knowledge that they can act with impunity, even in the face of a clear message from the United Nations Security Council, and clear evidence of a weapons of mass destruction program."[37]

It was Saddam's persistence in pursuing these programs that had caused the Clinton and Bush regimes to regard his regime as an intolerable threat. When Bush's weapons inspector David Kay could not locate stockpiles of weapons of mass destruction after the victory in Iraq, he explained, "We know there were terrorist groups in [Iraq] still seeking WMD capability. Although I found no weapons, Iraq had tremendous capabilities in this area. A marketplace phenomena was about to occur... sellers meeting buyers. And I think that would have been very dangerous if the war had not intervened." When asked by interviewer Chris Wallace what could be sold if there were no weapons, he replied, "The knowledge of how to make them, the knowledge of how to make small amounts, which is, after all, mostly what terrorists want. They don't want battlefield amounts of weapons.... Iraq remained a very dangerous place in terms of WMD capabilities, even though we found no large stockpiles of weapons."[38] Of course, if there had been no war and the United States had withdrawn its invasion force, Saddam could have reconstituted the programs and begun producing weapons within a matter of months.

In addition to ignoring these considerations, the Democrats' attacks misrepresented the intelligence assumptions on which the war policy had been based. In their attacks the Democrats focused on the intelligence errors of the Bush White House, when they were in fact the shared assumptions of every intelligence agency in the Western world, including the Germans, the Russians, and the French—not to mention the U.N. weapons inspectors themselves. The rationale for the war was not based on a particular stockpile or estimate of Saddam's arsenal but on Saddam's failure to comply with seventeen U.N. resolutions including Resolution 1441, which had given Saddam a "final opportunity" to make good on the truce he had signed twelve years before. The resolution was passed unanimously on November 8, 2002, and breached by Iraq on December 7. In other words, the rationale for the war was articulated *before* the State of the Union address with the now famous sixteen words about Niger uranium and *before* Secretary of State Colin Powell's presentation to the General Assembly concerning Saddam's weapons programs. The factual claims in these statements were not rationales for the war but attempts to answer objections of the Left, which was determined to appease Iraq.

It was the nature of the war itself, however, that made the Democrats' attacks most difficult to understand. Unlike Vietnam, which had gone badly and had resulted in the loss of more than 50,000 American lives and seemed to have no end when the criticisms began, the war in Iraq was a relatively painless and spectacularly successful conflict. It could easily be said to have been one of the most efficient and beneficial wars on record. Hundreds of American soldiers had sacrificed their lives so that 25 million Iraqis could be free. The United States had secured a military base bordering two terrorist states, Syria and Iran, and the Iraqis had gained a democratic constitution for the first time in five thousand years.

Given these facts, the attacks on an administration that had won such a war were difficult to explain, particularly in light of the encouragement that such internal attacks would provide to the terrorist forces on the other side. Yet during the spring, summer, and fall of 2003, the Democrats hammered the president just as though the war had been a disaster, and in doing so they damaged his credibility and undermined his ability to consolidate the peace.

As the Democratic primary campaign moved into high gear, even the candidates who had supported the war joined the attack. One week after the Niger uranium issue surfaced, the *New York Times* reported: "Democratic presidential candidates offered a near-unified assault today on President Bush's credibility in his handling of the Iraq war, signaling a shift in the political winds by aggressively invoking arguments most had shunned since the fall of Baghdad. Even Democratic candidates who had supported the war, the *Times* noted, "[now] declared that President Bush's credibility had been harmed because of his use of unsubstantiated evidence in supporting the looming invasion of Iraq in his State of the Union address in January. They also criticized the administration for what has happened in postwar Iraq, especially the continued deaths of American military personnel, which many attributed to Mr. Bush's failure to enlist the help of the United Nations in conducting the war. They questioned the failure to uncover the nuclear, chemical, or biological weapons Mr. Bush had cited in pressing for war."[39] Although American troops were still consolidating their recent victory, these political attacks, according to the *Times,* had put the White House "on the defensive." Jennifer Palmieri, a spokeswoman for prowar Democrat John Edwards, told *Times* reporter Adam Nagourney, "It's the first time we've seen them sweat . . . It's the first time anything has ever stuck."[40]

Leading the attacks was Howard Dean, a newcomer to national politics. Dean had been an obscure governor of Vermont whose unorthodox campaign had begun with seven staffers and $147,000 in the bank. He had built a movement that included more than a hundred thousand volunteers and a $45 million war chest, more money than any Democrat in history had raised including Bill Clinton when he was president.[41] Most observers attributed his remarkable rise outside the formal structures of the party to his ability to tap the power of the Internet, which had provided three-quarters of his funding.[42] But it was a very specific Internet community that Dean was able to mobilize, namely, the political activists and organizations of the anti-war Left. His senior adviser, Gina Glantz, was a consultant to the anti-war website MoveOn.org, and before the Iowa primary Dean would be endorsed by the most prominent anti-war Democrats, former President Jimmy Carter and former vice president Al Gore, and by the farthest Left unions in its political base, AFSCME and the SEIU, for whom Glantz was also political director. The SEIU was headed by former sixties leftist and anti-Vietnam activist, Andrew Stern.

MoveOn.org was typical of the organizations whose members were galvanized by Dean's blunt rhetoric against the war.[43] A "progressive" website with 1.4 million members, MoveOn.org was one of the most important political forces in the Internet world that had an agenda of moving the Democratic Party to the left. It had been created during the Clinton impeachment controversy and had raised more than $4 million for Democratic congressional candidates in the 2002 mid-term elections. In the 2004 primaries its focus was entirely on winning the Democratic nomination for an anti-war candidate. To this end, Democratic funder George Soros had provided it with a $15 million gift.[44] Through a second website at EU-Moveon.org, the organization was able to raise campaign money from the international anti-war Left until the practice was stopped in December 2003 after being exposed in the press.[45]

MoveOn's "organizing director," Zack Exley, was the creator of a satiric left-wing site, GWBush.com which had achieved a degree of public notoriety through the venom of its "satires." One prank included a doctored photo of the president with cocaine on his nose and upper lip and the caption, "GWBush, Not a Crackhead Anymore!" Exley's first media production for MoveOn.org was a political commercial based on the infamous "Daisy" ad devised by Bill Moyers to defeat Barry Goldwater in the 1964 presidential campaign. In Exley's ad an ominous voice-over warned that the war in Iraq could spread and terrorists could take over countries with nuclear weapons, leading to the unthinkable. It finished with an image of a mushroom cloud. Exley created a public uproar a third time when he held a political ad contest for the presidential campaign in which one of the finalists featured at the MoveOn site compared Bush to Adolf Hitler. During the campaign the site featured bumper stickers and T-shirts with slogans like "Imperialism: A Way of Life Worth Bombing For," "Regime Change Starts At Home," and "Capitalism: It's Great in Theory, It Just Didn't Work in Practice."[46]

On June 24, MoveOn.org held a "virtual Democratic primary" that Dean won. All the top finishers were candidates of the anti-war Left. The runner-up, trailing Dean by twenty points, was congressman Dennis Kucinich.[47] Senator John Kerry came in third. After the vote, prowar Democrats like Congressman Richard Gephardt complained that MoveOn.Org had failed to mail their responses to its issues questionnaire to MoveOn members. Among other things, the submitted questions described the Patriot Act as "dangerous" and "frightening," and asked if the candidates agreed. Gephardt was further "alarmed by the fact that Zack Exley, MoveOn's organizing director, had taken a two-and-a-half-week leave of absence to work on Howard Dean's Internet campaign."[48]

Moveon.org also played an important role in putting together the anti-war electoral coalition. It created and funded Win Without War, a celebrity-driven coalition of leftist organizations, some of which were heavily involved in anti-Israel and anti-American campaigns on college campuses, and which had components that bore names like "Peace Action," "American-Arab Anti-Discrimination Committee," and "Global Exchange" (Medea Benjamin's radical front).[49] Win Without War was formed by members of the group of radical activists who had met in the offices of People for the American Way on October 25, 2002 to form an anti-war coalition that would appear moderate to the American public, the meeting that had resulted in the creation of the umbrella group United for Peace and Justice, led by veteran Communist Leslie Cagan.

Eight of the activists present at the meeting, including Eli Pariser, the "international campaigns director" of MoveOn.org, went out to dinner afterward to discuss ways to create yet another front organization to make the anti-war appeal user-friendly to labor and liberals. "Right from the beginning," Pariser told the *New York Times*, "we tried to frame it as a message that would go down well in broader communities than just the anti-war crowd." The organizers agreed to create a parallel group to United for Peace and Justice called Win Without War. The new group "announced itself in December with a news conference and a Web site identifying itself as the 'mainstream' voice against the war. Doing so allowed it to win members like the N.A.A.C.P., the National Organization for Women, the Sierra Club and the National Council of Churches and gain access to their mailing lists and memberships."[50]

With the fighting in Iraq over, the anti-war Left turned to the Dean campaign and the electoral process to pursue its agendas. The Dean style and tone—uncompromising and confrontational—

reflected the passions of its political base. When Dean took up the Democrats' standard critique of unilateralism, it came across with an emotional edge. "If I as governor of Vermont can figure out the case is not there to invade Iraq, how can three senators and a congress-man who claim to have authority in public affairs manage to give the president unilateral authority to attack Iraq?"[51] "This president has used humiliation as a weapon, not only against our enemies but against our friends."[52]

Dean exploited the fact that even the pro-war Democrats among the presidential contenders were now willing to attack the case that Bush had made for the war. In attacking the rationale for a war they had supported, the prowar Democrats had put themselves in a bind. As one editorialist observed, "The logic is self-contradictory. If the justification for the war was invalid, then how can anyone claim the war itself to be justified?"[53] Dean resolved this dilemma by attack-ing the war itself. "We don't know whether in the long run the Iraqi people are better off," he said on June 22, and "we don't know whether we're better off."

Eventually, Dean's rhetorical extremes caused him to stumble and be overtaken by John Kerry, a candidate the press and the party regulars regarded as more electable in November. Kerry's decisive victory in the Iowa primary was made possible by the intervention of Kennedy, the Party's most famous "Liberal" and an icon to Iowa's elderly Democratic caucus goers, who flew into Iowa, dominated the local headlines, and provided Kerry as an acceptable left alternative to Dean, despite his vote for the war. But Dean's impact on the Democratic Party and on the direction of the race could not be denied. "On the War on Terror," the *Wall Street Journal* editorialized when the race was over, "[Howard Dean] has almost single-handedly pulled his party to the anti-war Left. As he often said on the stump, his main competitors all voted for the Iraq war. But as Mr. Dean climbed the polls by denouncing the war, he made opposition to it a party litmus test.... The candidates who stayed honorably hawk-ish.... went down to defeat."[54]

One of these candidates was Dick Gephardt, who had played a pivotal role in mobilizing a sufficient minority in his party to support the war in the first place. But now, in the wake of the Niger flap and Dean's surge in the polls, Gephardt did a 180-degree turn with a sweeping dismissal of the victory America had won. "When President Bush landed on an aircraft carrier and declared victory in Iraq," he told the San Francisco Bar Association on July 22, "I think he chose the wrong back-drop for his photo-op. If you ask me, if he really wanted to show us the state of affairs in Iraq, he should have landed on a patch of quicksand." Attacking Bush's "utter disregard for diplomacy," and referring to his alleged treatment of allies "like so many flies on the American windshield," he concluded, "I'm running for president, because I believe George Bush has left us less safe and less secure than we were four years ago."[55]

Writing in the conservative *Weekly Standard*, William Kristol wondered, "Were we safer and more secure [four years ago] when Osama bin Laden was unimpeded in assembling his terror network in Afghanistan? When Pakistan was colluding with the Taliban, and Saudi Arabia with al Qaeda? When Saddam Hussein ruled Iraq?... When our defense budget and our intelligence services were continuing to drift downward in capacity in a post–Cold War world?"[56]

Gephardt's words, Kristol concluded, were a turning point in American politics. They "change everything. They reflect the consid-ered judgment of a centrist Democratic presidential candidate, one who voted to authorize the war, that his party must stand in funda-mental opposition to the Bush foreign policy. They indicate the cap-ture of the Democratic party by the pace-setter in the presidential race, former Vermont governor Howard Dean." What they represented, in fact, was the capture of the Democratic Party by the political Left.

Within hours of Gephardt's speech, former President Bill Clinton appeared on *Larry King Live* and attempted to stop the party's plunge over what appeared to be a political cliff. Discussing the Niger controversy, King suggested that intelligence mistakes were understandable, Clinton agreed. "The most important thing," he said, "is we should focus on what's the best way to build Iraq as a democracy. How is the president going to do that and deal with continuing problems in Afghanistan and North Korea? We should be pulling for America on this. We should be pulling for the people of Iraq."[57] Directing his words to the growing fracture in the nation's foreign policy consensus, the former president said, "We can have honest disagreements about where we go from here, and we have space now to discuss that in what I hope will be a nonpartisan and open way."[58]

But the Democratic Party was too busy rolling over the cliff that Clinton seemed to be warning them against to take heed. On August 7, Al Gore appeared as the keynote speaker for an event sponsored by MoveOn.org at New York University. Before the speech, a Gore adviser told reporter Stephen F. Hayes, "We heard President Clinton's take on [the Niger controversy] a couple of weeks ago. Now we'll hear Gore's." Hayes described the ensuing scene:

> Eager students were distributing flyers and holding up signs—"Draft Clark" and "Draft Gore" and "Bush planned 9/11 as a pretext for Afghan/Iraq invasion and war against the Bill of Rights."... In a broad rambling lecture that began with and returned many times to Iraq, former Vice President Al Gore toyed with some of the very same conspiracy theories peddled by the crazies outside. In thirty-five minutes, he managed to squeeze in several bizarre accusations directed at the Bush administration—recycling the blood-for-oil claim, suggesting the Iraq war was conceived and conducted to

"benefit friends and supporters," labeling the administration "totalistic"..."[59]

Gore even suggested that the president had stabbed American troops in the back: "Too many of our soldiers are paying the highest price for the strategic miscalculations, serious misjudgments, and historic mistakes that have put them and our nation in harm's way." Nor was this performance the end of Gore's assault. Within months Gore was suggesting the president had committed treason. "He betrayed us," Gore ranted to a cheering crowd in Tennessee. "He took America on an ill-conceived foreign adventure, dangerous to our troops, that was preordained and planned before 9/11."[60]

No Democrat distanced himself from Gore's war cry against the president and his national security policy. On the contrary, the extreme standard he set had already been surpassed by Senator Edward Kennedy, the party's most powerful legislator and senior congressional statesmen, who had called the war in Iraq "mindless, needless, senseless and reckless" and a product of "pure, unadulter-ated fear-mongering."[61] In an interview with an AP reporter, weeks after Gore's speech—a setting in which there was no question of being influenced by the heat of a crowd—Kennedy laid out a view of the war that could have easily come from the conspiratorial Left: "There was no imminent threat. This was made up in Texas, announced in Janu-ary to the Republican leadership that the war is going to take place and was going to be good politically. This whole thing was a fraud."[62]

Kennedy's remarks took on greater significance because of his role as the senior advisor to the new front-runner in the race, his Massa-chusetts colleague John Kerry, who had emerged after the Iowa and New Hampshire primaries as the party's leader. The choice of Kerry as the party's titular nominee seemed a signal to many that the Democrats had drawn back from the political brink. But the weeks that followed showed that the standard Gephardt had set in July—and that Gore and Kennedy had raised even farther—was Kerry's as well. Kerry had voted in favor of the war in November, making a sound case for Iraq's central importance for the War on Terror.[63] But he was now fully on board for the anti-war crusade. He denounced the president for conducting, "the most inept, reckless, arrogant and ideological foreign policy in modern history,"[64] and called the allied forces a "coalition of the bribed, the coerced, the bought and the extorted."[65]

In retrospect, the party's new standard-bearer was well suited for the role he now assumed. A New England aristocrat and decorated Vietnam veteran, Kerry had launched his career by joining the anti-war Left, appearing before Congress to testify against his fellow soldiers and his own country. "We wish that a merciful God could wipe away our own memories of [our military] service," Kerry told the Senate after his return from Vietnam. Associating himself with pro-Communist activists like Tom Hayden and Jane Fonda and describing alleged atrocities committed by American soldiers, Kerry claimed that "these were not isolated incidents but crimes committed on a day-to-day basis with the full awareness of officers at all levels of command."[66]

In his first campaign for Congress, Kerry pledged to "almost eliminate CIA activity,"—a promise that was unintelligible without an accompanying view that America had no significant foreign enemies or was itself a global problem. Kerry's subsequent career exhibited a penchant for political equivocation, but also the consistent distrust of American power and purpose he had shown as a young man. In the years when al Qaeda bombed the World Trade Center, blew up two U.S. embassies, and attacked the USS *Cole*, Kerry supported deep cuts in U.S. intelligence services, including 25 percent of overseas operations, and proposed billions of dollars in cuts of his own.[67] Four years before 9/11, Kerry asked his congressional colleagues,

"Now that [the Cold War] struggle is over, why is it that our vast intelligence apparatus continues to grow?"[68] In a survey of legislators by the nonpartisan *National Journal*, Kerry was judged to have the most left-wing voting record in the United States Senate.

Defining his position as an anti-war presidential candidate in the 2004 campaign, Kerry said, "I've fought all my life for peace. I fought against the war in Vietnam when I came home. I fought against Ronald Reagan's illegal war in Central America."[69] But the war in Central America was illegal only in the eyes of the Left, and was an effort to contain the spread of Communism in the region. Regarding the current global conflict, Kerry signaled that he would turn away from the war the White House had declared on terror and attempt to reinstate the pre-9/11 policies that had treated terrorist attacks as primarily a law enforcement matter. The president, Kerry told a group of Oklahoma City firefighters, "doesn't understand the War on Terror. Fighting terror," he conceded, "will involve the military now and then," but he explained, "It's a great big manhunt. . . . it's primarily an intelligence and law enforcement operation that requires cooperation around the world—the very thing this administration is worst at."[70] Characterizing the president's domestic security policy as an "assault on our basic rights,"—many of whose victims he noted were those "of Arab descent"—Kerry also promised to "end the era of Ashcroft," a reference to the attorney general responsible for enforcing the Patriot Act. Among the provisions of the Patriot Act that Kerry promised to end was the "secret monitoring of attorney-client conversations," the provision which had allowed Ashcroft to indict Lynne Stewart for assisting her client's terrorist apparatus.[71] Consolidating his alliance with the political Left, Kerry placed MoveOn.org's Zack Exley in charge of his online communications.[72]

Epilogue:
Secessionists

The presidential contest began in earnest in March 2004—even before the Democratic primaries were officially concluded—with a campaign skirmish over two images of 9/11. As it became clear that Kerry was going to lock down the Democratic nomination, the Bush team ran a thirty-second ad called "Safer, Stronger." Against a rapidly changing kaleidoscope of images, which included scenes of the World Trade Center attack, the on screen text read, *"January 2001. The Challenge. An economy . . . in recession. A stock market . . . in decline. A dotcom boom . . . gone bust. Then . . . a day of tragedy. A test for all Americans. Today America is turning the corner. Rising to the challenge. Safer, stronger. George Bush, Steady Leadership in Times of Change."* It seemed an appropriate ad for a president whose defining moments were the attacks on 9/11 and his response to the War on Terror.

But the ad was immediately attacked as an abuse of those images. Within days of its release, a group of individuals representing themselves as relatives of the victims of 9/11 held a press conference to protest the ad. Even though the images of 9/11 were on screen for only five seconds, the protesters condemned what they

said was the president's "offensive exploitation" of 9/11.[1] "We're saying find some other way to run a campaign without stepping on the
bodies of our dead," declared one of the protesters, Rita Lasar, who
lost her brother in the attacks. The story was picked up by the
national media, including the *Washington Post*, which generally
described the group as "nonpartisan." The extensive coverage the
press conference received put the White House on the defensive and
forced the president to explain himself.

In fact the protest was less an expression of personal anguish than
it was political agitprop, a production of the same radical anti-war
forces and organizations that had been behind the Dean campaign
and now the Kerry campaign. The group holding the press conference was called the September 11th Families for Peaceful Tomorrows, a faction of the anti-war movement with a seat on the steering
committee of United for Peace and Justice and extensive ties to the
Democratic Party. Outside the conservative press, no journalists covering the story made an effort to look into the nature of the group,
but its agendas were not exactly obscure. As the *New York Times*
observed, the founder of September 11th Families for Peaceful
Tomorrows," David Potori, was a radical journalist with a public
record of opposing faith-based initiatives, nonunion companies, and
the "gaping inequities" in America. "Within three months of losing
a brother on September 11, [Portori] was protesting the War on Terror in a peace march sponsored by Voices in the Wilderness, one of
whose founders, Kathy Kelly, was recently sentenced to three
months in prison for breaking onto an army installation."[2]

The public relations firm behind the Peaceful Tomorrows conference was Fenton Communications, whose principal, David Fenton was a sixties radical with a thirty-year history of promoting
leftist causes, including public relations work for the Marxist regimes
in Nicaragua and Grenada. MoveOn.org was one of his current

clients. Arlie Schardt, a senior consultant for Fenton, served as Al Gore's press secretary in his first presidential campaign, while the Fenton Communications account executive assigned to the Peaceful Tomorrows project, Jessica Smith, formerly worked for the Democratic National Committee and for Al Gore's 2000 presidential run.[3]

The funding organization for Peaceful Tomorrows was the Tides Center, the central clearinghouse for radical left causes. Tides has provided funding for both the North Korea oriented Marxists of International ANSWER and the anti-war coalition led by Leslie Cagan, United for Peace and Justice. Tides is a money source for Win Without War, and MoveOn.org and the legal left, including the National Lawyers Guild, the Center for Constitutional Rights, and the Hamas-generated Council for American-Islamic Relations. The Democratic presidential candidate's wife, Teresa Heinz Kerry, is a multimillion-dollar donor to the Tides complex.[4]

According to its mission statement, the goal of Peaceful Tomorrows was to "turn our grief into action for peace." In practice this had meant systematic opposition to America's actions to defend itself both domestically and abroad. Since its creation shortly after 9/11, Peaceful Tomorrows "condemned the 'invasion' of Afghanistan, supported Dennis Kucinich's bill to gut the Patriot Act, and sent a delegation to Iraq to meet with Foreign Minister Tariq Aziz and participate in a peace demonstration organized by Saddam Hussein's government. During the demonstration Kristina Olsen, who was also present at the protest over the Bush campaign ad, sang, "Being kind is all the sad world needs."[5]

This battle over the images of 9/11 was an almost perfect emblem of the political state of the nation as it entered a presidential season that would define the war against its enemies for years to come. It revealed, as John Edwards said during the primary campaign, that there were "two Americas," whose destinies would have a profound impact on the nation's future. But not in the sense that Edwards had made into his campaign theme.

The two Americas that matter in the War on Terror are not those of rich and poor, or even of the blue states and the red. In cherishing a nation that offers more opportunity and freedom to its citizens both rich and poor or right and left than any other, these Americans are still fundamentally united. The two Americas that matter in the decisions ahead are an America that embraces its heritage and purposes, and an America that has seceded from both.[6]

The secessionists are persuaded that America is the adversary of what is decent and good in the world, that its heritage is one of inequality and injustice, and that its purposes are expressed in an arrogant will to dominate and oppress. They believe that America is the root cause of the forces that assault it and that its adversaries are actually its victims. Consequently, the secessionists want to make a separate peace with America's enemies, even in the midst of a War on Terror in which the enemy has condemned every American—regardless of race, gender, age, or creed—to death. They want to disown the courageous and generous acts of their own government in defending the powerless against oppressive regimes like the Taliban or tyrants like Saddam Hussein. In conducting their internal war against America's war on terror, they reveal a loathing—which is really a self-loathing—for their country and its citizens.

Writing on the morning of America's liberation of Baghdad—an event that saw the closing of prisons for children, the opening of mass graves, the provision of food and medicines (which the toppled regime had denied), the closing of torture chambers, and the creation of a system of individual rights for Iraqis—one of these secessionists, Howard Zinn, asked this question:

Should we not begin to redefine patriotism? We need to expand it beyond that narrow nationalism which has caused so much death and suffering.... At some point soon the United States will declare a military victory in Iraq. As a patriot, I will not celebrate.... I will mourn the Iraqi children who may not die, but who will be blinded, crippled, disfigured, or traumatized like the bombed children of Afghanistan who, as reported by American visitors, lost their power of speech.[7]

In other words, in the repellent phrase of the Vietnam generation, America is a nation of baby-killers. This is the anti-American voice of an "internationalism" that goes back more than a century to Marx's idea that radicals should have no country, that their only loyalty should be to the revolutionary future and the forces presumed to embody it. The secessionists are the heirs of Marxism and Communism who believe they are "citizens of the world"[8] rather than of the nation that guarantees their survival and their freedoms.

"Are we truly internationalist?" one secessionist—a professor of journalism at a major American university—challenged his political peers shortly after 9/11. "Can we get beyond patriotism? Or, in the end, are we just Americans?"[9] Asking these questions, he wrote, "is a way... of asking whether we are truly for peace and justice.... If we are not truly internationalist in our outlook—all the way to the bone—then I do not think we can truly call ourselves people committed to peace and justice." In other words, only by being disloyal to America can one be loyal to humanity:

For me, all this means saying goodbye to patriotism.... We must give up our "love and loyal or zealous support of one's own country" and transfer that love, loyalty and zealousness to the world, and especially the people of the world who have suffered most so that we Americans can live in affluence.[10]

The writer concludes, "We must say goodbye to patriotism because the world cannot survive indefinitely the patriotism of Americans."[11] It is a sentiment identical to the words spoken by Nicholas De Genova, the Columbia professor who wished for a million Mogadishus and America's defeat in the war on terror, saying that a world in which there is peace and justice is "a world where the U.S. would have no place."

The human mind is an interesting organ. It is capable of building vehicles that can reach outer space or of developing weapons that can kill millions of people. It can employ the power of reason to argue almost anything and deny the existence of the most obvious facts. And these denials can provide the central themes of national movements for "peace" and "social justice," and can even influence mainstream political campaigns. But if the United States did not exist, the Communist empire would still be standing, the Taliban would rule Afghanistan, Saddam Hussein would be in power, and the world would be a place of infinitely greater cruelty, injustice, and tragedy than the world that confronts us today.

Acknowledgments

I want to thank my executive assistant, Elizabeth Ruiz, for helping me locate documents and sources for this text, and for taking care of details that would have distracted me from this labor. My daughter Sarah, who is critical of the war for worthy reasons, kept me aware that there are others like her and that it was important to reach them. My wife April has been a shelter in the storms that inevitably surround me; I am daily blessed by her love and support.

Notes

INTRODUCTION

1. *New York Review of Books*, Oct. 23, 2003.
2. Commencement speech at West Point, June 1, 2002; cited in Ivo H. Daalder and James M. Lindsay, *America Unbound: The Bush Revolution in Foreign Policy*, (Brookings: Washington D.C., 2003), 121.

PART I

1. www.legalservicesindia.com/osama/edicts.htm.
2. Ibid.
3. During the first six weeks following the attacks, there were more than 500 demonstrations worldwide involving more than a million demonstrators. www.protest.net/Peace/protest_numbers.html.
4. That there would be such attacks was indisputable. An al Qaeda manifesto explained the calculus of the terrorists: "We have not reached parity [with America's alleged attacks on Muslims]. Therefore, we have the right to kill 4 million Americans—2 million of them children—and to exile twice as many and wound and cripple hundreds of thousands. Furthermore, it is our right to fight them with chemical and biological weapons, so as to afflict them with the

fatal maladies that have afflicted Muslims because of the [Americans'] chemical and biological weapons." www.memri.org, Abu Gheith, "Why We Fight," Special Dispatch 388, June 12, 2002.

5. *The New Yorker*, Sept. 24, 2001.

6. Oct. 8, 2001.

7. Katha Pollitt, "Put Out No Flags," *The Nation*, Sept. 20, 2001.

8. *London Review of Books*, Oct. 4, 2001.

9. www.memri.org, Abu Gheith, "Why We Fight," Special Dispatch 388, June 12, 2002.

10. http://www.whitehouse.gov/news/releases/2001/09/20010920-8.html.

11. Anemona Hartocollis, "CUNY Chief Repudiates Forum Remarks," *New York Times*, Oct. 4, 2001. The statement was made by mathematics professor Walter Daum. For other quotes, including those at the University of North Carolina, see Jerry L. Marin and Anne D. Neal, *Defending Civilization: How Our Universities Are Failing America and What Can Be Done About It?* a report of the American Council of Trustees and Alumni, 2001.

12. Andy Golodny, "Students, Profs Walk Out of Class to Protest Air Strikes," *Brown Daily Herald*, Oct. 10, 2001.

13. Harvey Klehr, *The Heyday of American Communism: The Depression Decade* (New York: Perseus, 1984).

14. Leon Trotsky, *The Revolution Betrayed* (New York: Pathfinder Press, 1973).

15. The famine was predicted by Noam Chomsky. See David Horowitz and Ronald Radosh, "Noam Chomsky's Anti-American *Jihad*," in Peter Coller and David Horowitz, eds, *The Anti-Chomsky Reader* (San Francisco: Encounter Books, 2004).

16. *Wall Street Journal* editorial, March 22, 2004.

17. A case for Saddam's complicity in these attacks has been made by terrorism expert Laurie Mylroie in *The War Against America: Saddam Hussein and the World Trade Center Attacks, A Study of Revenge* (New York: Harper Collins, 2001).

18. H.R. 4655.

19. There were 37 abstentions (16 Republican, 20 Democrats).

20. These events are described in Kenneth L. Pollock, *The Threatening Storm* (New York: Random House, 2000), 92-95. Pollock was a member of the National Security Council in the Clinton administration.

21. The Oil for Food program, administered by the U.N. was established in 1995 and provided $50 billion in food aid to alleviate any food shortages created by the sanctions program. This did not prevent the Iraqi regime and anti-war activists from claiming that 500,000 Iraqi children had starved because of the sanctions. After the war it was revealed that Saddam had skimmed $10 billion from the program to use as bribes, particularly to the French and Russians, to provide him diplomatic support.

22. For a list documenting Iraq's defiance of UN resolutions, see: www.whitehouse.gov/infocus/iraq/decade/sect2.html

23. Richard O. Spertzel, "Iraq's Faux Capitulation," *Wall Street Journal*, Sept. 24, 2002. Spertzel was chief weapons inspector for the years 1994-1998.

24. *Washington Post*, Sept. 5, 2002.

25. Al Gore, "Iraq and the War on Terrorism," Sept. 23, 2002 at the Commonwealth Club, San Francisco, CA.

26. Bernard Lewis, *The Crisis in Islam* (Modern Library: New York, 2003), 70.

27. On the connections between the Saddam regime and al Qaeda, see Stephen F. Hayes, "The Saddam-Osama Memo," www.weeklystandard.com, Nov. 11, 2003; Stephen F. Hayes, "The Clinton View of Iraq-al Qaeda Ties," www.weeklystandard.com, Jan. 5, 2004.

28. Michelle Goldberg, "A Day For Peace—And Fury," *Salon.com*, Oct. 27,2002.

29. Barbara Marx "Notes on the Anti-War Movement," *Monthly Review* vol. 55, no. 3, July-Aug. 2003.

30.   David Horowitz, "America Under Siege," www.frontpagemag.com,
       Jan. 20, 2003. The speech was televised live on C-SPAN on Jan. 18,
       2003.

31.   Ibid.

32.   The Republican was Ron Paul, a libertarian.

33.   Communication to the author. Cf. also, Alan Colmes, *Red, White
       and Liberal* (Regan: New York, 2003), 53.

34.   *New York Times*, Feb. 4, 2003. See Horowitz, "The 'Anti-War' Move-
       ment is a Bigger Problem Than You Think," *The War Room*, Feb. 13,
       2003. Available at www.frontpagemag.com. Cagan was the head of
       United for Peace and Justice, a coalition created in the headquarters
       of People for the American Way, for the express purpose of provid-
       ing a more reasonable message to the American public. *New York
       Times*, Feb. 4, 2003

35.   www.dcindymedia.org. See *"Who Is the Peace Movement?"* op. cit., 77.
       Also Horowitz, "Sabotage: The Peace Movement's Plans for War,"
       The War Room, March 18, 2003.

36.   Margaret Hunt Gram, "Professors Condemn War in Iraq at Teach-
       In," *Columbia Spectator*, March 26, 2003.

37.   Andrew Boyd, "The Web Rewires the Movement," *The Nation*,
       Aug. 4, 2003.

38.   www.protest.net

PART 2

1.   For a description of this organization, see Greg Yardley, "Historians
      Against History," www.frontpagemag.com July 11, 2003.

2.   "It is unthinkable . . . that American Negroes would go to war on
      behalf of those who have oppressed us for generations . . . against a
      country [the Soviet Union] which in one generation has raised our
      people to full human dignity of mankind." *New York Times*, April 4,

1949. Philip S. Foner, ed., *Paul Robeson Speaks* (Citadel Press: Seacaucus, NJ), 1978, 537 n.1.

3. John P. Diggins, "Fate and Freedom in History: The Two Worlds of Eric Foner," *The National Interest*, Fall 2002; available at www.nationalinterest.org/ME2/dirmod.asp?sid=92CC3CD26692 45CFBCA1759C59.

4. Theodore Draper, "Freedom and Its Discontents," *New York Review of Books*, Sept. 23, 1999. Foner even "pays tribute to Communists for enlarging the scope of American freedom."

5. Albert Vetere Lannon, *Second String Red: The Life of Al Lannon, American Communist* (Lexington: Lanham, MD, 1999), 151. The author is Lannon's son.

6. Lewis refused to take a "no strike" pledge, while A. Philip Randolph refused to call off the 1943 March on Washington. Lewis Coser and Irving Howe, *The American Communist Party* (Praeger: New York, 1974).

7. John Earl Haynes and Harvey Klehr, *Venona: Decoding Soviet Espionage in America* (Yale Press: New Haven, 1999). See Appendices A and B for lists of "Americans and U.S. Residents Who Had Covert Relationships with Soviet Intelligence Agencies."

8. Maurice Isserman and Ellen Schrecker, "'Papers of a Dangerous Tendency': From Major Andre's Boot to the Venona Files," in Cold War Triumphalism, (New Press: New York, 2004), 157. Of course, no one who knew or understood Communists would be surprised by this.

9. I have myself in *The Politics of Bad Faith*, (Free Press: New York, 1998).

10. Gerhart Niemeyer, *Deceitful Peace: A New Look at the Soviet Threat*, (Arlington House: New York, 1971), 205. Cited in Aileen Kraditor, *"Jimmy Higgins," The Mental World of the American Rank-and-File Communist 1930-1958*, (Greenwood: New York, 1988), 2.

11.   Cited in John Earl Haynes and Harvey Klehr, *In Denial: Historians, Communism and Espionage*, (Encounter Books: San Francisco, 2003), 53; See Aileen Kraditor, op. cit.

12.   Haynes-Klehr, *In Denial*. The statement is from a book written by one of the Communist Party's leading trainers of cadre.

13.   West's comment is on the jacket cover of an anthology by the magazine's editors, Noel Ignatiev (a sixties Maoist) and John Garvey. *Race Traitor*, New York, 1996. In the words of Amazon.com's reviewer, "The journal *Race Traitor* began in 1992 with one lofty ambition: to serve as an intellectual center for those seeking to abolish the white race." West was a political consultant to the Democratic Party campaigns of former Senator Bill Bradley and Al Sharpton.

14.   *Witness*, (Regnery: Washington, D.C.: 1952), 524.

15.   Of course, they do not apply the same standard to revolutionary movements and regimes, which are struggling to bring a just society to birth. The failures of revolutionary movements and regimes are to be explained by the opposition of the old regimes, and their efforts to strangle the revolutionary utopia at birth.

16.   Gerhart Niemeyer, *Between Nothingness and Paradise*, (St. Augustine Press: South Bend, IN: 1998), 96-7.

17.   Niemeyer, ibid.

18.   Kraditor, 60-61.

19.   Herbert Aptheker, *History and Reality*, (Cameron Associates: New York: 1955), 112. Cited in Kraditor, 62. The book was by author Cleveland Amory.

20.   Kraditor, 62.

21.   Also present were Communist professor Angela Davis, and history department member Manning Marable who is a member of the Committee of Correspondence, a faction of the American Communist Party led by Davis that was expelled because of its opposition to the attempted *coup* against Mikhail Gorbachev in 1991.

22. Horowitz, "America Under Siege," op. cit. The speaker was Malik Shabazz, a graduate of Howard University, a lawyer and the leader of the New Black Panthers.

23. Stephanie Courtois and Mark Kramer, *The Black Book of Communism*, (Harvard: Cambridge, 1999).

24. "The Road to Nowhere," in Horowitz, *The Politics of Bad Faith* (Free Press: New York, 1998); Martin Malia, *The Soviet Tragedy*, (Free Press: New York, 1994).

25. Hollander, 272.

26. See Horowitz, "The Road to Nowhere," *The Politics of Bad Faith*.

27. Of course, after 1956, their defense of Communism was qualified. New Leftists generally referred to their "critical support" of the Soviet bloc to signal its qualified nature. Such support was summed up in a famous article of the Sixties by Andrew Kopkind called "Two Cheers for the Soviet Union." See discussion below.

28. E.g., Daniel Singer, "989: The End of Communism?" in George Katsiaficas, *After the Fall*, (Routledge: New York, 2001), 13, 15, 128, 130, 134, 144. Again the caveat must be made that not all leftists took this view, in particular those who had supported the anti-Communist Cold War effort of the United States and the Western powers.

29. Paul Hollander, *Discontents: Post-Modern and Post-Communist*, (Transaction: New Brunswick, NJ, 2002), 281. See also two typical collections (with the same name): Robin Blackburn, ed. *After the Fall*, (Verso, 1991), and George Katsiaficas, *After the Fall*.

30. *Wall Street Journal*, Nov. 25, 1991.

31. Verbal communication from Christopher Hitchens to the author. Hobsbawm was piqued by the fact that the Party had not sent him a request for renewal.

32. Author David Caute, for example, has called him "arguably our greatest living historian—not only Britain's, but the world's." Jacket

blurb, Eric Hobsbawm, *Interesting Times: A Twentieth Century Life*, (Knopf: New York, 2002).

33. A reference to Hobsbawm's four-volume history of industrial capitalism, from a review by Joseph Keppler, *Seattle Times*, April 16, 1995.

34. An analysis of the book is contained in Horowitz, *The Politics of Bad Faith*, 17.

35. Hobsbawm, *Interesting Times: A Twentieth Century Life*, 55-56.

36. See Haynes and Klehr, *In Denial: Historians, Communism and Espionage*, which analyzes the responses of American historians to the fall of Communism and the opening of the Soviet archives. Tony Kushner's *Perestroika* is a cultural expression of the indulgence and nostalgia progressives feel for their failed past.

37. *Interesting Times,* op. cit. See also Geoffrey Wheatcroft's review of the autobiography in the *New York Times*, Sept. 5, 2003, titled "Still Saluting the Red Flag After the Flag Pole Fell."

38. This is evident both in his final work, *The Age of Extremes*, in his post-Communist articles (see following footnote) and in the interviews he has given in the last decade.

39. "After the Fall," in Robin Blackburn, ed. *After the Fall: The Failure of Communism and the Future of Socialism*, (Verso: London, 1991), 122-3. *Interesting Times*, 280.

40. *Interesting Times*, 280-81. During World War I, Luxemburg famously said that mankind was faced with a choice between "socialism or barbarism."

41. Yardley, "Historians Against History," www.frontpagemag.com, July 11, 2003.

42. Gerda Lerner, *Fireweed, A Political Autobiography*, (Temple University: Philadelphia, 2002), 369.

43. Technically, of course, the United States was neutral. But American sympathies clearly lay with Hitler's victims, while the aim of the

Communist peace movement was to keep America neutral. See, Harvey Klehr, *The Heyday of American Communism*, op. cit.

44. Lerner, *Fireweed*, 370. Lerner includes "idealism and heroism" in her catalogue of utopian ideas, but this is just typical radical bad faith. The idea of human perfectibility–of a society embracing the ideals of social justice—is integrally connected to the Communist catastrophe. But in what way do a belief in the possibility of individual heroes and/or noble aspirations lead to Marxist gulags? They don't. Nor are they concepts specific to Marxism and Communism.

45. For example, Leo Pannitch and Sam Ginden, "Transcending Pessimism: Rekindling Socialist Imagination" in Kastiaficas, ed. *After the Fall, 179*. "The socialist 'utopian' goal is built around our potential to be full human beings."

46. Interview with Joan Fisher, *Wisconsin Academy Review*, Spring 2002 vol. 48, no. 2. http://www.portalwisconsin.org/gerdalerner02.cfm.

47. Op. cit., p. 371, Lerner.

48. E.g., Martin Malia, *The Soviet Tragedy*, (Free Press: New York: 1995) and Leszek Kolakowski, *Main Currents in Marxism: The Breakdown*, vol 3, (Oxford Press: Oxford, 1981).

49. On the new terminology as an attempt to speak American, see James Miller, *Democracy Is In The Streets* (Simon & Schuster: New York, 1988). On the similarity in the meaning of the concepts, see Horowitz, "The Port Huron Statement and the War on Terror," Glazov, ed. *Left Illusions: An Intellectual Odyssey* (Spence: Dallas, 2003).

50. See Oglesby's speech "Name the System," in Miller, *Democracy is in the Streets* and Horowitz, "Hand-Me-Down-Marxism," in *Left Illusions*.

51. I was also an editor of *Root and Branch*. The other journals were *Studies on the Left and New University Thought*.

52. Robert Scheer and Maurice Zeitlin, *Cuba: Tragedy: in Our Hemisphere* (Grove Press: New York, 1961). I helped to edit this book.

Scheer is a also a lecturer at the Annenberg School of Communications at USC.

53. *Root and Branch,* issue 1, Berkeley 1960. Only two issues of the magazine were published.

54. The present writer was one of the *Root and Branch* editors.

55. This was true for all but a handful of leftists who had been anti-Communist all along. For example, those grouped around Irving Howe's magazine, *Dissent.*

56. *CIA World Fact Book,* www.photius.com/wfb1999/rankings/gdp_per_capita_0.html.

57. Argiris Malapanis, UCLA Symposium, "LA Symposium Debates Che and the Cuban Revolution," *The Militant,* Nov. 24, 1997. *The Militant* is an organ of the pro-Castro Socialist Workers Party (SWP).

58. An appropriate term for these groups might be "paleo-communists."

59. Chris Hedges, "A Longtime Anti-war Activist, Escalating the Peace," *New York Times,* Feb. 4, 2003

60. Kate Zernike and Dean E. Murphy, "A Nation at War: Dissent–Anti-war Effort Emphasizes Civility Over Confrontation," *New York Times,* March 29, 2003, and Michelle Goldberg, "Peace Goes Mainstream," *Salon.com,* Jan. 20, 2003.

61. Leslie Cagan, "It Should Be Possible, It Has to Be Possible," *Zmag.net,* June 1998; communication from Ronald Radosh who was familiar with Cagan in the 1960s.

62. Cagan, op. cit.

63. For the lengths Cagan is willing to take her alliance see discussion below.

64. *The Fight Is for Democracy: New Liberal Unorthodoxies,* edited by George Packer. (Harper Collins: New York, 2003).

66. Ibid., 119.

66. This is a curious slip. The Vietnamese flags present in the anti-war demonstrations were Vietcong flags – the flags of the Communist-

controlled South Vietnamese National Liberation Front, not North Vietnam flags. There would not have been North Vietnamese flags since the Left maintained (falsely) that the Vietnamese liberation struggle was a struggle for self-determination by the Vietnamese in South Vietnam.

67. E.g., Bui Tin, *From Enemy to Friend: A North Vietnamese Perspective On The War*, (Naval Institute Press: Annapolis, 2002); Truong Nhu Tang, *A Viet Cong Memoir* (Vintage Books: New York, 1985). Truong was minister of justice for the NLF. Colonel Bui Tin was one of the architects of the Ho Chi Minh Trail, the path of the Communists' conquest of the South. He was a leader of the Hanoi regime and a personal friend of Ho Chi Minh. Truong Nhu Tang was a founder of the National Liberation Front.

68. Bui Tin, *Following Ho Chi Minh*, (Univ. of Hawaii Press: Honolulu, 1995), 192.

69. Peter Collier and David Horowitz, "A Decade Overrated and Unmourned," in Collier and Horowitz, *Deconstructing the Left*, (Univ. Press of America: Los Angeles, 1995), 9.

70. Gitlin, "Varieties of Patriotic Experience," op. cit. 133.

71. Ibid., 134.

72. A response to the general radical indictment of America is to be found in Dinesh D'Souza, *What's So Great About America?* (Regnery: Washington, 2002). America accounted for less than 1% of the world slave trade in Africans. For data on American slavery, see Horowitz, *Uncivil Wars: The Controversy Over Slavery* (Encounter Books: San Francisco, 2001), 111.

73. What graves are Gitlin talking about? There were indeed isolated massacres of Indians just as there were isolated massacres by Indians. But "mass graves" has connotations of actual genocides committed by Nazis and Communists (not to mention Saddam Hussein) that are merely outrageous distortions and a group libel when placed in the

historical context of the American frontier. This is a charge more readily put to the Aztecs, who regularly sacrificed as many as 80,000, virgins than to the European settlers in North America.

74. Larissa MacFarquhar, "The Devil's Accountant," *The New Yorker*, March 31, 2003; *Guardian* quote cited in Keith Windschuttle, "The Hypocrisy of Noam Chomsky," *The New Criterion*, May 2, 2003.

75. Chomsky, *9-11*, (New York: Seven Stories Press, 2001).

76. Noam Chomsky, *Class Warfare*, reprint edition, (Common Courage Press, 1996), 122-3.

77. Barry Loberfeld, "The Coercive Anarchism of Noam Chomsky," www.frontpagemag.com, Jan. 31, 2003. Loberfeld is a libertarian.

78. Op. cit., p. 73.

79. Op. cit., p. 64.

80. See H-DIPLO March 2003 logs. Confronted by John Williamson with the untenability of his statements, Chomsky claimed that he had never made them and that the *New Yorker* reporter Larissa Mac-Farquhar had merely made them up. In fact the entire event, including the exchange cited by MacFarquhar was videotaped by C-SPAN, which showed that Chomsky was lying. John Williamson, "Chomsky, Linguistics and Me," Peter Collier and David Horowitz, eds. *The Anti-Chomsky Reader*, (San Francisco: Encounter Books, 2004)

81. Werner Cohn, "Chomsky and the Holocaust Deniers," in Collier and Horowitz, eds., *The Anti-Chomsky Reader*.

82. Noam Chomsky, *What Uncle Sam Really Wants* (Ododian Press: New York 2002).

83. Ibid.

84. Ibid.

85. E.g., "It is likely to prove to be a crushing blow to Palestinians and other poor and oppressed people," because of the adverse American reaction. Noam Chomsky, "A Quick Reaction," www.counterpunch.com, Sept. 12, 2001. Christopher Hitchens, "Of Sin, the Left and Islamic Fascism," *The Nation*, Oct. 8, 2001.

86. Interview, Sept. 19, 2001. www.zmag.org. Pearl Harbor doesn't count in Chomsky's calculus of attacks on the national territory because Hawaii was a "colony" at the time. The fact that it was a benignly run colony and that it is now a proud state of the Union counts for nothing, of course, in Chomsky's view.

87. Transcript available at http://www.zmag.org/GlobalWatch/chomskymit.htm.

88. Cited in David Horowitz and Ronald Radosh, "Noam Chomsky's *Jihad* Against America," in Collier and Horowitz, *The Anti-Chomsky Reader*. The relief agencies' alarm was not unrelated to the left-wing politics of the relief community and the charges of Chomsky himself.

89. Chomsky's remarks were also reported in the November 6 edition of the *Teheran Times*.

90. An impressive array of left-wing media outlets provide platforms for Chomsky's views. In addition to bibliographical Internet sites devoted to his work, they include *The Nation, The Progressive, The Boston Review of Books, Zmag.org,* Indymedia.org, Counterpunch.org, Commondreams.org, Anti-war.com, the Pacifica Radio network, and PBS, to name a few. Chomsky's influence is discussed in Richard Posner, *Public Intellectuals*.

91. Howard Zinn, *Terrorism and War*, (Seven Stories Press: New York, 2002). Like Chomsky's *9-11*, which sold 200,000 copies and was translated into many languages, Zinn's tract is a one (small) volume interview about these themes.

92. MIT professor Joshua Cohen. Cohen told the author this in a private communication.

93. Zinn, *A People's History*, 646. "Objectivity is impossible, and it is also undesirable. That is, if it were possible it would be undesirable, because if you have any kind of a social aim, if you think history should serve society in some way; should serve the progress of the human race; should serve justice in some way, then it requires that you make your selection on the basis of what you think will advance causes of humanity." Cited in Dan Flynn, "Master of Deceit," a review of Zinn's book. www.frontpagemag.com, June 3, 2003

94. Zinn, *A People's History*, 23.

95. Zinn, ibid., 658-9.

96. "Scattered Soviet materials have shown that Soviet involvement in preparing and planning an invasion after Stalin gave his reluctant endorsement in January 1950 was higher than previous writers had thought." Bruce Cumings, *Korea's Place in the Sun* (Norton: New York, 1998), 263. As it happens, Cumings is a left-wing historian.

97. Zinn, *A People's History*, 59.

98. Zinn, ibid., 73.

99. "Varieties of Patriotic Experience," 120.

100. Haynes and Klehr, *In Denial: Historians, Communism and Espionage* (San Francisco: Encounter, 2003), 1.

101. Robin West, *Progressive Constitutionalism: Reconstructing the Fourteenth Amendment* (Duke University: Durham 1994), 17-18.

102. Gitlin, "Varieties of Patriotic Experience," 122.

103. Gitlin, ibid.,120.

104. Stephen Morris, "Chomsky on Communist Vietnam and Cambodia," in Collier and Horowitz, eds., *The Anti-Chomsky Reader*.

105. Norman Mailer, "The White Man Unburdened," *New York Review of Books*, July 17, 2003, http://www.nybooks.com/articles/16470.

106. James Weinstein, *The Long Detour: The History and Future of the American Left*, 225. Weinstein was a founding editor of *Studies on the Left* and the founder and publisher of *In These Times*.

107. "Chomsky on War," *Zmag.org*, March 31, 2003.

108. "Daniel Ellsberg on Iraq," *Zmag.org*, Jan. 31, 2003.

109. Willam Blum, *Rogue State: A Guide to the World's Only Superpower* (Common Courage Press: Monroe Maine, 2000), 1.

110. William Blum, *Killing Hope: U.S. Military and CIA Interventions Since World War II* (Common Courage Press: Monroe. Maine), 1995, 1. Blum has a website called "The American Holocaust" and speaks widely on American campuses and abroad.

111. *Rogue State*, 1.

112. Andrew Boyd, "The Web Rewires the Movement," *The Nation*, Aug. 4, 2003. http://www.thenation.com/doc.mhtml?i=20030804&s=boyd.

113. Chomsky, *What Uncle Sam Really Wants*, 15.

114. For an analysis of this movement, see discussion below.

PART 3

1. Bernard Lewis, *The Crisis of Islam: Holy War and Unholy Terror*, especially, 70-71. See also Paul Berman, *Terror and Liberalism* (W. W. Norton: New York, 2003), and Stephen Schwartz, *Two Faces of Islam*, (Anchor: New York, 2002).

2. Translated with an introduction by Hamid Algar, (Islamic Publication International: Oneonta, New York, 2000). It was originally published in 1950.

3. Gilles Keppel, *Jihad: The Trail of Political Islam* (Belknap Press: Cambridge 2002), 23 et seq.

4. Berman, 95.

5. Berman, 97. For jeopardizing the security of the state, the penalty under Islamic sharia is exile, dismemberment, or crucifixion. The purges conducted under various forms of Marxist rule have been no less severe.

6. The translator was Ali Shariati. Keppel, 36 et seq. Berman, 106. Among those who celebrated Khomeini as a great liberator was Princeton professor and *Nation* contributor Richard Falk, who thirty years later was one of the outspoken opponents of the war in Iraq.

7. Laden Boroumand and Roya Boroumand, "Terror, Islam, and Democracy," in *The Journal of Democracy*, Feb. 13, 2002.

8. For an extensive discussion of this issue and analysis of relevant texts, see Robert Spencer, *Onward Muslim Soldiers* (Regnery: Washington, D.C., 2003).

9. Ibid.

10. Qutb, op. cit. p. 2

11. Lewis, 80.

12. Qutb, 71: "It is a civilization which permits the American conscience to acquiesce in the systematic eradication of the Red Indian race." As noted in the text above, there are more "Red Indians" alive in America today than there were when the European settlers first arrived.

13. Islam's role in the African slave trade predates America's by 1,000 years and exceeds it in numbers by a factor of roughly 15-1.

14. Lewis, 80-81.

15. Jerusalem Media & Communication Center—Public Opinion Poll Unit Poll #49, October 2003.

16. Berman, 143.

17. Neither, of course, would they be able to recognize the pathology in their own political passion.

18. Berman, 131.

19. Ibid.

20. Ibid., 125; 21 et seq.

21. Karl Marx, *Introduction to A Contribution to the Critique of Hegel's Philosophy of Right*.

22. For Marx's formulation, see "On the Jewish Question," http://csf.colorado.edu/psn/marx/Archive/1844-JQ/

23. *Village Voice*, April 11, 1980. Reprinted in Andrew Kopkind, *The Thirty Years War* (Verso: London, 1995), 348.

24. As a result of Turkey's defeat in World War I, its empire had come under the control of the British and French. In the interwar years, the empire was divided and the states of Jordan, Syria, Lebanon and Iraq were created by the powers victorious in World Wars I and II in exactly the same fashion as Israel. Details in David Fromkin, *The Peace to End All Peace*, New York, 2001.

25. Barry and Judith Rubin, *Yasser Arafat: A Political Biography*, (Oxford University: Oxford, 2003), 31.

26. Ibid., 40.

27. Ibid., 26. Nasser even created an abortive "United Arab Republic" joining Syria and Egypt.

28. PLO Charter. http://www.us-israel.org/jsource/Peace/cove1.html.

29. Rubin, 187, http://www.us-israel.org/jsource/Peace/cove1.html.

30. Cited in Theodore Draper, "Israel and the Arabs," *Commentary*, August 1967, 34.

31. Rubin, 14, 19.

32. Keppel, 118-123.

33. See discussion of al-Arian below.

34. http://www.islam.org.au/articles/15/LADIN.HTM

35. Keppel, 144-147.

36. As revised in December. Arafat continued to negotiate for several months while launching his new military offensive. Cf. Yossef Bodansky, *The High Cost of Peace: How Washington's Middle East Policy Left America Vulnerable to Terrorism*, (Prima: New York, 2002) Chapter 17, "The Outbreak of the Intifadah (2000)."

37. Rubin, 208.

38. The pretext of this eruption was Ariel Sharon's visit to the Temple Mount. Sharon was at the time the leader of the Israeli opposition (Bodansky).

39. Rubin, 203. Palestinian propaganda presented the Intifada as a response to the visit by Israeli Prime Minister Ariel Sharon to the Temple Mount. But testimony by Arafat's own aides establish that the Palestinian offensive was planned in July when Ehud Barak was

still Israel's Prime Minister, and that Sharon's visit had been cleared with the Palestine Authority.

40. Bodansky, 345.

41. Bernard Lewis, *The Assassins: A Radical Sect in Islam*, (Basic Books: New York, 2003).

42. Stephen Hayes, "The Saddam-Osama Memor," *The Weekly Standard*, Nov. 11, 2003; "The Clinton View of Iraq-Al Qaeda Ties," *The Weekly Standard*, Dec. 29, 2003.

43. Rubin, 6.

44. Keppel, 116-117. See Kenneth L. Pollock, *The Threatening Storm*, Kanan Makiya, *The Republic of Fear (Univ. of California Press:* 1990).

45. http://abcnews.go.com/sections/world/DailyNews/miller_binladen_980609.html.

46. http://ict.org.il/Articles/Hiz_letter.htm#note.

47. MEMRI Special Dispatch (No. 268), Sept. 17, 2001.

48. See www.un.org/WCAR, the official site of the conference. In the Rwandan genocide, Hutus slaughtered a million Tutsis. The genocide could have been prevented by a U.N. intervention, but no U.N. action was taken. Philip Gourevitch, *We Wish to Inform You That Tomorrow We Will Be Killed With Our Families: Stories From Rwanda* (Picador USA: New York, 1999). See also http://www.pbs.org/wgbh/pages/frontline/shows/evil/.

49. For a summary of the conference failure from a moderate left-wing source, see Chris Greal, "UN Conference Ends In Acrimony," *Guardian*, Sept. 8, 2001

50. www.adl.org/durban/durban_083101.asp.

51. Herbert Keinon, "Festival of Hate," *Jerusalem Post*, Sept. 7, 2001, cited in Ken Timmerman, *Prophets of Hate*, (New York, 2003) 25.

52. www.hri.ca/humanrights/racism/daniels.shtml. The American NGO delegation was funded by the Ford, Rockefeller, MacArthur and Charles Stewart Mott Foundations.

53. John Fonte, "Liberal Democracy vs. Transnational Progressivism: The Future of the Ideological Civil War Within The West," *Orbis*, Summer 2002. The American NGOs also deplored the "denial of economic rights" in the United States and demanded the recognition of the "right" to an adequate standard of living.

54. Abigail and Stephan Thernstrom, *America in Black and White*, (Simon & Schuster: New York, 1999).

55. The anti-American agendas of the reparations movement are analyzed in Horowitz, *Uncivil Wars: The Controversy over Reparations for Slavery* (Encounter Books: San Francisco, 2001).

56. Robert Fogel, *Without Contract or Consent*, (W.W. Norton: New York, 1995).

57. Thomas Sowell, *Conquests and Cultures*, (Basic Books: New York, 1999).

58. To institute "social justice" requires state control of civil society and the private economy, and a pervasive political control of social life. See Friedrich Hayek, *The Mirage of Social Justice and The Road to Serfdom*, and Barry Loberfeld, "Social Justice: Code for Communism," www.frontpagemag.com, Feb. 17, 2004

59. Since the fall of Communism this goal is usually not articulated, or is articulated as a "socially just" social order. But such an order is of necessity totalitarian since it is the remedy for a totalistic fault rather than a specifically unjust law or institution . E.g., see Horowitz, *The Politics of Bad Faith*, op. cit.

60. Joe R. Feagin, *Racist America* (Routledge: New York, 2001), 6.

61. Ibid., 16.

62. "Declaration of the Asia Pacific NGO Forum," Tehran, Iran, Feb. 17-18, 2001. http://www.hri.ca/racism/meetings/teheran.shtml

63. A similar observation is made by Timmerman, *Prophets of Hate*.

64. E.g, Chomsky *Hegemony Or Survival* (Metropolitan: New York, 2003), 235; on the role of communist intelligence agencies, see Peter

Collier and David Horowitz, *Destructive Generation*, New York, 1989, 157 et seq.

65. Alex Cockburn and Jeffrey St. Clair, *Five Days That Shook the World: Seattle and Beyond*, (Verso: London, 2000), 3.

66. The World Trade Organization is a group that negotiates agreements to lower or eliminate tariffs.

67. A call to oppose the policies of the WTO had been sent out from approximately ninety nations and a thousand nongovernmental organizations including AIDS activists, human rights and animal rights activists, and environmental and "indigenous peoples" activists, who had engaged for years in disputes over labor regulations, policies on modified foods policies, and other issues impacted by the WTO and international institutions like the World Bank. John Nichols, "Now What?" *The Progressive*, Jan. 20, 2000.

68. http://www.socialismtoday.org/44/seattle.html. The phrase was from a 1965 speech by SDS president Carl Oglesby who had named the system, "corporate liberalism."

69. Naomi Klein, *Fences and Windows*, (Picador USA: New York, 2002), 4.

70. *New York Times*, Oct. 13, 1999; www.corpwatch.org/news/PRT.jsp?articleid=314; www.globalpolicy.org/socecon/bwi-wto99/protst99.htm

71. Cockburn and St. Clair, *Five Days That Shook The World*.

72. Marc Cooper, "After Seattle," *Los Angeles Weekly*, March 24, 2000.

73. *The Nation*, April 21, 2003.

74. William F. Fish and Thomas Ponniah, *Another World Is Possible: Popular Alternatives to Globalization at the World Social Forum*, (Zed Books: New York, 2003), 4. This text was prepared with the cooperation of the World Social Forum. The foreword was written by Michael Hardt and Antonio Negri, a convicted Italian terrorist. On Ford Foundation funding, see Greg Yardley, Fifth International, www.frontpagemag.com, June 26, 2003.

75. Ibid.

76. Naomi Klein, "World Social Forum–A Fete for the End of History," www.thenation.com, March 19, 2001

77. Ibid.

78. Chomsky, *Hegemony Or Survival*, 235; Yardley.

79. Ibid.

80. Ibid.

81. A reference to "identity politics" and race, gender and gender-orientation issues.

82. Fisher and Ponniah, 12.

83. Ibid., 14.

84. Naomi Klein, "World Social Forum."

85. Fisher and Ponniah, 342-47 for the full text.

86. Ibid., 346.

PART 4

1. Naomi Klein, *Fences and Windows* (Picador USA: New York, 2002). This is a journalistic record of these protests written by a radical employed as a reporter by the Toronto *Globe and Mail*.

2. Chomsky is here deliberately forgetting the history of the Communist movement which sent its agents to Spain during its civil war in the thirties. The only significant difference was that these international efforts were not exclusively organized under the control of the Communist Party, but what would once have been called "fellow travelers" of the Communist Party.

3. Noam Chomsky, *Hegemony or Survival: America's Quest for Global Dominance* (Metropolitan: New York, 2003), 217 et seq., 235.

4. Chomsky, *Hegemony or Survival*, 236.

5. Teresa Gutierrez, "Anti-war Forces Call For National Action," press release. www.workers.org/ww/2001/sept290927.php

6.   Ibid.

7.   Ryan O'Donnell, "Steering Committee for Peace," in David Horowitz and John Perazzo, "Who Is the Peace Movement?" Los Angeles, 2003; Michelle Goldberg, "Peace Kooks," *Salon.com*, Oct. 16, 2002;

8.   Manny Fernandez and David A. Fahrenthold, "Police Arrest Hundreds in Protests," *Washington Post*, Sept. 28, 2002; Knight Ridder, "Summit Activists Protest War," Sept. 28, 2002; Manny Fernandez and Monte Reel, "Against War, a Peaceful March," *Washington Post*, Sept. 30, 2002

9..   John Perazzo, "NION: Maoists for Peace," www.frontpagemag.com Feb. 28, 2003 in Horowitz and Perazzo, "Who Is the Peace Movement?", 2003. Goldberg, "Peace Kooks," *Salon.com*, Oct. 16, 2002.

10.   Michelle Goldberg. See David Corn, "Behind the Placards: The Odd and troubling origins of today's anti-war movement," *Los Angeles Weekly*, Nov. 1, 2002.

11.   Horowitz, "100,000 Communists March on Washington to Give Aid and Comfort to Saddam Hussein" www.frontpagemag.com Oct. 28, 2002 and "America Under Siege," www.frontpagemag.com, Jan. 20, 2003. The second article describes a demonstration also organized by International ANSWER, shown on C-SPAN.

12.   The *New York Times*, for example, assigned the leftist Chris Hedges to profile United for Peace and Justice head Leslie Cagan. See Chris Hedges, "A Longtime Anti-war Activist, Escalating the Peace," *New York Times*, Feb. 4, 2003.

13.   Kate Zernike and Dean E. Murphy, "A Nation At War: Dissent–Anti-war Effort Emphasizes Civility Over Confrontation," *New York Times*, March 29, 2003.

14.   The Trotskyists controlled the Mobilization to End the War (the Mobe), and the Communists controlled the People's Coalition for Peace and Justice (PCPJ). These two groups organized all the

national anti-war demonstrations. In a column reproving the critics of the anti-war movement, veteran Leftist Alexander Cockburn made a similar point. See Alexander Cockburn, "The Anti-War Movement and Its Critics," Counterpunch.org, Nov. 14, 2002.

15. Michelle Goldberg, "Peace Goes Mainstream," *Salon.com*, Jan. 20, 2003: quote.

16. Zernike and Murphy, "A Nation At War: Dissent–Anti-war Effort Emphasizes Civility Over Confrontation," op. cit.

17. Jan Pearce, "Code Pinko," www.frontpagemag.com, March 26, 2003. Its chief spokesperson, Sand Brim and key organizer Kirsten Moller had worked with Benjamin in close association with the Communist guerillas in El Salvador and the Sandinista government in Nicaragua during the 1980s.

18. *The Nation*, April 21, 2003.

19 Jan Pearce, "Code Pinko," www.frontpagemag.com, March 26, 2003.

20. Ibid. Cockburn and St. Clair, op. cit.

21. John Perazzo, "The Anti-American," www.frontpagemag.com, Nov. 15, 2002.

22. *The Nation*, April 21, 2003.

23. E.g, Indymedia.org, anti-war.com, commondreams.org, zmag.org, counterpunch.org. Indymedia.org is translated into ten languages.

24. Laura Flanders, "Interview with Occupation Watch Staff and Military Families Speak Out," July 10, 2003. www.occupationwatch.org and Daniel Mandel, "Saddam's Press Lackey," www.frontpagemag.com, March 4, 2004.

25. Grant McCool, "Worldwide Protests Demand Iraq Pullout," YahooNews! March 21, 2004; Global Exchange was also one of the sponsors. www.UnitedforPeace.org. "UFPJ is pleased to have played a vital role in initiating and building support for a broad-based, global day of action against war and occupation on March 20th.... Many member groups on UFPJ's Steering Committee are

already actively building March 20th...Not In Our Name, and other anti-war forces have expressed strong interest in joining this call. ANSWER recently announced they will participate...."

26. www.unitedforpeace.org/articlephp?id=2136

27. www.internationalanswer.org/campaigns/m20/index.html

28. Jess Bravin, "Judge Deals Blow to the Patriot Act," *Wall Street Journal*, Jan. 27, 2004.

29. Eric Lichtblau, "Citing Free Speech, Judge Voids Part of Antiterror Act," *New York Times*, Jan. 27, 2004.

30. Op. cit.

31. Liberation Tigers of Tamil Eelam.

32. U.S. Court of Appeals, Ninth Circuit, *Humanitarian Law Project et al v. Reno et al* http://www.ca9.uscourts.gov/ca9/newopinions.nsf/ 044DE357BD726D7288256DF10063BDE4/$file/0255082.pdf? openelement

33. A dossier of cases can be found in Jules Lobel, *Lost Causes*, New York, 2004. Lobel is vice president of the Center for Constitutional Rights.

34. In the early seventies Arthur Kinoy met with the author who was then editor of the radical magazine Ramparts and handed him a 35 page manifesto written by Kinoy and Kunstler calling for the formation of a "new Communist Party."

35. Lobel, 186.

36. Ibid., 187.

37. George Packer, "Terrorist Lawyer," *New York Times*, Sept. 23, 2002

38. Eric Lichtblau, who covered the case for the *New York Times*, explained in a phone interview with the author that this was the *Times'* standard practice.

39. Michael Radu, "Terrorism Is Free Speech," www.frontpagemag.com, Feb. 3, 2004. Radu is a terrorism expert at the Foreign Policy Research Institute.

40. Jean Pearce, "Humanitarian Law Project," www.frontpagemag.com, April 14, 2004. Aris Anagnos, the funder of the Anagnos Peace Center is a pro-Castro real estate magnate who funded the Christic Institute's RICO suit against the CIA for alleged drug trafficking and support of assassinations in Nicaragua. The suit was thrown out when most of the "witnesses" turned out not to be real people. Ralph Fertig, the principal director of the Human Law Project, is a lawyer for the far Left Americans for Democratic Action and a board member of the Pacifica Foundation, a radical public radio network whose board Cagan chaired. Lydia Brazon, the number two executive at the Humanitarian Law Project is also on the Pacifica board and like Fertig a radical anti-war activist.

41. Lichtblau, *Times*, op. cit.

42. www.ombwatch.org. Tim Visser and Kay Guinane, "Patriot Games: The USA Patriot Act and Its Impact on Nonprofit Organizations." This article covers the cases from a left-wing perspective.

43. *Washington Times*, Jan. 8, 2004

44. Radu.

45. Ibid.

46. Timmerman, 276 et seq.

48. Steven Emerson, *American Jihad: The Terrorists Living Among Us* (Free Press: New York, 2002), 37.

49. William R. Hawkins and Erin Anderson, *The Open Borders Lobby and National Security After 9/11*, Los Angeles 2004, a Center for the Study of Popular Culture book. The original article is available at www.frontpagemag.com

49. Ibid.

50. Emerson, 2, 84.

51. Ibid., 128 et seq. See also, Gilles Kepel, *Jihad: The Trail of Political Islam*, 144 et seq.

52. Emerson, 130.

53. Ibid., 131.

54. Ibid., 134.

55. Packer, "Terrorist Lawyer," op. cit.

56. *Monthly Review*, Nov. 25, 2002. Reprinted in www.frontagemag.com/Articles/Printable.asp?ID=4764

57. *New York Times*, June 28, 1995.

58. Emerson, 121, 122.

59. Ibid.

60. Cited in State of Michigan, Washtenaw County Circuit Court, Case 02-1150CZ, *Richard Dorfman and Adi Neuman v. University of Michigan.*

61. David Tell, "Al-Arian Nation," *The Weekly Standard*, Feb. 3, 2003.

62. http://www.usdoj.gov/usao/flm/pr/022003indict.pdf

63. Emerson, op. cit., 109 et seq.

64. Robert Spencer, "Al-Arian: Terrorist Professor and His Campus Allies," www.frontpagemag.com, Feb. 26, 2003.

65. *Salon.com*, Jan. 19, 2002. http://archive.salon.com/tech/feature/2002/01/19/bubba/.

66. The AAUP's position is analyzed in Nathan Giller, "American Association of University Professors: Lobby for the Left," www.frontpagemag.com, June 4, 2003.

67. Ken Timmerman, *Preachers of Hate*, 273; Ron Radosh, "The Case of Sami Al-Arian," www.frontpagemag.com, Feb. 8, 2002; Jonathan Schanzer, "Professors for Terrorist Al-Arian," www.frontpagemag.com, Feb. 24, 2003.

68. Sarah Shields, "Sami Al-Arian and the Dungeon: A Fable for our Time," www.CommonDreams.org, Nov. 16, 2003.

69. Heather Mac Donald, "Why The FBI Didn't Stop 9/11," *City Journal*, Autumn 2002.

70. The rule was called, "Procedures for Contacts Between the FBI and the Criminal Division Concerning Foreign Intelligence and Foreign Counterintelligence Investigations."

71. Ibid.

72. *The State of Civil Liberties: One Year Later, A Report Issued By the Center for Constitutional Rights*, 2002.

73. Michelle Goldberg, "The Peace Movement Prepares to Escalate," *Salon.com*, March 14, 2003 http://www.salon.com/news/feature/2003/03/14/war/index.html

74. Ibid.

75. Christine Pelisek, "The List," *Los Angeles Weekly*, July 4, 2003.

76. The relocation, whatever its faults, was planned after intelligence reports showed many Japanese immigrants, loyal to the Japanese emperor, were involved in anti-war activities and spying for the enemy. See Michelle Malkin, *In Defense of Internment: The Case for "Racial Profiling" in World War II and the War on Terror* (Regnery: Washington, D.C., 2004).

77. Bill Perkins, New York City council member and sponsor of a resolution condemning the Act. Michelle Garcia, "NY City Council Passes Anti-Patriot Act Measure," *Washington Post*, Feb. 5, 2004. Perkins was also the sponsor of a bill to name a New York Street after Communist Party leader Benjamin Davis, who was ousted from the City Council after being convicted under the Smith Act in 1949. "Benjamin Davis is a predecessor of mine who followed Adam Clayton Powell and was a progressive force for social justice," Mr. Perkins said. "I'm looking into his story, ideally, to resurrect his contributions to the city, the black community and the cause of social justice." Errol Louis, "Perkins Seeks to Name Street for Communist, Would Honor Davis, Who Backed Stalin." *New York Sun*, April 9, 2004; Richard Leone, president of the Century Foundation and editor of *The War On Our Freedoms: Civil Liberties in an Age of Terrorism*. Cited in Heather Mac Donald, "Straight Talk About Homeland Security," *City Journal*, Aug. 11, 2003. This is a thoroughgoing critique of the critics of the act.

78. As of February 19, 2004. A complete list is posted on the website of the Bill of Rights Defense Committee, www.bordc.org.

79. http://www.aclu.org/SafeandFree/SafeandFree.cfm?ID=11256&c=206

80. Peter Collier and David Horowitz, *Destructive Generation*, contains a history of the Weather Underground.

81. Dohrn is a member of two important committees of the American Bar Association and was appointed to a project of the Roger Baldwin Foundation of the ACLU. In 2004, she was the commencement speaker at Pitzer College, a top-tier liberal arts school in California.

82. *Monthly Review*, July-August, 2003. http://www.monthlyreview.org/0703dohrn.htm

83. Timmerman, 276 et seq.

84. Ibid. p. 277; Michael Tremoglie, "Stanley Cohen: Terrorist Mouthpiece," www.frontpagemag.com, December 17, 2002.

85. Timmerman, 277, et seq.

86. Ibid.

87. Packer, "Terrorist Lawyer."

88. Erick Stakelback, "Cheerleaders for Terrorism," www.frontpagemag.com June 17, 2003; *New York Lawyer*, May 2, 2003.

89. Lynne Stewart, "Law for the People 2003: Demand Democracy!" Closing speech at the National Lawyer's Guild Convention, Minneapolis, Oct. 26, 2003. Text available on the National Lawyers Guild website, www.nlg.org www.nlg.org/members/convention/stewart.html

90. *Monthly Review*, Nov. 25, 2002

91. John W. Sherman, *A Communist Front at Mid-Century: The American Committee for the Protection of the Foreign Born, 1933-1959* (Praeger: Westport, 2001).

92. *Boston Review of Books*, December 2002/January 2003. http://bostonreview.net/BR27.6/contents.html.

93. Sherman. According to Sherman, the initiative for founding the ACPFB originated within the Communist Party and the organization itself was only a nominally independent successor to the more explicitly party-controlled National Council for the Protection of the

Foreign Born founded in 1923. Sherman shows that the members of the organization's staff were either secret members of the Party or were fellow travelers who accepted party guidance and control. The policy positions of the ACPFB faithfully followed the party line. Sherman's research does not even take into account the files in the Soviet archives. Cf. the review of Sherman's book by John Earl Haynes, in the *Journal of American History*, v. 90, issue 2, Feb. 3, 2004.

94. Sherman, 93.

PART 5

1. Feb. 4, 1998.
2. Jan. 28, 2002
3. Todd S. Purdum and the editors of the *New York Times*, *A Time of Our Own Choosing* (Times Books: New York, 2003), 22.
4. Al Gore, "A Commentary on the War Against Terror: Our Larger Tasks," Feb. 12, 2002. Emphasis added.
5. Purdum, et al, 40.
6. WallStreetJournalonline.com, Aug. 15, 2002.
7. Text available at www.nion.org. Other signers included Ramsey Clark, Tom Hayden, Barbara Kingsolver, Toni Morrison, Martin Sheen, Danny Glover, Noam Chomsky, Howard Zinn, Katha Pollitt, Representative Jim McDermott (D-Wash.) and Mumia Abu Jamal.
8. The policy, including the doctrine of pre-emption had been made explicit in presidential speeches going back to the State of the Union; it was formally articulated in a white paper three days prior to Gore's speech. See "The National Security Strategy of the United States," Washington D.C., Sept. 20, 2002.
9. "In fact, though a new U.N. resolution may be helpful in building international consensus, the existing resolutions from 1991 are sufficient from a legal standpoint." Gore.

10. Bob Gibson, "Carter Criticizes Bush For Policy Against Iraq," *The Daily Progress* (Charlottesville), Sept. 24, 2002

11. www.cnn.com/2002/WORLD/europe/10/11/carter.nobel. This was nothing new for the Nobel committee which had previously awarded the prize to several left-wing "peace" groups, and even to terrorist spokeswoman Rigoberta Menchu and terrorist leader Yasser Arafat.

12. Ibid.

13. Hans Blix, *Disarming Iraq* (Pantheon: New York, 2004), 108.

14. Ibid., 197.

15. Ibid., 108, 117. A month after the declaration, a U.N. inspection team found "a crate of warheads designed for chemical weapons," which were unarmed.

16. Ibid., 109, 112. On the other hand, Blix like many others on the political Left was unprepared to consider that force was required when diplomacy failed to bring the dictator to heel. A diary entry written on New Year's Eve 2002 contains these revealing words: "It has been an intense year. The inspections path must be and must be seen to be, as an alternative not a prelude to armed action."

17. Kenneth L. Pollock, "Saddam's Useful Idiots," *Wall Street Journal*, March 15, 2004.

18. Shawcross, 19, 131.

19. "Iraq appears not to have come to a genuine acceptance – not even today – of the disarmament which was demanded of it and which it needs to carry out to win the confidence of the world and to live in peace." Blix, 106 et seq. On his opposition to the use of force under any circumstances see his diary note quoted on p. 109: "The inspection path must be and must be seen as an alternative, not a prelude to armed action."

20. Bob Muehlenkamp, "War and Peace are Union Issues," Nov. 25, 2002.

21. Shawcross, 133.

22. Ibid.

23. Purdum, et al., 77.

24. Shawcross, 148.

25. Shawcross, 149.

26. Jimmy Carter, "Just War – Or a Just War," *New York Times*, March 9, 2003.

27. "Daschle: Bush Diplomacy Fails 'Miserably.'" Associated Press, March 18, 2003. Its president, Gerald McEntee, had been a featured speaker at the anti-World Trade Organization demonstration in Seattle in 1999 and member of Al Gore's kitchen cabinet.

28. Stephen Dinan and Amy Fagan, "Pelosi Stands By Vote Against Iraq War," *Washington Times*, April 11, 2003; Todd S. Purdum, 212.

29. Mark Trevelyan, "Al-Qaeda Switches Tactics, Seeks New Targets," Reuters, Sept. 10, 2003.

30. NationalReviewOnline, July 11, 2003 9:40AM www.national review.com/york/york.asp. The ad was designed by former Clinton-Gore advisors.

31. Ibid.

32. John Podhoretz, *Bush Country*, (St. Martin's Press: New York, 2004), 221 et seq.

33. "The Yellowcake Con," editorial *Wall Street Journal*, July 15, 2004. The quote is from the 511-page report of the Senate Intelligence Committee. The Journal editorial concluded: "All of this matters because Mr. Wilson's disinformation became the vanguard of a year-long assault on Mr. Bush's credibility. The political goal was to portray the President as a 'liar,' regardless of the facts. Now that we know those facts, Americans can decide who the liars are."

34. Stephen F. Hayes, "The Imminence Myth," *The Weekly Standard*, Feb. 16, 2004.

35. It had been made two months earlier, in *The National Security Strategy of the United States White Paper*, September 2002.

36. Shawcross, 233.

37. Shawcross, 215.

38. Cited in George P. Schultz, "An Essential War," *Wall Street Journal*, March 29, 2004.

39. Adam Nagourney, "Democrats Attack Credibility of Bush," *New York Times*, July 14, 2003

40. Ibid.

41. Joe Trippi speech at Emerging Technology Conference, Feb. 9, 2004. Text at www.smartmobs.com/archives/002592.html

42. Don Hazen, "MoveOn and Dean Make the Big Leagues," Alternet.org July 1, 2003. Alternet is an anti-war website.

43. Discussions among radical activists about influencing the coming elections were taking place while the war was on. See Michelle Goldberg, "Rage or Reason/ Activists Debate: Should They Take Over the Streets or Work to Defeat Bush in 2004?" *Salon.com*, March 27, 2003.

44. http://www.frontpagemag.com/Articles/ReadArticle.asp?ID=11703

45. www.drudgereport.com, Dec. 15, 2003 Late last week, a Swedish website removed an "EU-MoveOn.org Fundraising Appeal," claiming MoveOn.org "No Longer Accepts Contributions From Non US Citizens/Permanent Resident Aliens." Former U.S. Vice President Al Gore, who has been headlining moveone.org events, is said to have vocalized serious concerns about the website accepting cash from foreign sources, the *Drudge Report* has learned. See also Jimmy Moore, "Brewing MoveOn Scandal Over Foreign Contributions Involves Dean, Clark Campaigns," *Talon News* Dec. 16, 2003

46. Shawn Macomber, "Kerry's New Hate-America Man," www.frontpagemag.com April 8, 2004.

47. Michelle Goldberg, "Progressive Popularity Contest," *Salon.com*, June 24, 2000.

48. Ibid.

49. www.winwithoutwarus.org.

50. Kate Zernike and Dean E. Murphy, "A Nation At War: Dissent – Antiwar Effort Emphasizes Civility Over Confrontation," *New York Times*, March 29, 2003.

51. Nagourney.

52. Reuters, May 19, 2003.

53. Chris Weinkopf, "Politicizing the War," frontpagemag.com July 16, 2003. Weinkopf is an editorial writer for the *Los Angeles Daily News*.

54. Editorial, "Dean the Dream," *Wall Street Journal*, Feb. 19, 2004.

55. Richard Gephardt, "American Engagement and the War Against Terror," July 22, 2003.

56. William Kristol, "Gephardt's Sixteen Words," *Weekly Standard*, July 24, 2003.

57. Quoted by Kristol, ibid. The interview was on *Larry King Live*.

58. Stephen F. Hayes, "Gore Goes Gaga: The Paranoid Style In Democratic Politics," *The Weekly Standard*, Aug. 18, 2003.

59. Ibid.

60. Associated Press, "Gore Says America 'betrayed' by Bush," *USA Today*, Feb. 8, 2004.

61. Senator Edward Kennedy, "On the Administration's Failure to Provide a Realistic, Specific Plan to Bring Stability to Iraq," www.commondreams.org, Oct. 16, 2003.

62. Associated Press, "Kennedy Says Iraq War Case a 'Fraud.'" Sept. 18, 2003.

63. Kerry outlined his position in a speech delivered on Oct. 9, 2002.

64. Patrick Healy, "Senator Attacks Bush War Stance," *Boston Globe*, Dec. 12, 2003.

65. Kenneth L. Pollock, "Saddam's Useful Idiots," *Wall Street Journal*, March 15, 2004.

66. "Vietnam Veterans Against the War Statement by John Kerry to the Senate Committee on Foreign Relations," April 23, 1971.

67. C.W. Bill Young and Porter Goss, "Need Intelligence? Don't Ask John Kerry," *Tampa Tribune*, March 10, 2004. Goss is chair of the Permanent Select Committee on Intelligence.

68. Ibid.

69. Cited in William J. Bennett, "The Democratic Party and the Politics of War," *Claremont Review of Books*, Spring 2004.

70. John Kerry. . . . Johns Hopkins. Carl Limbacher, "Kerry Pledges Return to Clinton Terrorism Policies," Newsmax.com. March 13, 2004; In one of the televised primary debates Kerry reiterated that the battle against terror was "far less of a military operation and far more of an intelligence and law enforcement operation." *FOX Sunday Morning* news clip, March 11, 2004.

71. www.johnkerry.com; cf. also "Transcript Democratic Candidates Debate in South Carolina," Jan. 29, 2004 FDCH e-Media, Inc. On Stewart, see above.

72. Macomber.

EPILOGUE

1. William Schneider, "9/11 Families Make Their Voices Heard," *Inside Politics*, CNN.com March 12, 2004. But see David Broder, "Would FDR Run Those 9/11 Ads?" *Washington Post*, March 11, 2004. Broder showed that the use of events like 9/11 in partisan ads was a well-worn American political tradition. After reviewing Roosevelt's use of the war to promote his reelection campaign, Broder concluded, "If you accept President Bush's premise that this nation is at war with terrorism, then you have to applaud the restraint his campaign has shown so far in exploiting the attack that began the war."

2. Editorial, *Wall Street Journal*, March 10, 2004; Peaceful Tomorrows' actions are described on its website at www.peacefultomorrows.org. The site contains a statement denying Teresa Heinz Kerry's involvement in funding the organization. It does not deny, however, that Kerry is a multi-million dollar donor to the Tides Foundation which provided $230,000 to set up the Tides Center which has an interlocking directorate and staff. See the profile of Tides in www.searchthenetwork.org

3. Tim Ryan, "Peaceful Tomorrows, Leftist Todays," www.frontpagemag.com, March 17, 2004; *Wall Street Journal.*

4. Ben Johnson, "Teresa Heinz Kerry: Bag Lady for the Political Left," www.frontpagemag.com. Feb. 13, 2004.

5. Jay Bryant, "Extremists Behind Attack On Bush Ad," Townhall.com, March 10, 2004.

6. David Horowitz, "Secessionists Against The War," www.frontpagemag.com, Feb. 10, 2004.

7. Howard Zinn, "My Country: The World," *Newsday*, April 13, 2003. The article was produced on many leftist websites including www.commondreams.org and www.unitedforpeaceandjustice.org.

8. An American socialist Eugene Victor Debs used the phrase to express his own internationalism: "I have no country to fight for; my country is earth, and I am a citizen of the world."

9. Robert Jensen, "Saying Goodbye to Patriotism," Counterpunch.org, Nov. 12, 2001. Jensen is a professor of journalism at the University of Texas, Austin.

10. Ibid.

11. Ibid.

Index